# TEEN TV

*Teen TV* explores the history of television's relationship to teens as a desired, but elusive audience, and the ways in which television has embraced youth subcultures, tracing the shifts in American and global televisual teen media.

Organized chronologically to cover each generation since the inception of the medium in the 1940s, the book examines a wide range of historical and contemporary programming: from the broadcast bottleneck, multi-channel era that included youth-targeted spaces like MTV, the WB, and the CW, to the rise of streaming platforms and global crossovers. It covers the thematic concerns and narrative structure of the coming-of-age story, and the prevalent genre formations of teen TV and milestones faced by teen characters. The book also includes interviews with creators and showrunners of hit network television teen series, including *Degrassi*'s Linda Schuyler, and the costume designer that established a heightened turn in the significance of teen fashion on the small screen in *Gossip Girl*, Eric Daman.

This book will be of interest to students, scholars, and teachers interested in television aesthetics, TV genres, pop culture, and youth culture, as well as media and television studies.

**Stefania Marghitu** is a visiting faculty member at Pitzer College. She has also taught courses at Chapman University, California State University Northridge, and Columbia College Hollywood. She received her PhD from the University of Southern California's Division of Cinema and Media Studies. Her primary interests deal with critical and cultural studies of television, the showrunner and modes of authorship, production cultures, and feminist media studies. Her dissertation is titled *Women Showrunners: Authorship, Identity, and Representation in US Television*. She has published in *Feminist Media Studies*, *Communication, Culture and Critique*, *New Review of Film and Television*, and *The Spectator*.

# ROUTLEDGE TELEVISION GUIDEBOOKS

The Routledge Television Guidebooks offer an introduction to and overview of key television genres and formats. Each guidebook contains an introduction, including a brief history; defining characteristics and major series; key debates surrounding themes, formats, genres, and audiences; questions for discussion; and a bibliography of further reading and watching.

**REALITY TV**
*Jonathan Kraszewski*

**THE SITCOM**
*Jeremy Butler*

**FAIRY-TALE TV**
*Jill Terry Rudy and Pauline Greenhill*

**SPORTS TV**
*Victoria E. Johnson*

**TEEN TV**
*Stefania Marghitu*

For more information about this series, please visit: https://www.routledge.com/Routledge-Television-Guidebooks/book-series/RTVG

# TEEN TV

*Stefania Marghitu*

NEW YORK AND LONDON

First published 2021
by Routledge
605 Third Avenue, New York, NY 10158

and by Routledge
2 Park Square, Milton Park, Abingdon, Oxon, OX14 4RN

*Routledge is an imprint of the Taylor & Francis Group, an informa business*

© 2021 Taylor & Francis

The right of Stefania Marghitu to be identified as author of this work has been asserted by her in accordance with sections 77 and 78 of the Copyright, Designs and Patents Act 1988.

All rights reserved. No part of this book may be reprinted or reproduced or utilised in any form or by any electronic, mechanical, or other means, now known or hereafter invented, including photocopying and recording, or in any information storage or retrieval system, without permission in writing from the publishers.

*Trademark notice*: Product or corporate names may be trademarks or registered trademarks, and are used only for identification and explanation without intent to infringe.

*Library of Congress Cataloging-in-Publication Data*
A catalog record for this title has been requested

ISBN: 978-0-415-31585-2 (hbk)
ISBN: 978-1-138-71389-5 (pbk)
ISBN: 978-1-315-22964-5 (ebk)

Typeset in Perpetua
by codeMantra

In Memory of Thomas Russel Parten, 1991–2020

# CONTENTS

*Acknowledgments* viii

Teen TV Introduction 1
1 Baby Boomer Teen TV 23
2 Generation X Teen TV 65
3 Millennial Teen TV 105
4 Gen Z Teen TV 159

*Discussion Questions* 213
*Teen TV Filmography* 215
*Index* 225

# ACKNOWLEDGMENTS

The process behind this book often mirrored the rollercoaster of adolescence. I could not have done it without the support and encouragement of so many wonderful people, professionally and personally.

My husband Conor kept me grounded and never doubted me throughout all of this.

My grandparents didn't know our *Beverly Hills 90210* nights would be so influential, just one of the many ways they helped shape who I am. My patient and selfless parents, for letting me indulge in my teenage fandom.

I thank those who took the time to be interviewed for the book: Kathleen Bedoya, Eric Daman, Winne Holzman, and Linda Schuyler.

My dissertation chair, Henry Jenkins, encouraged me to pursue every project I felt passionately about, and he made the work balance seem possible. Aniko Imre, an incredible mentor, always took time to listen to me and to offer advice and positive reinforcement. Christine Acham reminded me to be valued for the work I have done. Jennifer Holt told me to "write my best," and spoke of the gaps in scholarship that the field needs.

My academic community spans across the US and abroad. Friends as well fellow early career scholars lifted me up to write this book: Elisa Jochum, Kelsey Moore Johnston, Erendira Espinoza-Taboada, Katie Panhorst Harris, Caroline and Chandler White, Matthew Parten, Qui Ha Nguyen, Rachel Fullmer, Anna Strand, Leslie Streicher,

ACKNOWLEDGMENTS

Nadia Bhuiyan (from watching and talking about *The O.C.* from our teens to thirties), Sabrina Howard, Courtney Cox, Perry Johnson, Rachel Summers (rehashing *The O.C.* and discussing new teen shows), Megan Connor, Katie Walsh, Lydia Burt, Sigi Priessl, Anne Mette Jaeger Hansen, Filipa Marques, Lydia Burt, Andy Enkeboll, Lina Nguyen, Rossen Sanchez-Baro, Michelle Doman, and Manish Agarwal. Marley Thrower for always willing to discuss *Normal People* summer 2020. Ben Stevens and Conrad Ng always listened to me and let me know "I got this." Denise Reyes for her pride and support and willingness to discuss teen shows. Stephanie Mendonce, for always supporting my writing a bright star. Alexa Altman, for her unconditional friendship and encouragement. Thank you to Meg O'Connell for her design advice and warmth.

Friends and mentors in academia who took the time to help me and express enthusiasm about my work and provide advice and insight: Andrea Kelley (and of course Izzy), Michael Newman, Elana Levine, Gry Rustad (the leading expert on *Skam*), Alfred Martin, Sarah Louise Smyth, Shelley Cobb, Sarah Banet-Weiser, Harvey Cohen, Tanya Horeck, Linde Murugan, Elizabeth Affuso, Emily Carman, Erica Aguero, Dianah Wynter, Frances Gateward, René Bruckner, Alyx Vesey, Amanda Keeler, Daniel Murphy, Joan Hawkins, Lee Griveson, Melvyn Stokes, and Justyna Beinkek.

My Irish-Korean family, the O'Neills, The Crawfords (The original Derry girls), and to Rosie: XOXO *Gossip Girl*.

I thank my undergraduate students at USC, Chapman, and Pitzer who provided engaging discussions and helped fuel my writing.

My undergraduate research assistant Livi Edmonson, who was always there to discuss teen media and helped me along the process. To Erica Wetter for her initial guidance as editor at Routledge.

Finally, my thanks to Emma Sheriff at Routledge for supporting the project, particularly during a global pandemic.

# TEEN TV INTRODUCTION

When I first began this book project in 2016, many people asked me two recurring questions: "Does Teen TV even exist anymore?" and "Do teens even watch TV anymore?" Many assumed the guidebook would be a purely historical endeavor. By this time, I had already spoken with Kathleen Bedoya, co-creator and showrunner of *East Los High* (2013– 2017), one of Hulu's first original series that broke many barriers of the genre in terms of on and offscreen inclusion. The Norwegian series *Skam* (2015–2017, NRK) was a grassroots global hit through fans sharing subtitled episodes on the platform Tumblr, which led to several national adaptations. The summer of 2016, Netflix began tapping into the teen market with one of its most valuable original series, the 1980s-set blockbuster *Stranger Things*, which would appeal to a multi-generational audience. In 2017, the CW premiered its new spin on *Archie Comics, Riverdale* (2017–) and Netflix released another one of its most watched series that would focus on teens, *13 Reasons Why* (2017–2020). Teen TV was back for a new generation and for fans and scholars of the genre.

In summer of 2019, HBO's first teen centered series, *Euphoria*, became an enthralling and contentious topic among media critics, academics, and fans. What would we expect when the genre would be given its first prestige premium cable series? Who would watch? Who would be shocked, and who would relate? As someone writing a teen television book, I knew it would spark conversations for the genre.

What I didn't expect, once the school year began, was that *Euphoria* would become the most mutually watched series amongst my undergraduate students throughout University of Southern California, Chapman University, and Pitzer College. This common ground among viewing habits was rare, just as the nearly universal positive reviews and feedback. I also began to notice how the new Generation of Gen Z students all had very niche tastes and viewing habits. Film students who adhere to traditional cinephilia, or fandom for blockbuster releases, seemed to have more shared viewings. This was particularly true during the time before the Oscar awards. However, this did not apply to non-cinephiles. As we move further from the traditional network era and its distinct programming, and limited options for viewing in contrast to the contemporary era, I find it more difficult to explain early television to new students. This shift requires greater detail and expansion of the nature of US commercial television, programming and flow of broadcast, and the sheer monopoly networks held.

At the same time of this shift with Gen Z college students, there seemed to be greater multi-generational divides; 2019 was also the year of "OK Boomer," a viral retort to anyone who asserted anything that conveyed the conservatism of a certain percentage of the generation. The 2020 Covid-19 pandemic and presidential election further divided generations in the US through political viewpoints.

This book will present the history of television's relationship to teens as a desired, but elusive audience. Further, it will illustrate the ways that television has at times taken up youth subcultures and at others ignored them. By linking the historical and the contemporary, the intersections of social justice youth movements and teen media culture through the network era, multi-channel era and rise of cable, and expansion and dominance of streaming platforms, this book will both provide cultural specificity to each period and generational struggles, while also connecting the recurring themes and issues of American teens. Along with a chronological account of teen TV that also explores constructs and discourse of generation identity, the genre is approached in terms of the problems that the nature of series and serials pose to the concerns and narrative structure of the coming-of-age story. Second, the specificity of teen issues within the genre is investigated to understand how it alters and sometimes innovates genre conventions. Third, the book traces milestones faced by the teen characters, in terms of identity, to compare series across some of the best and most popular teen series of the last 60 years. While the focus is on US television, due to the nature of the American teenager, later chapters will reveal the influence of global television.

Genre is foundational to the study of television as a medium and has been a rich site of study of aesthetics, narrative, representation, and ideology. Early television scholars explored the role of the soap opera, which led to its roots in feminist television criticism. Television genre has also, in my experience, been a rewarding aspect of teaching undergraduate students across several disciplines.

First, it is critical to establish a succinct framework for analyzing genre.

While not an early foundational genre to television such as the soap opera serial, western, or episodic action series, teen television is mostly concerned with its targeted demographic. Yet teen television also comes from a strong lineage of the literary coming-of-age story.

Teen narratives are historical. Shorter life expectancy in past eras meant puberty and adolescence marked the shift from childhood to adulthood, marriage, and parenthood, rather than a period of transition for self-actualization. Literary teens are perpetual protagonists in high school English classes and theatre productions, from William Shakespeare's *Romeo and Juliet* to J.D. Sallinger's *Catcher in the Rye*. Readers of all ages delve into stories about teens, such as the *Harry Potter* and *Game of Thrones* series. Literary adaptations to film and television hold a strong historical trajectory that carry common traits to the teen coming-of-age genre. As James Gilbert has usefully demonstrated in *Cycle of Outrage*, teenagers have cyclically been the focus of media panics, whether because of the spread of subcultures that alarm the adult middle class or because of shifting patterns of mobility (automobile and motorcycle usage); adolescent sexuality; drug and alcohol usage; and tastes in music and dance.

Teen TV is understood here as a comedy or drama centered around adolescent characters with a focus on cultural milestones and rites of passages—from issues of finding the right romantic partner, rebelling against or conforming to adults rules, choosing a career path, coming to terms with one's parents, and establishing a secure identity. Rather than a comprehensive, chronological account of successful shows, we explore the unique storytelling conundrums challenges in storytelling that teen TV of series pose, how older genres are refreshed by recasting the main characters as adolescents or young adults, and how these incorporate reframing them as the stories of young adults, and serials pose to the thematic concerns and narrative structure of the coming-of-age story. Within the genre, character archetypes are chronicled and dissected as reflections of traditional, or non-conventional, attitudes, of the time. It examines the historical context of how teens have been targeted as an audience along with changes in generational identity. The book chronicles the genre from Baby Boomers to Gen Z, and the network era to multi-channel era to the current post-network digital streaming era.

Teen television is a historically transmedia storytelling endeavor. From early 1950s adaptations of popular novels and films (*The Many Loves of Dobie Gillis* and *Gidget*, respectively) to today's reboots, remakes, and prequels (*90210*, *Skins*, *Scream*, and *The Carrie Diaries*), multiple platforms are intrinsic to the teen TV viewing experience. The emphasis on franchises also favored what Todd Gitlin refers to as "recombinant culture" through spinoffs, reboots, and sequels.[1] While series like *Dawson's Creek*, *The O.C.*, and *Gossip Girl* incorporated fashion and music intentionally as cross-promotions and an attempt to display the precocious maturity of its protagonists, teen TV incorporates worldbuilding strategies to provide a total and immersive viewing experience for a variety of potential viewers, which also included adults to preteens.

In addition, the series discusses adhere to elements of the coming-of-age story. Certain narrative elements present themselves in nearly every teen series: the protagonist feels alienated from the adult world she is on the threshold of entering. This conflict is intertwined with a passionate story of first love and new discoveries during the transition from child to adult. Many teen dramas rely on aspects of the literary coming-of-age genre, in which the adolescent character leaves home, comes to know more about the adult social world and feels critical, dismayed, and unable to accept society on society's terms.

In teen drama, stereotypes emerge from the shifting pool of villains (*Beverly Hills 90210*, *Gossip Girl*, *Pretty Little Liars*) or each character can, in turn, eventually be filled out, made more complex, and challenged (*Degrassi*, *Freaks and Geeks*, *Skins*, *Euphoria*). In teen comedy, the classmates typically represent the range of stereotypes and are the group's reference in and of itself, the situation comedy convention of finding a happy unity in the group's differences at the end of each episode trumps the specificity of the coming-of-age genre. What will interest us in this analysis of teen TV is the ways that the characters' age creates a paradox for the narrative and the show's creators. These protagonists will be used up with each season; they time out on adolescence and young adulthood. Each new experience pushes them closer to the inevitable ending of the coming-of-age story. How TV series have dealt with this paradox and what innovations to the serialized drama have been devised for this problem will be examined. Teen TV creates considerable challenges for the writers to keep the story going for multiple seasons as well as for teen stars managing their transition to adulthood (From Sally Field of *Gidget*, Brandy Norwood of *Moesha*, Aubrey Graham AKA Drake of *Degrassi*, and Zendaya of *Euphoria*).

In ways more blatant than other genres, teen TV is a gender factory, much like high schools themselves, where the subject matter continually fixates on good and bad versions of masculinity and femininity. A central change has taken place in the genre over the last 20 years with popular homecoming queen types becoming the driver of much of the action in her cruelty and competitiveness. In Jane Austen (*Emma* and *Pride and Prejudice*), Emily Bronte (*Wuthering Heights*), and Louisa May Alcott (*Little Women*)—prime examples of the female coming-of-age genre in literature, the search for self takes place in a protected world of female friendship. The challenge is to find the appropriate partner while balancing domestic and social demands, and occasional artistic ambitions. In today's teen TV series with a focus on female characters, a strict hierarchy of social status replaces the supportive female group, and excessive consumerism and materialism are the base evil.

This produces the irony of shows showcasing brand name products for its audience through tie-ins and product placement, while simultaneously condemning teen girls for obsessing about consumer goods.

Teen television requires the need for both innovation and relying on formulas and narrative closure, that creates special difficulties for writers and producers. Some of these challenges are inherent in all series television; others are unique to teen TV genre. Where the TV series inevitably departs from, and lies in tension with the genre, is in the conundrum of all television series: with narrative closure, the definitive ending impossible given the commercial demands of television series running as long as an audience still exists to watch it, TV dooms every teen TV protagonist to outlasting their adolescence (sometimes spending an absurd length of time in high school, to physically age beyond adolescence (as many actors cast in teen series are 18 or 21 but able to play 5–8 years younger than their age, at least at the onset of the series).

Teen TV has had a direct relationship to advertising, product placement, tie-ins, and music sales and pioneered many of television's selling practices that have only gotten bolder in the post-network era and have replicated themselves in the new media environment. The allure of the teen market is exceptionally strong for marketers due to their influence over parents' consumer decisions and their future position as adult consumers, who could be forming lifelong patterns of brand loyalty.

## Genres as Cultural Categories: The Case of Teen TV

For Stuart Hall, one of the founding fathers of the Birmingham School of Cultural Studies, TV viewers are not the "cultural dupes" that the Frankfurt School decried all mass media audiences are. Two primary methodological tools dominated the core of cultural studies. The first consisted of ethnographic work that encourages the meanings of viewers' responses, known as "decoding." The second includes textual analysis related to ideology, cultural myths, identity politics, and other pertinent issues.[2] Cultural studies analysis of television, for example, used a three-part textual analysis: the primary text of the series that is produced by the industry; the sublevel that can still be made by the culture industry but also studio publicity and criticism; and the texts that the viewer adapts for themselves based on their background and relationship to a given series.[3] When it comes to genre analysis, cultural studies and television scholars agree that the text alone is not enough. Genres, like texts, do not exist in an artistic vacuum. As Jason Mittell asserts, "as many genre scholars have noted, there are no uniform criteria for genre delimitation-some are defined by setting (westerns), some by actions (crime shows), some by audience effect (comedy), and some by narrative form (mysteries)."[4] This is why genre is a particularly rich site of study for students, who can employ interdisciplinary methodologies to teen TV. Mittell states, by incorporating discursive practices to genres,

> To examine generic discourses, we should analyze the contextualized generic practices that circulate around and through texts. We might look at what audiences and industries say about genres, what terms and definitions circulate around any given instance of a genre, and how specific cultural concepts are linked to particular genres.[5]

John Fiske was one of the first US scholars to implement a British cultural studies framework to US television and genre, while applying the ethnographic and theoretical approaches to young female fans of Madonna.[6] British Cultural Studies first used their methods to make sense of issues surrounding race and class in the UK, and feminist scholars would follow by incorporating gender and sexuality. Feminist media scholars in the UK and the US also incorporated ethnographic work and social theory. Henry Jenkins, a founder of fan studies, was one of first to place fans as active cultural producers, and authors in their own right, from Trekkies who attend Comi-Con and write fan fiction, to early users of the Internet who used forums to discuss *Twin Peaks*.

## Interviews and Production Studies

This book includes interview material with several key creative personnel to illustrate changes in the television industry itself from network to cable and the constraints and pressures on writers and directors in the teen genre. The interviews are primarily with showrunners (creator, writer, producer hybrids) and a costume designer who contributed to the authorship of their respective series. Television, and radio before it, has always been viewed as a commercial endeavor. As representatives of the commercial interests of the industry, producers hold power over writers, creators, directors, and actors. Aware of the power of this role, radio and television author-writers who want to take control of their projects have learned to take up the managerial role of the producer. Creative writers learned the television business to assert their authorial presence throughout the making of a series.[7] This hybridity is what marks the role of the showrunner. As with the writer-director-producer trifecta in film, being a showrunner includes heightened income, cultural capital, and influence. Critics of US television and mass media since the Frankfurt School have argued that it purely serves to promote capitalism through consumption and consumerism. Some scholars, such as Mark Crispin Miller, go as far as to state that:

> In short, the modern history of America is, in large part, the history of an ever-rising flood of corporate propaganda—and also of our various responses to it, as We the People have obscurely struggled to reverse it, or resist it, or to live our lives in spite of it, or have simply let it carry us away.[8]

This book does not accept the notion that television is a monolithic and homogeneous medium when considering its multifaceted contributors and producers, from the strictly corporate networks, advertisers, and programmers to writers and producers. Within the ecosystem of television, public opinion—through cultural critics, audience and fan interventions, and government and nonprofit organizations—contributes to the cultural shifts of the medium, as well as to changes from within the industry via collective bargaining and unionization.

The interviews will highlight the use of production studies as a component of media industries that is often described as a cultural studies approach to production. It is largely rooted in history and/or ethnography and a subsequent critical analytical framework based on the empirical findings. While the nascent work on media authorship from Horace Newcomb and Todd Gitlin remains foundational, their focus on interviews and participant observation obstructs the opportunity for further detailed analysis.[9] This remains a problem in contemporary production studies with thorough ethnography and limited critical analysis. While authorship has been a fundamental component in film studies since the early 1960s, television authorship has been slower to emerge as a critical tool for understanding a program's origins, meanings, and reception, largely because television was previously considered an anonymous mass medium, and television directors do not have creative control over series. The director as *auteur* facilitated film's transition from mass medium to art form in the 1960s with the *Cahiers du Cinema* writers in France and, later, Andrew Sarris in the US being the major proponents of auteur theory.[10] The rise of *auteurs* in the 1960s also boosted new Hollywood marketing strategies based on filmmakers as public star personas. Auteur theory and star studies, both subfields of film studies, exist in parallel. The construction of the *auteur* mirrors that of the star image, as both are enacted by the branding and marketing strategies of the media industries:

> This kind of voluntarist and Romantic understanding of the agency of film authorship as encapsulating the possibilities for expression (especially male) artist's "personality" was immediately co-opted by film commerce, for the purposes of which the name of the author came in the post-war period, outside and inside Hollywood, to "function" as a "brand name," a means of labeling and selling a film and of orienting expectations of meaning and pleasures in the absence of generic boundaries and categories.[11]

For proponents of auteurism, demystifying the notion of a pure artist—one who pursues art for art's sake—seems to take away from the value of the art itself. Yet, hiding the process of cultural production (which in many ways reveals the struggles of the artist) eschews commodity fetishism and brings the issues of the industry's relationship to its treatment of art and artists based on branding, marketability, and supply and demand. These figures are not pure artists or activists; they are television's politicians who must negotiate and balance their goals and the interests of their constituents (audiences).

While media industries can often focus on the economy and methods of political economy scholarship, production studies are more interested in concentrating on the role of the creative worker, or certain creative groups, in relation to issues surrounding labor, history, and critical social theory. Production studies gathers empirical data on the intended producer or group, and then historicizes, theorizes, and analyzes the implications at large using an interdisciplinary framework. Most importantly, production studies as a methodology holds a strong grasp on the "situated authorship" of any creative producer.

Hall also incorporates Michel Foucault's concept of discourse, identified as the production of knowledge through language, as a key concept to understanding receptions of media texts.[12] Foucault studied discourse as a system of representation, and this nascent concept has since been applied to cultural studies and production studies as a way to make meaning of media cultures. Hall's encoding/decoding model of communication was used in his analysis of television discourse, an approach that looked at how media is produced, disseminated, and interpreted. A production study also considers the production, distribution, and reception of a media text. It also acknowledges that texts function as discourse within media industries on this three-tiered level. Moreover, just as cultural studies never placed viewers as passive cultural dupes, production studies do not believe creative workers are simply cogs in the mass media machine. Production studies considers encoding, the production of a text, as well as encoding. The ethnographic work and subsequent textual analysis of the industry lore or double speak of the media producer mirrors ethnographic work of reception and fan research that originated with the Frankfurt School.

Students have also enjoyed taking up issues of production studies and authorship, which is why these interviews will be particularly useful to engage with the field of study. Production studies aim to investigate how media producer also produce their own culture, while also making themselves into a specific type of worker in the new mediated societies. With this, production studies continue with the goal to:

> look up and down the food chains of production hierarchies, to understand how people work through professional organizations and informal networks to form communities of shared practices, languages and cultural understandings of the word.[13]

This book incorporates production studies methodologies applied to the Teen TV genre, which include direct interviews with showrunners, and a costume designer that have contributed to the world-building and authorship of key series addressed in each chapter (Linda Schulyer, co-creator of Degrassi (1979-2019, CBC/CTV/Much Music/Netflix) Winnie Holzman, showrunner of My So-Called Life, 1994-1995, ABC) Eric Daman, costume designer of Gossip Girl (2007-2012, The CW) and Kathleen Bedoya, showrunner of East Los High (2013-2017, Hulu). Industrially, these programs cover Canadian public service, and US commercial network/broadcast channels, and multi-channel and streaming-based niche casting. They also incorporate discussions of different forms of episodic and serialized storytelling, stardom, fandom, and shifts in representation of gender, sexuality, race, ethnicity and national identity within the genre.

Production studies research addresses that the idea of authorship is "one of both subjective identification and outsider objectification," supplemented with "organizational hierarchies of media labor, and reinforced by 'auteur' studies of film and television producers as the 'authors' of their creative projects."[14] Therefore, the goal is to address the self-reflexive industry talk that producers use in interviews and other outlets, while acknowledging the hierarchies in which they operate under. They assert that one of the challenges is that "the crisis of representing producers, their locations, industries and products is the burden of representation for production studies."[15]

Banks, Caldwell, and Mayer all provide thorough investigations of different below-the-line media laborers and the nature of their work. For example, Banks uses feminist theory and production studies to introduce feminist production studies, a framework for looking at labor practices and receptions from the highly gendered careers of stunt doubles and costume designers. Further, costume designers, such as the interviewed Eric Daman of *Gossip Girl*, serve as authors of a series as they determine the aesthetic tone. However, as they still answer to the showrunner and various other above-the-line personnel, this can be seen as an extension of another creator's authorship. Depending on how close a showrunner works with costume designing will determine the level of agency and authorship of a below-the-line worker. Production studies also addresses that most industry research is focused on above-the-line workers, neglecting the significant impact of the invisible labor of below-the-line workers. Focusing on above the line also privileges above-the-line workers as auteurs and below the line as "blue collar" workers who hold no creativity.

As production studies methodologies adapt to the changes in the media industries, new concepts help in applying the various ways in which media workers extend their agency and authorship outside of the text itself. Jonathan Gray, for example, uses the term paratexts to define all of the additional, accompanying texts besides the primary body of work.[16] While prominent showrunners are features in profiles in *Variety* magazine and hire assistants to manage their social media "brand," it is also necessary to study the digital ambitions of emerging creative workers whose work can be found online, and their promotional paratexts and savvy help elevate their popularity and potential crossover to mainstream media. Here, "paratexts" refers to all of Rhimes' additional, accompanying texts outside her primary body of work; that is, outside her television series.[17] Part of the paratextual analysis is the showrunner's relationship with fans. I emphasize how fans and their individual and collective actions (in the form of visibly passionate audiences who love their work) and the industry at large (in the form of studio and network heads, executives, and advertising sponsors) are all inherent in the development of the showrunner's career trajectory. Without the support of viewers and the business side of the industry, a showrunner cannot sustain their place within cultural memory and history. Further,

I show that the visibility of a series' fan following can be used to understand how burgeoning subcultural formations influence the ways network, cable, and streaming platforms all formulate programming based on targeted demographics and specific, previously ignored audiences.

Production studies remind scholars who research authorship that it is a multi-level process. The fight for autonomy and creative freedom is not solely a battle between the showrunner and the industry. Extended authorship through paratexts is a vital means to understanding a showrunner's politics and intentions as a creative professional and cultural influencer. Production studies also stresses the need to further study the labor of below-the-line workers, whose contributions to the collaborative nature of television-making is vastly underexplored. Lastly, empirical data and ethnographic research is the beginning of doing production studies research, but I will also need to historicize, theorize, and further analyze the implications for a rich study of authorship, agency, and identity of showrunners in the US cultural sphere.

## Stardom and Celebrity

Teen TV plays a special role in the creation of celebrity. Susan Murray states that it was not until 1955 that television standardized its production and programming, including the star system in which "merchandising of one's own persona had become an absolutely essential component of a television star's career."[18] Television's more nuanced and at times iconoclastic versions of masculinity and femininity have produced some of the most striking examples of actors catapulting from a television role to genuine movie or music stardom: Leonardo DiCaprio of *Growing Pains*; James Franco with *Freaks and Geeks*; Blake Lively from *Gossip Girl*; *Hannah Montana*'s Miley Cyrus; Selena Gomez of *Wizards of Waverly Place*; Nicholas Hoult, Dev Patel, and Jack O'Connell of the British *Skins*; and Aubrey Graham, AKA Rapper Drake of the Canadian *Degrassi*. Disney Channel's revival of *The All-New Mickey Mouse Club* from 1989 to 1995 fostered budding stars like musicians Justin Timberlake, Britney Spears, and Christina Aguilera, and future actors Ryan Gosling and Keri Russell. This book will explore the rise of the teen celebrity on YouTube. Recently, the grassroots success of YouTube teen stars that gain massive popularity from their fellow peers have no middle man in the form of a TV platform. The Internet as a competitor to traditional television and film viewing has been a constant problem for the entertainment business. In this case, teens taking control of their own media proves the independence, versatility, and acumen of the millennial in the digital 21st century. The purpose of analyzing the star personas of these showrunners is not to discern between their "real self" and their public persona, but to understand what these bifurcated representations reveal about the expectations of the television industry. Just as stars' careers are viewed as texts, star personas are viewed as performative.

Richard Dyer's *Stars* first introduced the framework of analyzing stars as their own texts based.[19] Dyer offered several ways to construct the star: first, as social phenomena of production and consumption, and through ideological forces. Second, he viewed stars through their images and as "types," including alternative or subversive types. Third, stars could be viewed as signs based on their characters and performance. Dyer also offers a useful definition of ideology, as applied pervasively to the analysis of stars, but that also influenced cultural studies methodology. For Dyer, ideology is defined by "how society is characterized by divisions of class and gender, and secondarily, but not reducible to them, by divisions between races and sexual, cultural, religious and other minorities and majorities":

> Ideology is the set of ideas and representations in which people collectively make sense of the world and society in which they live. It is important to distinguish between ideology in general and ideology in particular. Ideology is a characteristic of all human societies, but a given ideology is specific to a particular moment in its history. All ideologies are developed in relation to concrete, material circumstances of human life—
>
> They are the means by which knowledge is made out of those circumstances. There is no guarantee that this knowledge is true in an absolute sense—indeed, all ideology is by definition partial and limited (which is not at all the same things as saying it is 'false').[20]

Within the dominant western ideology of Hollywood, Dyer stresses the notion of polysemy, which allows for multiple meanings of stars. Therefore, he does not deem his, or any, textual analysis, as a "correct meaning," but what legitimate meanings can be scrutinized. He goes on to say:

> Ideological analysis of media text does of course make the political implications of what we are saying inescapable. Since we often seek to avoid facing such implications, preferring to believe that what we do has no political consequences, this is reason enough for such an approach. It is, however, also intellectually more rigorous—as I have suggested above, all textual analysis has to be grounded in sociological conceptualizations of what texts are, and since what they are is ideology, with all its contradictory complexities, it follows that textual analysis is properly ideological analysis.[21]

Dyer also suggests "four categories of star/audience relationship": emotional affinity, self-identification, imitation, and projection.[22] This can be seen as foundational to the understanding of fandom cultures and fandom studies, especially as teen audiences can essentially "grow up" with teen TV stars. It is also influential to "queering" a text.[23] Dyer presented how stars can reinforce dominant ideology, but also subvert them. Audiences, fans, and scholars subsequently can discern this from their own encoding and decoding of the star text, as they would a television series or film. Dyer states, "stardom is an image of the way stars live," and lifestyle branding is also critical to the construction of the star. Stars must balance the spectacular with the everyday, and the extraordinary with the ordinary.[24] Again, this is particularly true for the intimacy of TV stars, especially youth stars who come of age both on and offscreen. The balance of the average and exceptional is also used in lifestyle television and reality television, as Laurie Ouellette has detailed in *Lifestyle Television*.[25] Lastly, Dyer's analysis of stars as "types" is also useful for the on and offscreen stereotypes, and their potential subversion, for teen TV stars. For him, the conceptualizing of social types through ideology is also crucial, rooted in stereotyping and othering from dominant ideologies. This use of social types will also prove useful for correlating the archetypes found in teen TV, and the subsequent ways their stars can either reify or defy them throughout their career.

## Chapter Breakdown

Past studies of the teen TV credits film's influence over early manifestation of the genre.

For example, while Glen Creeber states that its archetypical stock character is "inherited" from teen movies like the *Breakfast Club*,[26] Chapter 1 will reveal how *The Many Loves of Dobie Gillis* (1959–1963, CBS) depicted these stock characters since the 1950s, establishing the teen television archetypes. Further, Sally Field's *Gidget* (1965–1966, ABC) is highlighted as a nascent series to feature the aspirational Southern California teen lifestyle. A case study of Field's career is provided for understanding early stardom. Conventional knowledge of television history also places the birth of progressive programming in the 1970s, catching up to the 1960s civil rights movements. While this decade indeed marked a boom as a result of wider social justice and civil rights movements, pervasive precedents occurred. In addition to fictional teen TV in the form of sitcoms with white central characters from middle-class to upper-middle-class backgrounds, Chapter 1 delves into the class and racial politics of music programs such as *The Ed Sullivan Show* (1948–1971, CBS), *American Bandstand* (1952–1989, ABC), and *Soul Train* (1971–2006).

While teen television is inextricably influenced by film, as well as literature, music, magazine culture, and digital media, it also initiates intertextuality to provide a site for examining youth culture's multiple of writhing factors.

Whereas early family-centered network series and early teen-oriented TV focused on morally upright lessons and clear delineations of good vs. bad choices, the post-network cable era showed new ambiguities and more complex lessons to learn. The family sitcom encouraged teens to conform to their parents' ideologies, while teen series shifted toward adapting to the rules of high school in order to survive the social landscape. Because teen shows deal in stereotypes, we see melodrama's conventional emphasis on female chastity especially clearly in these shows that young women are defined in the stereotype by their availability to males as a sexual partner (the tease, the bookworm, the good girl, the cheerleader). Television and popular music have closely intertwined histories: television needs music as a draw to bring teenagers to the set at the same time that the most ardent fans of music do not have time to watch television. Just as Rock 'N' Roll swept Baby Boomers, alternative rock, specifically grunge, defined the rebellious ethos of Gen X.

Chapter 2: Generation X teen TV delves into the multichannel era, including the rise of the cable network MTV. With the addition of FOX as a new network in 1986, *Beverly Hills 90210* (1990–2000) ignited the incorporation of the popular nighttime soap that both applied culturally specific issues of teens, aspirational settings, and a formula for a larger audience. Meanwhile, *Saved by the Bell* (1989–1993, NBC) reinforced standard archetypes and reflected the respectability politics and upper-middle-class lifestyle of the conservative Ronald Reagan administration. Before the rise of nichecasting and premium cable, the short-lived critically acclaimed cult series *My So-Called Life* (1994–1995, ABC) and *Freaks and Geeks* (1999–2000, NBC) marked hybrid genre conventions and representations of outsiders not assimilating to normalcy. This chapter also includes case studies of the stardom that spawned from these two series. For *Freaks and Geeks*, creator Paul Feig and Judd Apatow found success in comedy films. Apatow helped cultivate the careers of *Freaks* alum Seth Rogen and Jason Segel, while James Franco independently thrived and revisited collaboration with his former co-stars. In addition to an in-depth interview behind the development, reception, and legacy of *Life* with its showrunner Winnie Holzman, the chapter also looks at the image of Claire Danes since her role as the series protagonist.

Chapter 3: Millennial teen TV first explores the cultivation of showrunner Jason Schwartz through two of the era's most defining series:

*The O.C.* (2003–2007, Fox) and *Gossip Girl* (2007–2012, CW). The chapter also examines the influence of mobile technologies and digital spaces for the last generation that was not born with the Internet. Analysis of the nature of participatory culture and convergence becomes essential to understanding both this era of television, and the representations surrounding the multi-faceted and often polarizing image of Millennials. The chapter includes an interview with *Degrassi: The Next Generation* (2001–2015, CTV/Much Music/MTV Canada) creator and showrunner Linda Schuyler, as the long-running Canadian public service program that has been praised for its diversity and inclusion, and topical nature and relevance, is detailed in contrast to US commercial teen TV. From *Degrassi* came teen actor turned rapper/mogul Aubrey Drake Graham: a Millennial star known for his international and multicultural identity. Further, an interview with *Gossip Girl* costume designer Eric Daman reveals how fashion played a pivotal role in the identity of the series, and how it provided teen audiences a glimpse into the world of high fashion before the accessibility digital culture.

While many of the "least objectionable" early network teen TV series could not deal with sex and alcohol drinking without a Public Service Announcement, cable and streaming's loose censorship helped ease representations and outcomes. As cable and narrowcasting became more prevalent, teen-oriented channels filled the gap between children's programming on Nickelodeon and Disney and the remainder of adult programs. Now defunct broadcast network UPN (1995–2006), owned by CBS then later Viacom, began to air teen-oriented series like *Sweet Valley High* (based on the popular books) and the relatively unknown *Breaker High* (with Ryan Gosling) as an extension of its UPN Kids lineup. UPN's competitor The WB (1995–2006) premiered other staples such as its first success *Buffy The Vampire* Slayer, as well as *Dawson's Creek*, *Supernatural*, *Popular*, *Charmed*, *Smallville*, and *Gilmore Girls*, although the latter can be considered a family series. Followed by the WB and UPN's decline, the two networks ended, and parent companies CBS and Warner Brothers merged to form the CW, a youth centered channel. As a result, millennial programming began to break new boundaries in terms of representing sex and sexuality, and more inclusive representation. In addition to the influence of Canadian television through Degrassi, the UK's *Skins* (2007–2013) success and influence further addressed the rise of an increasingly globalized television landscape.

Chapter 4: Gen Z TV reveals the potential for new modes of production for teen TV that can further promote inclusivity, through the case study of Hulu's *East Los High* (2013–2017). Through textual analysis and an extensive interview with *East Los* co-showrunner, the hopes of Millennial teen TV are heightened through streaming potential. Streaming platforms such as Netflix, Hulu, and Amazon began to produce their own original programming, and teen TV became an expanding genre both within the US and internationally. This leads to an even savvier potential audience who is exposed to non-English speaking programming, and immigrants and second-generation Americans begin to see themselves represented onscreen. Further, with premium cable platform HBO's foray into its first teen TV series, *Euphoria* (2019–), the genre begins new discourses of "quality TV" for teen TV.

## Conclusion

One goal of this book is to incorporate representation and structures of power into each chapter rather than to assume they can be isolated cases. Since teaching television to university students beginning in my late twenties, I have witnessed a rise in late Millennial and budding Gen X students' outspoken interest in fostering inclusion and social justice in the media, both on and offscreen. The pervasiveness of streaming platforms has debunked the discourse of "television is dead," and the amount of content catered for teens and young adults prove them as a viable targeted demographic, and brings this academic faith in the future of industry creators and leaders.

For many college professors, instructors, and teaching assistants who entered the media studies field out of the same love for the impact of television on their lives, along with a discerning eye for its various problematic factors and structures of power, seeing a classroom of students who demand more from their political, social, cultural, and media landscapes is tremendous to witness.

Just as some of the most culturally significant teen television developed by adults not only considers their own past adolescence, but respects the nature of its young audience, this book is dedicated to maintaining its guidebook status for potential readers.

The chronological nature of this book serves several purposes. The plethora of contemporary television with high production values, and nature of the medium as adaptive to audience's viewing habits, has made younger viewers less willing to engage with historical television. In the past few years, students have also remarked the lack of representation in network TV, in contrast to more recent programming in which they feel they are included. My answer to this is not unlike history educators: understanding the past is essential to making sense of the present and future. And, the aphorism of "history repeats itself" proves true in the shifts in television landscape. While young adults are optimistic about the promises of streaming platforms and inclusion in contrast to the confinements of network TV, they must also discern what is still limited and what patterns persist. Although Netflix has brought a tremendous amount of past and original content catered to new generations, its cancellations of cult programming with limited viewership indicate its decision-making mirrors that of network TV that relied on ratings. Netflix is not a benevolent entity, but a company that seeks maximum profit and monopolization. As young viewers who were accustomed to certain content as a mainstay on certain platforms disappear, the ephemera of digital media becomes all too real. While my students have an extremely high media literacy, and discern the effects of social media consumption and consumerism in relation to mental health, body image, and many more, they must also be as self-reflexive of their position in the world in contrast to past generations.

The divisions of chapters by generations are not meant to cause further differentiation, but to provide entry points into common ground, as well as understanding generational specificity. As viewing demographics show, teen TV is not just for teens. Nostalgia plays a part. So does potential intergenerational viewership between family, friends, romantic partners, and hopefully, students and educators.

While the biological and physiological nature of puberty and adolescence is, to an extent, universal to humankind, the nature of humanity makes it so that constructions and realities of time period, class, nationality, race, ethnicity, religion, geography, gender, and sexuality for teens are vastly different. The notion of generational specificity is influenced by what Kristen Warner calls "cultural specificity."[27] So, along with issues and constructs of race, gender, sexuality, ethnicity, and national identity, among other, teen TV posits the specificity of not only adolescent characters and coming-of-age narratives, but the context of generation to critically engage with the genre and its texts. Teen television also provides entry points into the significance of the intersection of fashion, slang, and music, critical components of the genre. As Mittell states, there is "a need for the need for detailed specificity, not overarching generalities, in exploring media genres."[28] The study of genre is to "negotiate between specificity and generality."[29] Historical formations and genre conventions are thus just as important as burgeoning new media and theoretical approaches. Just as the study of teens, and their generational identity, is often a juxtaposition of the established and the progressive, genre is also both in flux and holds stable roots.

As this book is by no means an exhaustive history of teen TV, it encourages students and academics to pursue their own viewing, research, and analysis of other programming, and provide alternative perspectives on the content presented.

## Notes

1 Todd Gitlin, *Inside Prime Time* (Berkeley and Los Angeles: University of California Press, 2000).
2 Stuart Hall, "Encoding/Decoding," in *Culture, Media, Language: Working Papers in Cultural Studies, 1972–79*, eds. Stuart Hall, Dorothy Hobson, Andrew Lowe and Paul Willis (London: Routledge, 1980), 117–127.
3 John Fiske, "British Cultural Studies and Television," In *Channels of Discourse, Reassembled: Television and Contemporary Criticism*, 2nd ed. (London and New York: Routledge, 1992), 319.

4 Jason Mittell, "A Cultural Approach to Television Genre Theory," *Cinema Journal* 40, no. 3 (Spring 2001): 4.
5 Mittell, "Genre Theory," 8.
6 Ibid.
7 John Caldwell, *Production Culture* (Durham, NC: Duke University Press, 2008), 15.
8 Mark Crispin Miller, "Introduction," in *The Hidden Persuaders*, ed. Vance Packard (Brooklyn, NY: Ig Publishing, 2007), 10.
9 Horace Newcomb and Paul Hirsch, "Television as Cultural Forum: Implications for Research," *Quarterly Review of Film Studies* 8, no. 3 (Summer 1983): 45, https://doi.org/10.1080/10509208309361170; Todd Gitlin, *Inside Prime Time*.
10 Edward Buscombe, "Ideas of Authorship," *Screen* 14, no. 3 (Autumn 1973): 75–85, https://doi.org/10.1093/screen/14.3.75
11 Catherine Grant, "Secret Agents: Feminist Theories of Women's Film Authorship," *Feminist Theory* 2, no. 1 (April 2001): 113–130.
12 Michel Foucault, "What Is an Author?" *Language, Counter-Memory, Practice* (Oxford: Basil Blackwell, 1977). first published Paris, 1969.
13 Miranda J. Banks, John T. Caldwell, and Vicki Mayer, eds., *Production Studies: Cultural Studies of Film/Television Work Worlds* (New York and London: Routledge, 2009), 1.
14 Banks, Caldwell, and Mayer, *Production Studies*, 7.
15 Banks, Caldwell, and Mayer, *Production Studies*, 3.
16 Jonathan Gray, *Show Sold Separately: Promos, Spoilers, and Other Media Text* (New York: New York University Press, 2010).
17 Ibid.
18 Susan Murray, *Hitch Your Antenna to the Stars: Early Television and Broadcast Stardom* (New York and London: Routledge, 2005), 61.
19 Richard Dyer, *Stars* (London: BFI Publishing, 1979).
20 Dyer, *Stars*, 2.
21 Dyer, *Stars*, 3.
22 Dyer, *Stars*, 17.
23 Glyn Davis, Gary Needham, eds., *Queer TV: Theories, Histories, Politics* (London: New York, 2008).
24 Dyer, *Stars*, 34.
25 Laurie Ouellette, *Lifestyle TV* (London: Routledge, 2016).
26 Glenn Creeber, The Television Genre Book, Third Edition (London: BFI, 2015) 38.
27 Kristen Warner, "In the Time of Plastic Representation," *Film Quarterly* 71, no. 2 (Winter 2017).
28 Mittell, "Genre Theory," 16.
29 Ibid.

# 1

# BABY BOOMER TEEN TV

This chapter explores the converging histories of the concept of the American teenager and the emergence of television as a central mass media form—a form that went on to have a profound influence on this new demographic. The chapter places Baby Boomer teens as the first generation that grew up and came of age with the television medium. In this respect, television and popular music also have closely intertwined histories, with both attracting large teen audiences. The chapter sheds light on the type of teen TV shows Baby Boomers were first exposed to; these shows were some of the earliest examples of the genre and included teen serialized soap operas and episodic situational comedies. The chapter also establishes both the foundational teen archetypes and key narrative arcs in the genre, discussing how early iterations of teen TV balanced conforming to societal norms and subverting them so as to adhere to shifts in youth point of view. As such, the genre reflects both the ideological messages that the generation received from the type of programming targeting them during their adolescence, and the rebellious spirit of the burgeoning 1960s counterculture that cut against the grain of those messages.

In addition, the chapter reviews the initial association of TV with youth music, on such programs as *The Ed Sullivan Show* (1948–1971, CBS), *American Bandstand* (1952–1989, ABC), and *Soul Train* (1971–2006), which deal with men as stars and young girls as fans. As Susan J. Douglas argues, what is looked back upon as pathbreaking during the era in question are the boys—James Dean, Elvis, and

The Beatles. This is "because what film and TV recorded girls doing those years—teasing our hair, chasing The Beatles, and doing the watusi in bikinis—was silly, mindless and irrelevant to history".[1] By the same token, however, "we must reject the notion that popular culture for girls and women didn't matter."[2] The history of foundational teen situational comedy programs will also be reviewed here, with a focus on *Dobie Gillis* (1959–1963, CBS) and *Gidget* (1965–1966, ABC), in the 1960s, followed by *Welcome Back Kotter* in the 1970s (1975–1979, ABC). *Dobie* established the televisual archetypes in the genre that would dominate characterization in subsequent programming, while *Kotter* reflected 1970s socially conscious programming and a shift away from focusing on white, upper-middle-class teens. *Gidget*, for its part, reveals a girl-centered space where the Malibu teen was both mischievous enough to provide suitable material for a situational comedy, but also mature enough to be a rare example of a confident teen girl who is seeking to date boys and gain independence from her family. Further, as a surfer girl, Gidget engaged in the sport alongside boys, rather than looking at them admiringly from the sand; in this way, she defied the "beach bunny" trope. However, the short run of the series indicates how difficult it was to place Gidget in broadcast programming, although the revival of the franchise through re-boots, spinoffs, and remakes indicates the lasting influence that the independent teen had on young girls. *Gidget* is just one of many transmedia texts of the franchise that spanned from the 1950s to the 1980s, and it constitutes an early example of teen-girl media culture. In Pamela Robertson Wojcik's *Gidget: Origins of a Teen Girl Transmedia Franchise*, which uncovers the 40 years that the surfer girl character captured audiences through novels, film, television, comics, board games, parodies, and more, Wojcik also contextualizes the cultural specificity of Gidget by situating it in an intertextual network that included such competitors as the *Tammy* series, *La Dolce Vita*, and *The Patty Duke Show*. An approach of this sort allows us "to better understand Gidget's meaning at different points in time, and also its uniqueness as a representation of teen girlhood."[3]

From 1941 to 1945, radio was a key platform for Americans seeking out news about World War II, but it also broadcast early fictional programming. Radio established foundations for the soap opera, situational comedy, and variety show genres later broadcast on TV. Before television, radio established the blueprint for TV broadcasting, including its dominant situational comedy and serialized soap opera genres. *Meet Corliss Archer* (1943–1946) stands out as an early teen radio serial and transmedia example. F. Hugh Herbert introduced Corliss Archer in a magazine story series. This led to Shirley Temple playing Corliss in the 1945 film *Kiss and Tell*, followed by a 1949 sequel titled *A Kiss for Corliss*. Magazine stories, comics, and literary adaptations would become standard models for television formulas, including the teen TV genre.

Baby Boomers are defined as the generation born directly after World War II, between 1946 and 1964. This boom also coincides with the postwar prosperity of the suburbs in the US, which allowed for the proliferation of televisions in suburban homes. The increasing number of televisions would have a huge impact on teenagers, who were a burgeoning market due to their newfound income. The Boomer generation, then, coincides with the rise of television and advertising culture. Teen-specific clothing, magazines, books, music, film, and of course, television, began to be created specifically for this generation.

## Literary Precedents from the 1940s to the 1960s: *The Hardy Boys* and *Nancy Drew*

Twentieth-century literary precedents for teen TV are evident in the *Hardy Boys* and *Nancy Drew* book series, as well as Archie Comics, although their TV adaptations initially came in the form of animated programming. The first *Hardy Boys* installment was published in 1929, and *Nancy Drew*, centering on the Hardy Boys' female counterpart, was released the year after. This pattern of teen-boy original and girl spinoffs would be repeated in teen TV as well. The *Hardy Boys* took a new direction in 1959, with the series aiming both to eliminate its original racial stereotypes and to serve as a competitor to television. In 1969, *The Hardy Boys* animated program premiered on ABC, as a direct competitor to ABC's *Scooby-Doo, Where Are You!* (1969). The series only lasted a season, but it is known for including one of the first black characters on Saturday morning TV and for its incorporation of filmation, in which the opening credits were shot in live-action rather than animated. Designed to appeal to those who liked the co-ed ensemble cast featured in *Scooby-Doo* and subsequent programming, the crossover live-action *The Hardy Boys/Nancy Drew Mysteries* aired from 1977 to 1979 on ABC. By its third and last season, the series was only called *The Hardy Boys*. Just as *The Hardy Boys* book series endured from 1929 to 2005, *The Nancy Drew Mystery Stories* lasted from 1930 to 2003, but its onscreen adaptations never succeeded, despite several attempts in the 1950s, 1970s, 1990s, and 2000s. Most recently, the CW network premiered a new iteration of *Nancy Drew* in 2019 to mixed reviews and ratings; the second season will premiere in 2021. Later, in Chapter 3, I return to the trope of the teen girl detective in an analysis of the series *Vernonia Mars*.

The *Archie Comics* series proved to be more malleable to adaptations. The first Archie-based comic was released in 1941, featuring the characters of Betty Cooper and Jughead Jones. The (*Archie's Girls*) *Betty and Veronica* series premiered in 1942 and was based on the dual "best friends" and "enemies" positions the two girls shared, given that they were caught up in a love triangle with Archie. Jughead's own series (*Archie's Pal*), *Jughead Jones*, premiered in 1949. The spinoff comic *Sabrina the Teenage Witch* premiered in 1962 and was adapted into three different animated series across four decades—*Sabrina the Teenage Witch* (1970–1974, CBS), *Sabrina, The Animated Series* (1999–2000, UPN/ABC), and *Sabrina: The Secrets of a Teenage Witch* (2013–2014, The Hub Network)—as well as two live-action series, namely, *Sabrina the Teenage Witch* (1996–2003, ABC/WB) and *The Chilling Adventures of Sabrina* (2018–, Netflix). In Chapter 4, I further discuss the rebranding of Archie Comics and explore the synergy between the series *Riverdale* (2017–, CW) and Netflix's *Sabrina*.

By the 1960s, the influence of rock 'n' roll music, the counterculture, and the civil rights movement were evident in television programming. Aniko Bodroghkozy asserts that in order to cater to the Baby Boomer demographic, 1960s television essentially had to concede to calls to air programming that reflected youthful rebellion and social and political change through the hippie counterculture, the antiwar movement, campus protests, and guerilla civil rights.[4] Hence, despite broadcast TV's initial reluctance to show Elvis and The Beatles onscreen, their television appearances gave them exposure to a wide audience and led to subsequent success. At the same time, this chapter also delves into the complex racial politics of these popular music series. The battle for desegregation onscreen on *Bandstand* revealed how broadcast executives and their advertisers aimed to keep programming white due not only to political pressure but also to financial incentives. Although *Bandstand* eventually agreed to show popular Black musicians on the air, it was not until the late 1960s that they began to show white and Black teens dancing together onscreen. The racial politics of music programming were further highlighted by the difficulty of keeping any music program for Black youth on the air. In this context, *Soul Train* became the first music series run by a Black man, Don Cornelius; it propelled the careers of Black musical acts and also prominently featured Black dancers. The evolution of popular music shows from *Ed Sullivan* to *Bandstand* to *Soul Train* shows the progress made during the 1960s and 1970s.

Mark Paterson argues that consumption is a part of everyday life, and that consumers are often placed in the binary between "savvy" and "sucker."[5] Marxist theorists believed that consumer capitalism made all consumers suckers based on a system of desires, "false needs" rather than actual needs, creating a:

> consumer who is alienated, unreflexive, inward-looking and routinized, where there is no real separation between work and leisure, and where the most that can be obtained is a form of pseudo-enjoyment where we are constantly in thrall to a series of spectacles that are staged for us.[6]

Yet Paterson asserts that placing consumption within the domain of the everyday explored by cultural studies can "move us on from the 'taken-for-granted' quality of everyday life that we might have assumed."[7] Paterson argues for an analysis of the significance of consumption in everyday life that allows us "to move from economic to symbolic explanations," in order "to meld the material and the symbolic, to analyze consumption as material culture."[8]

Throughout Douglas' book on growing up with the mass media, she credits her exposure to such media as the source of her feminist principles. And as Ellen Willis and other feminist media and sociology scholars have suggested, early exposure to mass media and media literacy does afford young girls and teens a period of transition into adulthood that gives them space to discern and decipher media images and texts. While the 1940s and 1950s attempted to contain teens' behavior, Palladino writes, "there was a growing underworld of working-class teenage 'cats' who had no intention of following adolescent rules."[9]

The underground rebellion simmering in the 1940s and 1950s would foreshadow the youth movements of the 1960s. And while the 1960s saw an explosion of consumerism in their own right, they also brought a challenge to traditional culture with civil rights activism, feminism, and other social justice movements that followed. The period also heralded new subcultures for teens—starting with rock 'n' roll. Whether or not teenage females were "suckers" or "savvy," exposure to mass media and everyday consumption would soon become inevitable.

## Targeting the Teen Consumer and Early Broadcast TV

*Seventeen* magazine was first published in 1944, and magazine culture would become a key resource for teen girls on the subjects of beauty, fashion, media, and social behavior. *Seventeen* would also reveal the potential of the teen market before television. The magazine's first editor, Helen Valentine, had previously shown the value of targeting the college demographic in her role as promotion editor for *Mademoiselle*. Yet manufacturers viewed teens as a "low-wage" group, which they did not think would expand beyond "cokes, candy, record, and trinkets" when it came to marketing.[10] Valentine demonstrated teen buying power through the success of *Seventeen*'s initial edition: within two days,

400,000 copies were sold, and the magazine's circulation surpassed 1 million within 16 months.[11] Analogously, broadcasting had shifted away from sponsored series by the 1950s, modeling itself after the "magazine format" of advertising interspersed with original content.

Valentine had hired researchers to test whether teens would buy more than magazines. The upper-middle-class teen girl demographic was established through the fictionalized "every girl" Teena:

> Teena ... has money of her own to spend ... and what her allowance and pin-money earnings won't buy her, her parents can be counted on to supply. For our girl Teena won't take no for an answer when she sees what she wants in *Seventeen*.[12]

Further, *Seventeen* informed advertisers that 66% of their readers would become homemakers, the most lucrative and profitable market of the time: "*Seventeeners* want to get married, eventually ... naturally! They're dreaming of linens, silver, china—a home of their own."[13] The homemaker demographic was already well-established in daytime radio and television broadcasting, which revolved around the housewife; thus the name "soap opera" originated from the essential product as a sponsor for the daytime dramas.[14] Valentine's researchers also revealed that 77% of American teenagers influenced their parents' domestic buying choices, from groceries to furniture.[15]

Thus, with magazines and particularly *Seventeen*'s launch having set a precedent for advertising to teens, broadcast TV followed suit, with varying results. The daytime soap opera and family sitcom genres represented well-established and successful formulas by the 1950s; establishing teen TV meant taking into account the perspectives, tastes, and interests of the demographic, as *Seventeen* had done. As Eugene Gilbert's early marketing research indicates, "Teenagers with characteristics and outlooks unique to their age groups, cannot be effectively impressed with the same kind of advertising created for adults."[16] While this claim may seem obvious now, the case for individual teen taste had yet to be proven. Valentine would go on to convince fashion and beauty companies to target teens and collaborate with *Seventeen* on ad sales. She also took into account the teenage desire for freedom, and the magazine's early content was presented as wholesome yet understanding advice from a big sister. In essence, she took her teen readers seriously as budding adults. As Grace Palladino writes,

> Helen Valentine promoted an image of well-informed, well-rounded, and ultimately rational teenagers, adults-in-training who could see for themselves that personal discipline and respectable behavior were the quickest routes to teenage independence.[17]

Valentine's approach to teen girls negotiated a path between understanding their maturity and upholding a respectability politics that did not scandalize parents, in contrast to Helen Gurley Brown's more disruptive takeover as *Cosmopolitan*'s Editor-in-Chief in 1965.

Television would soon be a US domestic staple, and it would expand its appeal to future homemakers. As such, broadcast television established a set of rules for the representation of children that fit with the goals of Least Objectionable Programming (LOP). Specifically, the National Association of Broadcasters established that neither programming nor commercials would undermine "respect for parents, the home, or moral conduct."[18] Film, at the time, had more freedom to show teens engaging in rebellious behavior, although the industry's own Motion Picture Production Code of the 1930s also prescribed bad consequences for characters that diverged from moral standards. The Code would be loosened by the 1960s as a result of the counterculture and the civil rights movement, not to mention the influence of European cinema and films associated with the New American Cinema, such as *Bonnie and Clyde* (1967) and *Easy Rider* (1969).

On average, two-thirds of American families purchased TV sets between 1948 and 1955.[19] At the same time, the postwar gender norms of the US were designed to produce housewife-consumers from white middle-class teen girls. Mass culture showed what teenage independence might allow, but only as a stop on the way to domesticity. Upper-middle-class white girls would also go on to college, where their higher education became another respectable accomplishment before housewifery. The second-wave feminist movement, initiated by Betty Friedan's book *The Feminine Mystique* (1963), chronicled the stories of college-educated women who did not find the fulfillment that 1950s TV housewives did in their domesticity. Accordingly, one of the movement's demands was for women to be allowed to enter the white-collar workforce. Lower-class women, of course, were already working to provide for themselves and their families. The introduction of the birth control pill in 1960 and shifting social norms also gave young girls and women greater agency over their sexuality and reproductive rights. As a result, growing concern subsided over the decline in marriage and age at the time of first marriage became one of many moral panics.[20] TV series directly influenced by the second-wave feminist movement, including *That Girl* (1966–1971, ABC) and *Mary Tyler Moore* (1970–1977, CBS), which shifted from having domestic housewives to single career women as protagonists, catered to the new demographic that identified with these onscreen women. This feminist influence would also transfer to teen series such as *Gidget*.

In early radio-turned-television domestic sitcoms, from *The Goldbergs* (1949–1956, CBS/NBC) to *Father Knows Best* (1954–1958, CBS/NBC), teen characters were secondary to their parents. *Father Knows Best* exemplifies the father's patriarchal dominance over a subservient housewife and the couple's obliging teenagers. Any teen rebellions, such as daughter Betty's desire to take on a male-dominated profession in the 1956 episode "Betty the Engineer," would ultimately be squashed and coupled with a moral lesson, which in this case was that a teenage girl should focus on marrying future engineers, rather than trying to become one. While the father figure is also a source for comedy and can be shown as fumbling and awkward, he still reigns over the family, mirroring postwar anxieties over masculine dominance. During the war, women took over jobs traditionally held by men, but then the soldiers returned, and mass culture reinstated traditional gender norms. Whiteness, particularly the White Anglo-Saxon Protestant (WASP) identity, was the standard for sitcom families living in suburban bliss. Non-white characters were either absent from television or included as servants, background characters, or villains. While domestic network sitcoms such as *Leave it to Beaver* (1957–1964, CBS) emphasized the young boy protagonist in its title, the series is really about the idealized suburban family, which included Theodore "Beaver" Cleaver's older teenage brother, Wally. For its part, *The Adventures of Ozzie and Harriet* (1952–1966, ABC) established Rickie Nelson as a nascent teen idol who straddled both music and acting careers.

Before the rules of LOP and broadcast were established, *The Goldbergs* contrasted sharply with the WASP suburban image of American families. The teens in *The Goldbergs*, as first-generation Americans, taught their Jewish immigrant parents how to negotiate the surrounding culture. In both the radio and TV versions of the series, the teenage son, Sammy, has a Bar Mitzvah ceremony and celebration. The parents and their adolescent children discuss first loves as well. As the matriarch, Mollie says in her Yiddish-inflected dialect: "Oy, vhat's sweeter dan your foist love letter, ha?"[21] Such inclusion was threatened by the blacklist of the 1950s, however. This blacklist, inspired by fears of communism, pushed writers and producers from marginalized groups, as well as female writers and producers, out of the television industry.[22]

## Early Teen Soaps

An early daytime serial that catered to teens, *Never Too Young* (1965–1966, ABC), featured a fictional cast of adventurous Malibu-based adolescents, including Tony Dow of *Leave it To Beaver*, who congregate at their local beach hangout, the High Dive. The Dive also functioned as a venue, and the short-lived series featured performances by popular acts such as Marvin Gaye, Paul Revere and The Raiders, The Sunrays, The Castaways, and The Girls.[23]

Meanwhile, *Love Is a Many Splendored Thing* (1967–1973, CBS) was developed by Irma Phillips, who created the soap opera genre and its numerous hits (from *Guiding Light* to *As the World Turns*) during the heyday of radio. The series predated the premiere of long-running, youth-targeting soaps created by Phillips' mentee, Agnes Nixon, including *One Life to Live* (1968–2012, ABC) and *All My Children*

(1970–2013, ABC). In keeping with the transmedia nature of TV, *Love Is a Many Splendored Thing* was a spinoff of the eponymous 1955 film. The film also featured an eponymous song by the Aces, which won the 1955 Academy Award for Original Song, and which the TV adaptation used as its theme song. The story was adapted from Han Suyin's best-selling autobiographical novel, *Many-Splendoured Thing* (1952), about her life as a Eurasian physician who fell in love with a married British journalist. Suyin's account explores the sociopolitical context for issues of class and race in England and mainland China. The series, as a spinoff set in San Francisco, centers on Mia Elliot upon her arrival from Hong Kong to study medicine in the US. As in the original story, Mia's mother is a physician and her father is a war correspondent. In addition to love triangles and serialized romances, the series also features issues such as immigration, abortion, divorce, and drug addiction and overdoses. It remains distinct for its successful incorporation of young protagonists in college and their early career years, rather than domestic storylines catering to housewives. The series also featured an interracial love story, with an Asian character as the protagonist, and a score designed to appeal to a youthful target audience, dominated by jazz and pop rather than traditional orchestral compositions.[24] Overall, the series suffered from a lack of continuity after Phillips left as head writer, but it was a rare example of ethnic diversity and the inclusion of young characters in a daytime serial that reflected changing demographics.

## *The Many Loves of Dobbie Gillis*, *Gidget*, and Early Teen TV Sitcoms

Although teen characters in family sitcoms were more the norm than individual series about the lives of Baby Boomer teens, series such as *The Many Loves of Dobie Gillis* and *Gidget* stand out as early primetime teen TV examples that would help establish the genre. *The Many Loves of Dobie Gillis* (1959–1963, CBS) originated in stories published by Max Shulman in popular magazines and books, beginning in 1945. Before the television series, Shulman adapted his short stories into a screenplay for the 1953 musical film, *The Affairs of Dobie Gillis*. The cast featured vaudeville, stage, film, and TV star Bobby Van and Debbie Reynolds (the year following her breakout role in *Singin' in the Rain*). The film was also Bob Fosse's onscreen debut, which marked the beginning of the end of his budding acting career. Fosse would go on to become an illustrious choreographer and director for stage and screen, directing *Cabaret* (1972) and *Chicago* (1975).

Shulman was also involved in the television adaptation, which is cited as one of the first network programs featuring teenagers as the main characters. In the treatment archives, Shulman states that the show's popularity was pre-tested based on the stories' established popularity.[25] He also cites its rare teenager point of view and notes that the audience consists of younger teens and middle-schoolers, not the college-aged students it depicts; these older students had considerable social freedom and were less likely to have television sets in their dorm rooms. According to Shulman, the character of Dobie Gillis (Dwayne Hickman) is relatable because he is "normal" and an "everyman."[26] This normalness is somewhat undercut by Dobie's determination to go to college, which stands out as a rebellion against his father, who is blue-collar and would rather his son take over the family business, Gillis Grocery.

The sitcom formula of *Dobie Gillis* centers on the titular character's pursuit of a fledgling romance that backfires and leads to his breaking rules, and sometimes even laws. By the end of every episode, Dobie learns a moral lesson that rights his wrongs. This pattern, however, does not prevent him from breaking new rules in the future. The series thus serves as an early negotiation of teen Baby-Boomer rebellion: pursuing college and potential new career opportunities instead of settling for the family business; using these years as a period of freedom and mischief-making; meeting different girls rather than settling down and marrying at an early age. These moral lessons serve as proverbial, patriarchal "teaching moments" for younger viewers.

Although the series is episodic, based on the new girls Dobie falls for and attempts to woo, his persistent crush on Thalia (Tuesday Weld) is serialized. Thalia, in contrast, is interested in a "moneyed partner," and she is pursuing higher education to avoid her older sister's mistake of marrying a poor man. Here we see a common tendency for the upper-middle-class, privileged white women of the time: attending university as a means for marriage and upward mobility, not career training. With Dobie playing the role of the relatable everyman, his friend and sidekick, Maynard (Bob Denver), is a "beatnik" who evokes the popular music of the period. However, 1960s countercultures were not presented in fictional television programming as much as they were in the music and cinema of the time. *Gillis* and *Gidget*, though, reveal the beginnings of these countercultural trends and the initial adolescent, primarily apolitical context in which they emerged. (I discuss *Gidget* later in this chapter.)

Gillis and the gang returned in the 1977 Movie of the Week, *Whatever Happened to Dobie Gillis?*, which centered on the characters' 20-year high school reunion. Shulman's original script, however, contrasts starkly with what aired: he was fired as the writer. Mirroring the new socially conscious themes and drives of the 1960s and 1970s, the movie was a dark look at the consequences of conforming and rebelling. While Dobie conforms, Maynard the beatnik rebels. At the beginning of the film, Dobie learns that his counterpart left their hometown and committed suicide. Dobie, on the other hand, has married a woman named Zelda (Sheila James), and he is a pharmacist who operates his own business along with his wife. (In the original series, Zelda is depicted as an undesirable romantic partner and an ultimate "safe" choice.) He also has a son, Davey. Viewers learn that Dobie still thinks of, and pines for, his lost love, Thalia.

Eventually, Maynard returns, confessing that he faked his death to avoid confronting the successful people from his past at the high school reunion. He was briefly the school janitor but failed in this career due to his anti-establishment orientation, which is shown here as immature. Maynard is still portrayed as unkempt and rebellious, and he plays the bongos with Dobie's son. With rock music now an established genre for teenagers, Davey, in contrast to the younger Maynard, is not othered due to his tastes. Dobie states that his son is also "girl crazy," as he once was. So, while Maynard did not grow up enough, Dobie may have grown up too soon. The film provides little closure for these now middle-aged characters living in the 1970s. Maynard eventually moves in with the Gillis family, so they can look after him; this plot twist shows how new families can be formed outside the traditional nuclear family.

## Dobie Gillis' Lasting Influence on Teen TV

While Dobie may be primarily known by those who watched the initial run and syndication of the original show, *Gillis*'s influence can be traced in what evolved into a much bigger youth franchise, beginning with the animated CBS series *Scooby-Doo, Where Are You!* (1969). Most striking are the archetypes of the four characters: Fred can be directly compared to Dobie, Daphne to Thalia, Shaggy to Maynard, and Velma to Zelda.[27] These core, all-American popular boys and girls would surface in the future as the athlete/jock, the "preppie" student, and the cheerleader, along with the "nerdy" girl and the accompanying "nerd" boy, or the girl or boy who is a member of a music-driven subculture.

These four core archetypes, or stock characters, and their accompanying narratives and formulaic plotlines would be played out in many ensuing teen series, or family series with a dominant teen cast. Characters would either instantiate one of these four archetypes, fall into a hybridized form, or defy the norm, in a dynamic that reflected the juxtaposition of young people's progressive attitudes with the mass media's attempt to quell youthful rebellion by teaching moral lessons. For example, casting the "all-American" athlete as the perpetual hero leaves out of the picture other ethnicities, races, immigrants, and those who do not pursue sports. Further, insofar as marrying well is the norm for the Thalia or Daphne prototype, a young girl is identified only by her appearance and ability to become a promising partner. These two initial archetypes drove how teens in early domestic sitcoms were depicted. Further, in later teen series that portrayed sex and the loss of virginity, the Thalia and Zelda characters often fell into the virgin/whore dichotomy.

Meanwhile, several commentators have credited the *Gidget* literary, film, and television transmedia franchise with placing surfing into mainstream US culture. The multiple book installments and films, on both the large and the small screens, surpass the brief television program that lasted from 1965 to 1966 on ABC, and that consisted of a total of 32 episodes. *Gidget* initiated the type of teen TV series set in an idyllic Southern California, later exemplified by shows like *Saved by the Bell*, *Beverly Hills 90210*, and *The O.C.*

Gidget originated in a novel written by Frederick Kohner called *Gidget, the Little Girl with Big Ideas* (1957), about a teen girl, her friends, and surf culture in Malibu, the Los Angeles seaside enclave. Several subsequent novelizations defined the SoCal teen as mobile and independent, rather than confined to her home in preparation for a life of domesticity. These later installments included *Cher Papa* (1959), *The Affairs of Gidget* (1963), *Gidget in Love* (1965), *Gidget Goes Parisienne* (1966), and *Gidget Goes New York* (1968).

The *Gidget* films both preceded and became part of the proliferation of the "beach party" film genre, which is officially credited to American International Pictures, and which was dominant from 1963 to 1967. Like teen-oriented B movies before them, they were mostly low-budget affairs that fused comedy, romance, and music for teen entertainment, featuring teens or young adults as the main characters. Columbia Pictures released three *Gidget Films*, each with different young actors playing the titular role: *Gidget* (1959, Sandra Dee), *Gidget Goes Hawaiian* (1961, Deborah Walley), and *Gidget Goes to Rome* (1963, Cindy Caro). The made-for-TV films *Gidget Goes Hawaiian* (1961) and *Gidget Goes to Rome* (1963), written by Ruth Brooks Flippen, reveal that women could find entry points as writers for TV films and series. Flippen would go on to write for one of the first successful single-career-woman series, *That Girl* (1966–1971, starring Marlo Thomas).

## *Gidget* and Baby Boomer Stardom: Sally Field

Although the series was short-lived, *Gidget* helped launch the long and industrious career of Sally Field. Born in 1946, she first appeared as an extra in the 1962 film *Moon Pilot*. Although her first star project, *Gidget*, was short-lived, her television career escalated in the 1960s and 1970s with *The Flying Nun* (1967–1970) and *The Girl with Something Extra* (1973–1974). She won her first Emmy Award for her performance in the 1976 mini-series *Sybil*. Field's film acting career thrived in the 1970s, and she would not return to television until the 2000s. Field won the Academy Award for Best Actress twice, for *Norma Rae* (1979) and *Places in the Heart* (1984), and her film career continued to flourish throughout the 1980s and 1990s.

From the beginning of television to the 1990s, TV actors who moved on to film were discouraged from returning to their roots, as cinema generally promised greater prestige and profit. Stars who shifted from film to TV were generally perceived as failures. As later stardom examples will show, the implosion of the film industry in the late 1990s and the subsequent expansion of television, including higher production values, led to discussions of "quality TV" discourses and a new cache for the medium. Additionally, film stars who appear in television series add credibility to "quality TV," and are often followed by critical praise and accolades. For example, Field's own television return in 2001, on the critical and commercial success *ER* (1994–2009, NBC), gained her a Primetime Emmy Award for Outstanding Guest Actress in a Drama Series. In further defiance of the supposedly lowbrow nature of television and its negative effects on actors' reputation, Field made her stage debut on Broadway the following year, in Edward Albee's *The Goat, or Who Is Sylvia?* After 15 years, she returned to Broadway in 2017, for the revival of Tennessee Williams' *The Glass Menagerie*, which led to a Tony Award nomination. In the 2000s, Field pursued film, television, and stage roles. She depicted the family matriarch in ABC's *Brothers and Sisters* (2006–2011) and received a Best Supporting Actress Oscar nomination for her role in Steven Spielberg's *Lincoln* (2012). She was also featured as Aunt May in *The Amazing Spider-Man* (2012) and *The Amazing Spider-Man 2: Rise of Electro* (2014).

Just as Dobie Gillis is "girl crazy," Gidget is "boy crazy." Instead of being a midwestern everyman, Gidget is a Southern California "beach bunny." From her father's profession as a prominent UCLA professor to her clothes and surroundings, Gidget's upper-class background is clear. This is an early example of "aspirational" teen TV, in parallel with the marketing strategies used in *Seventeen*. Such shows often take place in Southern California, or in America's more populated and affluent suburbs.

The central relationship in the series is between Gidget and her widowed father, Russ, who provides her with moral wisdom. Their relationship is often perceived as "too close," and nearly co-dependent. In Episode 4, "Daddy Come Home," she initially encourages Russ to begin dating, but soon worries when he arrives home late. In Episode 22, "We Got Each Other," her jealousy once again increases as her father dates again.

With its depictions of Gidget's married sister, Anne, and brother-in-law, John, a psychology student, the 1960s program presents an alternative to the onscreen nuclear family. In Episode 9, "Is It Love or Symbiosis?," the couple encourage Russ to send Gidget to a boarding school in Paris, arguing that he and she have grown too dependent on each other. More generally, Gidget navigates her life through school, home, social gatherings, and, of course, beaches. Like Dobie, she is meant to provide a teenage point of view. Gidget directly addresses the audience, breaking the fourth wall, engaging in intimacy, and narrating her own story. Eighteen-year-old Field played the 15-year-old high school student.

In the pilot episode, Gidget is introduced to the sport of surfing, its culture, and its surfer boys. Instead of just ogling the boys' athleticism, she surfs alongside them. Of course, she also falls in love with several surfers throughout the season. Her first love, Jeff "Moondoggie" Matthews, is technically her boyfriend, but he is away at Princeton University, so she is free to date other boys. This premise of the show is clearly inspired by the new social norms of the free love movement and second-wave feminism. Yet, since Gidget and Moondoggie eventually marry, the show also adheres to the Baby Boomer understanding that marriage is looming, and that adolescent freedom is fleeting. And Gidget is also aware of a desire to remain in her same social class beyond adolescence. She soon learns that some surfer boys do not share her upward mobility, as in Episode 3, "The Great Kahuna." Here, her new romantic prospect is content with a squarely middle-class life, which is not aligned with Gidget's goals. While Moondoggie likewise goes through a surfer phase, he remains an upwardly mobile middle-class suitor, and he goes on to become an Ivy League college student who can provide for her. In this way, the show reflects the need for teenage girls, as potential future housewives, to ensure their financial security by carefully managing their romantic prospects. While Gidget can have other boys in the interim, her marriage to Moondoggie is essentially arranged. That said, in the different versions of her story made possible by a transmedia text, Gidget actually embarks on several careers. Across the books and films, Gidget becomes a waitress, a teacher, a travel guide, and a fashion model. As the franchise moved into the 1960s and 1970s, though, Gidget reflected upper-middle-class, and second-wave feminist, career aspirations.

The open relationship between Gidget and Moondoggie is indeed rare in the teen TV of this period—and, in general; this relationship can be seen as reflecting the idea that the cosmopolitan teenager is more mature than her suburban or rural counterpart. The teen girl in the city displays greater social and sexual maturity. This same trope will be highlighted in subsequent series like *Beverly Hills 90210* and *Gossip Girl*, among others. That said, Jeff debuts in Episode 15, "Too Many Cooks," when he comes home the same weekend Gidget has planned a date with someone else. While they are free during this time, it is clear they will be married soon (the two are wed in the 1972 film *Gidget Gets Married*). In Episode 22, "In and out with the In-Laws," she meets his parents.

Meanwhile, Anne and John's involvement is pervasive in the series. When Gidget asks her brother-in-law to a luau, his attempts to fit into surfer culture lead her friends to call him a "poseur," i.e., a phony or imitator. This episode relies on the coded language of Baby Boomer teens. John nearly functions as the "nerd" friend, as the studious academic who instructs the family on elements of child psychology. Yet the roles are reversed when Gidget counsels John and Anne on their relationship in Episode 5, "Gidget Gadget." While therapy and psychology were still taboo subjects at the time, Gidget and her family's engagement and openness suggest progressive tendencies. Likewise, in a slight nod to the political and socioeconomic climate, Gidget protests the rise of movie ticket prices in Episode 10, "All the Best Diseases Are Taken." This semi-rebellious spirit returns when she launches a campaign to keep her favorite restaurant, The Shaggy Dog, open in Episode 23, "Operation Shaggy Dog." Here she collides with her father, because the restaurant is set to be replaced with a new museum that he is supporting as a board member. Gidget's independence is further apparent when she takes up learning to drive at school and purchases a hearse in Episode 6, "A Hearse, a Hearse, My Kingdom for a Hearse."

Gidget also possesses a mature attitude about fashion trends and about love and courtship. Her best friend, Larue, whom Gidget gives a makeover in Episode 11, is the opposite. Larue has a nonexistent love life; she is coded as the "nerdy" girl who is less attractive and outgoing, although, because she is a year older than Gidget, she has more freedom, as indicated by her being able to drive. Gidget's new surfer friends find Larue uncool, particularly when she arrives at the beach modestly dressed. In Episode 19, "Gidget's Career," she accompanies a nervous Larue to her guitar lesson. Gidget is asked to join the band; they have a chance to appear on TV but want to kick Larue out. The nerd stereotype is further exemplified by a young, bespectacled Richard Dreyfus playing a boy version of nerdiness, Durf the Drag. In Episode 14, "Gidget's Foreign Policy," she transforms a shy and engaged Swedish college student into a provocative, "boy crazy" version of Gidget.

As the plot of this last episode suggests, Gidget's maturity often competes with inappropriate and potentially illicit behavior. In Episode 17, "I Love You, I Love You, I Love You, I Think," the teen falls for an older surfer over the summer, only to start her fall semester and find that this love interest is her new math teacher. In Episode 27, "Independence – Gidget Style," she starts a part-time job at a teen diner to buy her father a birthday present, but her family mistakenly believes she's taken up a position at a Gentleman's Club.

### *Welcome Back Kotter* (1975–1979, ABC)

Just as *Splendored Thing* stood out as a youth-centered daytime soap, *Welcome Back Kotter* featured high school teacher Gabe Kotter and his class of ethnically and racially diverse students, known as the "Sweathogs," in blue-collar Brooklyn. Created, written by, and starring burgeoning comedian Gabe Kaplan, the series was part of the socially conscious wave of 1970s primetime programming from Norman Lear and Mary Tyler Moore Productions. The series begins as Kotter is hired to return to his alma mater, where the vice principal is convinced the remedial class will either drop out or be expelled from school. Kotter, however, is himself a former Sweathog and remedial student, and the series thus explores the complexities of intergenerational classroom dynamics. These dynamics mirror how *The Goldbergs* established a mutually enriching relationship between parents and teens. A year before the premiere of *Kotter*, former Goldbergs writer and producer James Comack's series *Chico and the Man* (1974–1978, NBC) became the first network series to be set in a Mexican-American neighborhood. In this way, as was common in the teen genre, adult-centered series established the foundations that would later be used for shows with a viable adolescent audience. Hence, the teen genre is often a hybrid of other popular subgenres, including crime, fantasy, science fiction, and adventure, among others. Although it is not "purely" a teen series, the high school setting and predominantly adolescent characters make *Kotter* a significant contribution to the genre, as well as a prime representative of 1970s socially conscious programming. It also establishes those outside the high school social hierarchy as protagonists. *Kotter* was also influenced by socially conscious programming created, developed, and produced by Norman Lear. Lear's *All in The Family* (1971–1979, CBS) shows the generational political divide between the family patriarch, the satirical Archie Bunker (Carroll O'Connor) of the Silent Generation, and his liberal Baby Boomer daughter Gloria Stivic (Sally Struthers) and hippie son-in-law Michael ("Mike") Casimir Stivic (Rob Reiner). The series has been heralded for delving into social and political issues of the 1970s, from abortion to the Vietnam War. Gloria's mother, and Archie's wife, Edith (Jean Stapleton), serves as the warmhearted mediator, and less outspoken family member. However, when Edith does intervene, she imparts wisdom. Lear's *Family* (and his other series) also helped black writers and actors enter the television industry. As a franchise showrunner with several series under his domain in the 1970s, he would delegate to junior writer-producers. The popular black-cast sitcom *The Jeffersons* (1975–1985, CBS), for example, was a *Family* spinoff that came about in this manner.

*Kotter* propelled the career of future movie star John Travolta as Vincent "Vinnie" Barbarino. This set the tone for his on and offscreen Italian American lothario persona. After *Kotter*, Travolta would go on to become a Baby Boomer star. In 1977, he starred in the box-office success *Saturday Night Fever*. In his depiction of Tony Manero, Travolta once again played a working-class Italian American, part of a generational subculture. *Fever* was known for popularizing the disco genre, with songs by The Bee Gees such as "Stayin' Alive" and "How Deep is Your Love," and for Travolta's masterful dancing. The soundtrack remains one of the best-selling of all time, with 15 million copies sold, surpassed only by Whitney Houston's *The Bodyguard*, at 18 million. Other film soundtracks that compare with *Fever* include Prince's *Purple Rain* (13 million copies); *Dirty Dancing* and *Titanic* (11 million copies); and Travolta's other seminal 1970s film, *Grease* (eight million copies).[28] *Grease* (1978), a teen musical film, exudes the sort of 1950s nostalgia that was part of the contemporary sociopolitical conservative wave—a conservative wave also exemplified by *American Graffiti* (1973) and by domestic sitcoms with teen protagonists, such as *Happy Days* (1974–1984, ABC). In the 1980s, the popular comedy/drama series (with no live audience or laugh track) *The Wonder Years* (1988–1993) depicted the late 1960s to the early 1970s through the coming-of-age story of Kevin Arnold, a middle-class suburban teen. More generally, the 1980s was a high-water mark for primetime domestic sitcoms and soap operas, many of which had teen characters that largely upheld conservative family values.[29]

## Early Music TV for Teen Baby Boomers

Rock 'n' roll undeniably changed the teenage market and helped expand it beyond middle-class demographics. As a music genre for youth, one that distinguished teens from adults, it afforded new independence and an identity that was not inherently tied to consumerism and socioeconomic standing. The rock subculture and its fashion enabled teens to express this mutually shared individuality. *Gidget*, for example, revealed the surfing culture that popular "surf rock" musicians such as The Beach Boys personified. Maynard of *Gillis* was the resident Beatnik. Rock 'n' roll established a teenage lifestyle that could be televised. As Palladino puts it in her study of teenagers in the US, "Like the jitterbugs, zoot suiters, and teenage cats who preceded them, teenage rebels wanted to walk on the wild side while they were still young enough and free to enjoy it."[30]

Music, via rock 'n' roll and R&B, is central to Baby Boomer identity. While going to the cinema and attending concerts revealed teenagers' desire to escape the confines of their house and their family lives, television still provided a source of entertainment for young Boomers, especially those too young to go out on their own. Three dominant series known for their performances and dancing, *The Ed Sullivan Show* (1948–1971, CBS), *American Bandstand* (1952–1989, ABC), and *Soul Train* (1971–2006, CBS and various syndicated channels), showcased popular music culture on television. While Frank Sinatra had a teen cult following in the 1940s, Elvis and The Beatles marked the intersection of rock 'n' roll stardom and fandom, on the one hand, and the power of television performances, on the other hand. Elvis, in particular, broke broadcast records along with album sales, proving him to be a musician of the television era. Palladino states that Elvis made the youth market "the most dynamic component of the domestic economy."[31]

By the 1960s, advertisers were convinced of the teen demographic's buying power. In 1964, 22 million Baby Boomer teens lived in the US. Their own spending money based on jobs made up $12 billion of the market, while they also spent $13 billion of their parents' money. Music and fashion were embedded in the teen market, whose cumulative album purchases totaled $100 million; teen girls alone spent $3.5 billion on clothes.[32] Pepsi branded itself as the soda option "for those who think young." Beyond Gilbert's foundational book, *Advertising and Marketing to Young People* (1957), major magazines such as *Life*, *Time*, *Look*, *Esquire*, and *Newsweek* expanded their coverage of teen culture.[33]

Like the history of rock 'n' roll in general, Elvis' career emulated both the musical stylings and performance of Black blues and R&B musicians. His covers of Black musicians can be traced back to their original recordings through his album credits, but their visual influence is less apparent, since the Black performers Presley watched on Memphis's Beale Street were rarely if ever filmed for a mass audience.[34] David R. Shumway states that Elvis brought this Black subculture to the mainstream through his television performances, which began in 1955. While Elvis' pelvic shaking may appear mild to contemporary audiences, at the time it marked an unprecedented display of sexuality. His early 1956 concerts led to police threats of arrest for "disorderly conduct."[35] Known as "Elvis the Pelvis," he was banned from *The Ed Sullivan Show* after his rendering of Big Mama Thornton's "Hound Dog" on *The Milton Berle Show* in June 1956. In previous performances, Elvis was confined to his acoustic guitar, yet Berle encouraged him to play without his instrument, advising, "Let them see you, son."[36] With 40 million viewers watching Elvis perform, "Hound Dog" on Berle brought the musician both fame and infamy: "The episode horrified parents and press, delighted the youth, and made Elvis a star."[37] His July 1956 "Hound Dog" performance on *The Steve Allen Show* was a stark contrast: to prevent any further perceptions of obscenity, the song was slowed down to a ballad, in which tuxedo-clad Elvis crooned to a basset hound wearing a top hat. This appearance can, and has been, interpreted in several ways. Some believe Elvis appeased the mainstream audience to become a star; others view the act as humiliating. These kinds of negotiations and push-and-pull between norms and their subversion are integral to any artist who crosses over to the mainstream.

Following his undeniable ratings success, Sullivan withdrew his Elvis ban and offered $50,000 for three performances, triple the amount he was given by *Allen*.[38] His *Ed Sullivan* debut in 1956 was the most-watched broadcast of the decade, drawing an estimated 60 million viewers, or 82.6 percent of the potential TV audience.[39] After negative responses to his full-body thrusting, including crowds who burned his effigy in Nashville and St. Louis, Elvis's third *Sullivan* performance in 1957 was tamer, and recorded from the waist up. Yet by this point, Elvis had already contributed to turning rock 'n' roll into pop, after selling 10 million records in the first 10 months of 1956 and topping the rock 'n' roll, Rhythm and Blues, Country and Pop charts.[40] His sex appeal drew teenage fans, but curbing it was necessary to reach an even wider audience. Elvis would give credit to the Black artists he emulated, but his reputation remains contentious based on questions of his appropriation or stealing of black culture.

Elvis, who modeled himself after another immortalized teen icon, James Dean, was not initially understood as a teen performer; but once his demographic was understood, "teenagers would be his major market"—though, as David Shumway notes, "cause and effect are hard to disentangle here, and we cannot safely assert either that Elvis' persona was designed to attract his teen audience or that the audience was attracted to a persona that emerged without conscious design."[41] That said, Shumway reports that Elvis' concerts and early TV performances were filled with predominantly teen-girl audiences whose responses are characterized as "scream, faint, and otherwise enact ecstasy."[42] This fanbase was foundational for Elvis and would become the marker of success for future rock stars. Before Elvis, no blueprint existed for the rock 'n' roll star, as the position and career did not exist. Elvis's manager, Colonel Tom Parker, had a clear goal to make him a popular musician/pop star. As Shumway writes, "if the teen audience was to be Elvis' base, the peak he would try to reach would be a mass audience of white middle class [viewers] of all ages."[43] Elvis' approach thus mirrored broadcast television's goals for ratings. Although he hoped to become a film star like Dean, Elvis' success did not translate to the box office. Fox, in an attempt to "capitalize on the teenage craze," sped the release of his film debut, which ultimately flopped.[44] Although Elvis would go on to make several films, he did not achieve movie star status.

As it unfolded in the 1960s, Beatlemania can be "best understood as a reprise of the reaction to Elvis but on a much grander scale."[45] While The Beatles did not engage in the sexualized dancing of their predecessor, their perceived effeminate nature (long hair, bangs, slim figures) stood in stark contrast to US norms for masculine identity. The hippie subculture that pervaded the 1960s and 1970s was defined by this feminization via long hair. Thus the 1969 film *Easy Rider*, in a diner scene set in rural America, shows teenage girls and young women fawning over this new counterculture, while elders and other local residents are visibly disgusted by the hippies' "queer" looks and their rock music, even if the teen music lovers are infatuated. While Elvis was influenced by Black R&B, The Beatles took their cue from the girl groups of the 1960s, like The Shirelles, The Shangri-Las, The Chiffons, The Dixie Cups, The Ronettes (The Spectrum Sound), and The Cookies, followed by Motown's The Marvelettes, Martha and the Vandellas, and The Supremes.

### *American Bandstand* and *Soul Train*

As Palladino discusses, TV broadcasters as well as the companies paying for advertising spots were initially skeptical of the teen consumer. The postwar 1940s was a period of experimentation for tapping into the adolescent market. The 1946 show *Teen Canteen*, a sponsored series that modeled itself on successful music radio shows, quickly failed on television. Palladino states, "in 1946, both advertisers and television executives thought that teenagers were more trouble than they were worth in the marketplace."[46] It was not the formula that led to this flop, however, as *American Bandstand*'s success would show a decade later. Teen girl fandom and consumerism capitalized on the crossover success of rock 'n' roll and televisual culture.[47]

*Bandstand* (1952–1989) initially aired as a local Philadelphia series in 1952, before going nationwide in 1957. Andrea Kelley notes that *Bandstand* originally catered to maturing audiences, but as the influence of youth culture and rock 'n' roll increased, it began accommodating its new, younger viewers by 1956.[48] Matthew F. Delmont cites *Bandstand* as the first national daily television series targeted at teens.[49] Popular bands would perform with local teen dancers who became stars in their own right, a set-up that allowed for a more inclusive and modern spin than *Sullivan*. *Bandstand*'s host, Dick Clark, also symbolized a newer generation of hosts younger than the traditional Sullivan. The teen experience was on display; thus, as Ilana Nash writes, *Bandstand* "fostered a united point of identity for teens around the country, exhibiting the clothing and dancing style of distant peers."[50] Its live broadcast encouraged the intimacy and immediacy necessary for fans to be involved in the new consumer landscape. This format would be a clear precedent to the culture MTV later created on cable television, through live performances, music videos, and various programming catering to youth culture.

Whereas *Bandstand* excluded Black teenagers from participating in the series, its counterpart, the local Philadelphia series *They Shall Be Heard* (1952–1953), was a forum-style live program that assembled an inclusive group of teens to discuss racial and religious prejudice.[51] The contrast between the series illustrates the lack of educational and public support that was (and is) characteristic of US commercial broadcast television that prioritizes advertisement-based programming.[52] In essence, *Bandstand*'s emphasis on the white teen demographic "fit neatly into the ethos of postwar consumer culture."[53] *They Shall Be Heard*, by contrast, exemplifies television's attempted innovation in the direction of inclusion and civil rights; but its short life foreshadows similar teen programming that faced cancellation when it did not meet the expectations of the network and advertisers. The multi-channel expansion and streaming era, based on subscriptions rather than advertisements, would better facilitate such innovation. The expectations of audiences would also change, and even network television adapted to the shifts in genre and format due to the influence of its cable competitors.

The battle between progress and profit is one of the most defining elements of television programming, and teen TV continues to be a telling lens through which to examine this relationship. Rock 'n' roll viewed as both a genre and a subculture, and *Bandstand* taken as a case study, show "the complex mix of community and commerce" that intersected, in turn, with US sociopolitical issues.[54] *Bandstand* became a site for debates about civil rights in the 1960s, as desegregation laws were enacted. Delmont writes that *Bandstand* producers incorporated a "color blind" casting rhetoric as a means to avoid conversations about race.[55] Colorblind casting specifies race or ethnicity when selecting an actor for a role and is partly meant to convey a fantasy based on meritocracy, which subsequently eschewers issues of inequality and cultural specificity. In this case choosing white teens as the "best" option was an attempt to circumvent racist casting practices. This tactic excluded Black teens as a means to appease advertisers who wanted to cater to white audiences.[56]

While *Bandstand* was a national phenomenon that exuded whiteness despite influence from black musicians, local Philadelphia civil rights activists such as is such as Georgie Woods, a local deejay, attempted to break down racial barriers in music and television programming. Delmont writes that by incorporating his critiques of the media industry with civil rights work in support of the Black teenagers who supported his career, Woods "offered a model for what music could achieve beyond commercial success."[57] Woods spoke out against the moral panic of early rock 'n' roll criticism that saw the music as synonymous with juvenile delinquency. As cited by Delmont, Woods stated that:

> Many of the teenagers who patronize these shows find in them an outlet for their emotions. And while previous single shows have been attended by as many as 30,000 teenagers we have never had any serious trouble. This proves, as far as I am concerned, that there might be less delinquency if there was more healthy entertainment such as that offered by our shows.[58]

In other words, rock 'n' roll, and the image of *Bandstand*, offered what Josh Kun refers to as auditopia, a concept that, along with Richard Dyer's theory of utopia, will be further explored in subsequent chapters. As Kun puts it,

> Music functions like a possible utopia for the listener[:] music is experienced not only as sound that goes into our ears and vibrates through our bones but as a space that we can enter into, encounter, move around in, inhabit, be safe in, learn from.[59]

On television, *The Mitch Thomas Show* (1955–1958) was a parallel to *Bandstand* when it was still local to Philadelphia, but it featured a Black host and a Black studio audience. As *Bandstand* went nationwide, Thomas' program continued to provide a space for non-white rock 'n' roll fans, even as fan clubs that called for the desegregation of *Bandstand* served as early civil rights and media activists.[60] Yet Delmont reveals that network affiliates ran *The Mitch Thomas Show* mainly for purposes of economic gain, in hopes that it could attract Black and white teens in the same way Black radio could.[61] From Ray Charles to Little Richard, Thomas could help catalyze an artist, album, and single's success.[62] Unsurprisingly, *Bandstand* was influenced by the music and dances of *Thomas*, which showed how Black culture would be appropriated and commodified for mainstream white consumerism, while Black citizens themselves remained excluded from this wider visibility, exposure, and recognition. Like *They Shall Be Heard*, *The Mitch Thomas Show* was short-lived, due to the racial dimensions of television economics. Not even *The Nat King Cole Show* could attract a wide audience: it only lasted from 1956 to 1957.[63]

As Woods and Thomas fostered the multi-racial rock 'n' roll community in Philadelphia that influenced *Bandstand*, its national host, Dick Clark, would be the white face of the program, beginning in 1956. ABC, a newer network than CBS and NBC, attempted to cater to a younger audience, which led to the *Bandstand* collaboration and the long-running relationship it held with Disney.[64] With *Bandstand* being the first show of its kind to go national, Clark also became the only non-regional disc jockey. He became synonymous with the program, which moved to Los Angeles in 1964 as it gained greater recognition. School segregation became illegal in the 1954 landmark Supreme Court case Brown v. Board of Education.[65] However, integration would only gradually be achieved over the next several years, not overnight. Ten years after the Brown case, and with the move to Los Angeles, the integration of *Bandstand* was finally implemented. Although the change was in part a result of activism, the immediate impetus for the shift seemed to be a decision made by Clark, who was also the producer of the series. That decision turned him into a music and media mogul. The power of such individuals, along with the power of authorship, is essential to understanding how teen TV has evolved. Clark hosted the show until its final airing in 1989.[66]

*Soul Train* was a significant and long-running music program that highlighted Black performers and Black subculture(s). Its creator, Don Cornelius, modeled the show after the *Bandstand* formula, but it provided unprecedented visibility and agency for Black Americans. Musician and author Questlove defines *Soul Train* as "a transformative cultural moment" that played, simultaneously, the roles of "a sibling, a parent, a babysitter, a friend, a textbook, a newscast, a business school, and a church" when he was coming of age in the 1970s. PBS's educational children's program *Sesame Street* was the only other TV series his parents allowed him to watch.[67] Popular soul and funk music embraced in the 1960s and 1970s by the Baby Boomers evolved into the hip hop and R&B embraced in the 1980s and 1990s by Gen X, and this whole tradition would be capitalized upon in cable programming and subsequent stylings of network TV. Expanding music subculture, from punk to hip hop, and programming, from *Soul Train* to *Saturday Night Live* (1975–, NBC), contributed to the demand for youth-centered programming in the 1980s, when Gen Xers and MTV would be synonymous.

## Linda Schuyler, Co-Creator and Showrunner, *Degrassi*

### *Transcribed Interview*

Conducted June 14, 2017

| | |
|---|---|
| Stefania Marghitu: | First of all, I was thinking, what are the predecessors of *Degrassi* for you? I know you worked as a teacher and then did the after school special, *Ida Makes a Movie*. Were the after-school specials themselves influential, were there other components? |
| Linda Schuyler: | I think they were. The biggest influence on my life was, of course, being a junior high school teacher. And also, while I was teaching, not being able to find any—we used to call them "audio visual works" in those days—any film or TV that had been designed for adolescents. |

And you're right, the closest thing to it was after-school specials. But there wasn't a lot of them, and there messaging wasn't really directly talking to the kids. So there was really nothing out there. And I had one of those light bulb days when I said, "You know I think I'd like to make that stuff."

SM: And how long were you a Jr. High School teacher?

LS: I taught for eight years. But you know I was young when I became a teacher, so I was 29 when I left.

SM: How did the goals and public funding for *Degrassi* allow you to do what commercial teen shows couldn't? What were you most proud of accomplishing?

LS: When you look at the early *Degrassi* (*Degrassi High* and *Degrassi Jr High*), and this was a time before the Internet, not only were those shows used on television, they were used in the classroom. We had a double mandate to entertain and educate. We worked with WGBH Boston, and they got funding to do teachers guide for every episode of *Degrassi High* and *Degrassi Jr. High*. So the show was designed for each episode to be a discussion starter. So because we had that double mandate working with our Canadian public broadcaster and WGBH Boston in the states, it allowed us to go after funding that some basic television shows couldn't go after.

SM: And were there any other mandates as far as what the Canadian government wanted for you? Did they push for anything? Was there a collaboration, or did they give you full autonomy from the get go?

LS: The Canadian government funding is more about counting if your key creative personnel are Canadian. There are rigorous tests for allowing for the funding. The content was more worked on by our [aforementioned] broadcasters in Canada and the US for those early episodes. The broadcasters

SM: Was there any pushback from the broadcasters during the early seasons of Degrassi about the content being to risqué, or too real, for a teen show?

LS: (Laughs). There were definitely discussions about it. It was very important to me that we not talk down to our [teen] audience. Like I said, I spent eight years in the classroom and I really respected these young people. I didn't want to make things seem too trivial or have to easy a fix. We had a mandate to reassure young people they were not alone. And if they were talking about it in the schoolyard or on our show, we wanted to talk about it on our show.

And we also didn't want to deal with in a way with all the kids would have a problem, and then some soft, warm friendly adult would solve the problem for them.

The kids would make choices, and some of them would not be good, but then they had to live with the consequences of those decisions and those actions. And sometimes the broadcasters thought that it got too messy, and they wanted to have neater solutions. But we said, if we really are going to gain the respect of those young people, we have to tell our stories this way.

SM: We talk a lot now in the digital era about fan responses and how immediate and visible they are in the Internet era. What were those initial responses like for the series, from critics, adults, and from teens? Do you recall what it was like initially?

LS: Well, we were fortunate to have received critical acclaim from the beginning. And no, there was of course no Internet in those days, but we used to get stacks of mail. The mail main that used to come our little modest office, he would literally come with bags of mail.

And one of the earlier episodes we did in *Degrassi Jr. High* was the teen mother, Spike, who had her baby and kept it and kept going to school. And we got sent teddy bears and all kinds of baby clothes asking if we could please give these to Spike and her baby. We right from the beginning seemed to touch a chord with teenagers.

SM: And that baby became a character in a later season if I'm not correct?

LS: You're so correct, Emma. We named her Emma because we won an Emmy for the episode that spike got pregnant. And my partner at the time was accepting the award and at the end he said, "and we're gonna' call her Emma after the Emmys!"

And then, when we finished *Degrassi Jr.* and *Degrassi Jr. High*, we actually thought we were done with *Degrassi*. My partner at the time went off to do certain things, I went off and did other things. And there came a point when we said, my goodness, maybe we're ready to bring them back. And Emma became the really critical character. We did the math, and she would be going into Jr. High. So she became the character that we went into *Degrassi: The Next Generation* with.

SM: That's incredible!

LS: It was so wonderful, and it allowed us when we did the first new episode, we did a reunion special. We brought in some of the older characters, and then also introduced Emma and all of the gang that would be brought throughout the series. And with next generation, we were working with different distributors. We were now working with CTV in Canada, and with Noggin at the time, and then they became Teen Nick. But it's all part of Viacom family.

*SM:* Was it always a conscious effort to interweave the teens and their family life? Because you know a lot of times, criticisms of American teen TV are surrounded by the idea that it's as if they didn't have parents, or the parents look the same age as the kids. But that earnestness and verisimilitude is something that I think was also so important about *Degrassi*. Was it something you always wanted to include?

*LS:* Well it's interesting, because adults have a very particular role in our series. And of course they're there—they're the teachers, the adults, the caretakers of our young people. But, every scene, even if it's got adults written into it, is from the perspective of the young person. So you would never see a scene with two adults talking about our young characters. You might have two adults talking about our characters, but they would be overhearing it from the other room. Adults are important to our world, they give it credibility, they help us understand some things, but every scene, every story line is driven by the young protagonist. And when we do have adults, they are cast like are teens, age appropriate.

And that's another thing we've done form the get go, is that we cast age appropriate. I think that's what sets us apart too. My theory is you can find a 25-year-old that looks 15, but the actor brings ten years of life experience to that role. Whereas you cast a 15-year-old to play a 15-year-old, they've only got those years of life experience. And that just makes the performance that more authentic.

Now it's also harder [to cast child actors], because of union rights. You can't work them the same hours as adults. And you also have to provide them tutoring on set. So, it's challenging, but it's absolutely worth it for the end result.

SM: Was meeting [the cast] of the next generation influential at all to the issues you talked about? After teaching, did you feel like you had to stay in touch? How did you approach that?

LS: Well, I feel like, in what we call "*Degrassi* Classic," which is *Jr. High and High*, I was fresh out of teaching, and was very much connected to youth. When we moved into next generation, it was really all about my writers. They were all younger than me. And they would go visit schools and be very connected. We also involve our cast. Every single episode we produce is workshopped with writers, producers and cast before we publish the script. So there is a lot of input from young people.

SM: How did working on a teen show allow you to introduce characters that were different and more challenging than adults, or family dramas? Do you find that the teen specific issues would be more challenging?

LS: I don't think so necessarily. But one of the issues that is very important to us surrounds sex and sexuality, because it's crucial for teenagers. And it's very interesting to watch *Degrassi* over the years. In *Degrassi High* and *Jr High*, we had some characters that thought they might be gay. And the closest thing to it was Snake had a gay brother. Whereas by the time we got to *Next Generation*, we had gay and straight characters, and bi. I was very proud when we later introduced a transgender character. She was with us for four years on the show.

So, as society has changed, we've been able to embrace those changes and talk about them in the show. I don't know how to compare it to adult television, but it's about keeping ourselves very mindful of where teenagers are with their own developing body and sexuality, and also [mindful] of the times. And it's important to reflect all of that as authentically as we can.

*SM:* Were there any characters coming-of-age stories that were particularly memorable or powerful to you? And with that, their issues surrounding sexuality?

*LS:* I was really proud when we did the transgender story, and it launched such good discussions in our workshop. And whenever it's like that then, it's the same after the episode airs. And last season, we introduced a character that doesn't identify by male or female, and wants to be identified with the pronoun "they." That caused a whole of discussion. Again it's just knowing that society is morphing as well as teenagers, and we have to be respectful that they are going through changes and the world is going through changes, and to look at all that.

*SM:* Can you talk about the workshopping and the aftermath, reception, and responses of the famous shooting episode?

*LS:* That's a perfect example of seeing the consequences of people's actions and choices. That's what's one of the joys about working on a show with longevity. It was bad enough that there was a school shooting, and Jimmy (Aubrey Graham/Drake) got shot, but then it gave us all kinds of opportunities to explore what happened when this young athlete who had really good potential as a basketball player has his life broken. So it's about how he gets his life back. It's not just the shooting that makes the headline in one day. The shooting was in season four, and he stayed with us until Season 8, so we got to show all of that. The plot for the next four years of that character's life, we were able to see the consequences.

*SM:* I know the US had problems with school shootings and continues to, but was that something going on in Canada at the time as well? Was there a headline story?

LS: I would say, obviously, with Canada being such a close neighbor to the US, we are shocked and horrified every time we hear a school-shooting story. We had one or two coming out of Canada, but it was just shocking enough that we felt we had to deal with it. And we flew out Barbara Coloroso, who wrote *The Bully, the Bullied, and the Bystander*, based on the Columbine shootings, to be a consultant for the show. We wanted to make sure, as with any of these topics we take on. We don't do it for a ripped from the headlines sensationalism; we do it because we really want to try to understand it from the youth perspective. She was really helpful in working with our writers, and making sure we were doing it right. Because you see, the character that did the shooting was being bullied. And we wanted to show that, and that bystanders have a responsibility as well.

SM: How would you say *Degrassi* fits into the Canadian national TV landscape?

LS: Well, that's a very hard question for me to answer. We just celebrated our 500th episode, and I think we carved out a very niche place in the Canadian landscape. There's no other show really like ours. And I'm pretty proud of it to tell you the truth.

SM: Was there any research involved in considering under 12 or over 25 viewers? How do you think about those viewers?

LS: Well first of all we are storytellers. And we did our best to be honest about those teenage years. And what's interesting is, we found that are viewership, we had some younger, it really started around 12, and went up to about 35.

Even if we were writing the show specifically for adolescents, we found there were so many *Degrassi* fan clubs on University campuses. They would have martini nights and get together and watch *Degrassi*. I think part of that appeal was, *Degrassi* was all about first time experiences. Well, sometimes people get away to college and university and they haven't had those experiences just yet, so it's kind of a cool way to look at it.

And then, for a lot of young parents, it was great for them to watch the show as well. So we had a very diverse audience. And with next generation, we had a split. We had the teens, and the thirty somethings who had been fans of the original shows. It's quite lovely, we definitely picked up more than teenagers as fans of the show.

SM: With the transition now in the digital space, and the show being on Netflix and other platforms, has it changed the way you look at doing the show at all? Has that initial reaction from fans been different?

LS: The mandate of the show still remains the same, but it was interesting when we moved to Netflix. We were used to telling our stories as half hour episodes week after week, and a week in between. And on Netflix when they release it as a binge watch, we realized how we parceled out the narrative had to change. How we parceled out the narrative was affected by changing to Netflix, we had to realize people were going to watch ten episodes in one sitting.

SM: How do you go about finding writers, do you look to have them to be as diverse as the actors involved? For example, the transgender story.

LS: Yeah, no question, we try to find as much diversity as we can in the writers room. We also take a chance on some very young writers. We had the biggest success in writing by performing from within. I've done this a number of times, and someone fresh out of school to be our story coordinator, which is a secretarial type

| | |
|---|---|
| | job pretty much. But, they get to be in the room, see the story being broken, so many of our writers started there and the next year came on as a Jr. story editor, and then as a story editor. We've had great success growing writers that way. |
| SM: | When the Manny abortion episode aired, it did not air in the US. I know it's the network's decision, but is there anything you are allowed to speak about? |
| LS: | Well, I think what happened was, we worked with some incredible executive broadcasters at the N, and they were with us all along with the storyline. And it wasn't until the show was completed and approved. It then went up the chain in Viacom, and there were people very close to the top that thought the subject matter was too dangerous. And it was heartbreaking not just for us as the producers, but for the broadcast executives who had worked so hard on the show as well.<br><br>Now to their credit, our broadcast executives didn't give up. It was two or three years later, they actually did air that episode with follow up episodes. And they had a wrap around with it where they did a segment with some experts. So they were eventually able to get it on air. But it was a lot of cry from our American fans who couldn't watch it, and knew they were airing it in Canada! |
| SM: | And American television has rarely covered abortion. You first had Maude in the 1970s, and there hasn't been much since. You have Shonda Rhimes series now. Even the discussions you have about showing diverse issues and characters, and the desire to have a diverse writing staff, these are all some of the major problems in US television now, but you've been able to get it right. |
| LS: | And actually, last month, *Cosmo* did a special on abortions in television. They had *Degrassi* in their twice, and *Maude*, it was quite expansive. |

## Notes

1 Susan Douglas, *Where the Girls Are: Growing Up Female with the Mass Media* (New York: Random House, 1995), 5.
2 Douglas, 9.
3 Pamela Robertson Wojcik, *Gidget: Origins of a Teen Girl Transmedia Franchise* (New York: Routledge, 2020).
4 Aniko Bodroghkozy, *Sixties Television and the Youth Rebellion* (Durham, NC: Duke University Press, 2001).
5 Mark Paterson, *Consumption As Everyday Life* (London and New York: Routledge 2006), 6.
6 Paterson, Consumption, 6–7.
7 Paterson, *Consumption*, 7.
8 Paterson, *Consumption*, 11.
9 Grace Palladino, *Teenagers: An American History* (New York: Basic Books, 1996), 114.
10 Palladino, Teenagers, 103.
11 Ibid.
12 Palladino, *Teenagers*, 104.
13 Ibid.
14 There is a rich history of feminist television scholarship on the relationship between housewives, television, and domesticity. For more information about the soap opera genre, see Robert C. Allen, *Speaking of Soap Operas* (Chapel Hill: University of North Carolina Press, 1985); Dorothy Hobson, *Soap Opera* (London: Polity, 2003); and Elana Levine, *Daytime Soap Opera and US Television History* (Durham, NC: Duke University Press, 2020).
15 Palladino, *Teenagers*, 104.
16 Palladino, *Teenagers*, 113.
17 Palladino, *Teenagers*, 107.
18 Palladino, *Teenagers*, 112.
19 Lynn Spigel, *Make Room for TV: Television and the Family Ideal in Postwar America* (Chicago, IL: The University of Chicago Press, 1992).
20 James Gilbert, *A Cycle of Outrage: America's Reaction to the Juvenile Delinquent in the 1950s* (Oxford: Oxford University Press, 1988).
21 Gertude Berg, "Sammy's Bar Mizvah," in *The Rise of the Goldbergs Scripts*, ed. G. Berg (New York: Barse & Co, 1931), 237.
22 Carol A. Stabile, *The Broadcast 41: Women and the Anti-Communist Blacklist* (London: Goldsmiths Press, 2018).
23 Episodes of *Never Too Young* are available at the University of California Los Angeles Film and Television Archive.
24 *Love is a Many Splendored Thing* is available for free, public domain streaming online at Archive.Org: https://archive.org/details/1967_PD_Soapie
25 Max Shulman, Writers Guild Foundation Archive, Los Angeles California.
26 Ibid.
27 For further details about these parallels, see https://www.metv.com/stories/the-characters-of-scooby-doo-were-based-on-the-many-loves-of-dobie-gillis

28 *Chicago Tribune*, "The Best-selling Movie Soundtracks of All Time," *The Chicago Tribune*, April 19, 2017, https://www.chicagotribune.com/entertainment/movies/ct-15-best-selling-movie-soundtracks-of-all-time-20170419-photogallery.html
29 Alice Leppert, *TV Family Values: Gender, Domestic Labor, and 1980s Sitcoms* (New Brunswick, NJ: Rutgers University Press, 2018).
30 Palladino, *Teenagers*, 157.
31 Palladino, *Teenagers*, 195.
32 Ibid.
33 Ibid.
34 David R. Shumway, "Watching Elvis: The Male Rock Star as Object of the Gaze," in *The Other Fifties: Interrogating Midcentury American Icons*, ed. Joel Foreman (Urbana: University of Illinois Press, 1997), 132.
35 Tim Gray, "How Elvis Presley Started a 'Riot' and Changed the Music Industry," *Variety*, August 14, 2015, https://variety.com/2015/music/news/how-elvis-presley-started-a-riot-and-changed-the-music-industry-1201567745/
36 Jordan Runtagh, "Elvis Presley on TV: 10 Unforgettable Broadcasts," *Rolling Stone*, January 28, 2016, https://www.rollingstone.com/music/music-news/elvis-presley-on-tv-10-unforgettable-broadcasts-225225/
37 Ibid.
38 Ibid.
39 Ibid.
40 Ibid.
41 Shumway, "Elvis," 134.
42 Shumway, "Elvis," 137.
43 Ibid.
44 Gray, "Music Industry."
45 Shumway, "Elvis," 139.
46 Palladino, *Teenagers*, 102.
47 For more on the relationship between teen girls, gender, and rock music, see Norma Coates, "Teenyboppers, Groupies, and Other Grotesques: Girls and Women and Rock Culture in the 1960s and Early 1970s," *Journal of Popular Music Studies* 15, no. 1 (2003): 65–94.
48 Andrea Kelley, *Soundies Jukebox Films and the Shift to Small-Screen Culture* (New Brunswick, NJ: Rutgers University Press, 2018), 121.
49 Matthew F. Delmont, *The Nicest Kids in Town: American Bandstand, Rock 'n' Roll, and the Struggle for Civil Rights in 1950s Philadelphia* (Berkeley: University of California Press, 2012), 1.
50 Ilana Nash, *American Sweethearts: Teenage Girls in Twentieth-Century Popular Culture* (Bloomington: Indiana University Press), 179.
51 Delmont, *Bandstand*, 50.
52 Delmont, *Bandstand*, 52, 66.
53 Delmont, *Bandstand*, 65.
54 Delmont, *Bandstand*, 126.
55 Delmont, *Bandstand*, 69.
56 Ibid.

57 Delmont, *Bandstand*, 127.
58 Delmont, *Bandstand*, 149–150.
59 Josh Kun, *Auditopia: Music, Race and America* (Berkeley: University of California Press, 2005), 2.
60 Delmont, *Bandstand*, 133.
61 Ibid.
62 Delmont, *Bandstand*, 134.
63 Delmont, *Bandstand*, 135.
64 Delmont, *Bandstand*, 140.
65 Brown v. Board of Education, 347 U.S. 483 (1954).
66 The NBC program, *American Dreams* (2002–2005), chronicled a family in Philadelphia in the 1960s, and *Bandstand* was a recurring narrative element for teen daughter Margaret "Peg" Pryor (Brittany Snow).
67 Questlove, *Soul Train: Peace, Love, and Soul* (New York: Harper Design, 2013).

# 2

# GENERATION X TEEN TV

Generation Xers are loosely defined by their emergence after the declining birth rate in 1965 and the cut-off in 1976 as the rate increased. Also known as "Baby Busters," Generation Xers seem to suffer from the repercussions of their preceding age group, which led to economic turmoil. Sherry B. Ortner asserts that Xers represent the first generation that is not inherently capable of surpassing their parents' living standards. She suggests the defining characteristic of Gen Xers is based on economics: "There are not enough jobs, there are certainly not enough well-paying jobs, and there are particularly not enough quality jobs available for the level of education and qualification many members of the cohort have achieved."[1] This is reflected in the discourse on Millennials, which suggests that they represent the first generation not to surpass their parents in terms of upward mobility. As mentioned in the introduction, each generation endures branding as the narcissistic "me" generation during individuals' teenage years, but Xers, in particular, were the first to be hit with the apathetic "slacker" archetype. To a large extent, this stereotyping dealt with heavy television consumption as well as alternative lifestyles based on grunge, recreational drug use, and skateboard culture. The alternative Gen Xer defied the all-American jock and cheerleader stereotypes and brought new light to the "nerd" and "outsider" as validating, as such individuals were not seen to be succumbing to social hierarchies and teenage peer pressure to assimilate.

In his 1991 novel *Generation X: Tales for an Accelerated Culture*, Douglas Coupland coined the term "Generation X" and also used economics to define the generation's character. Generation Xers frequently worked in "McJobs": low caliber occupations in the service industry reserved for the overeducated, overqualified, and utterly underwhelmed.[2] Ortner also remarks on the social conditions Xers suffered: "[a] soaring divorce rate, high rates of working mothers and latchkey children, ecological disaster, the AIDS epidemic, and so forth." The combination of the breakdown of the nuclear family and increased television viewing initiated the generation's antagonism toward their Baby Boomer parents.

Jonathon I. Oakes suggests that Gen Xers "are more usefully defined as spectatorship rather than as a group of individuals with common practices and rituals," further postulating that this is specifically rooted in "a unique relationship with media—particularly visual media—rather than a visual style (e.g., dress and music tastes)."[3] Oakes argues that Generation X is inherently dependent on media, but as spectators and not active participants. A report published in the *Journal of Consumer Marketing* in 2000 cites several characteristics that led to the dependency of Generation X on media, particularly on TV. Generation Xers were the first generation to have cable access in their early years and were subsequently exposed to an average of 20,000 commercials per year. To realize the huge contrast between the viewership of these generations, the report stated that "the average household television viewing grew from five hours and six minutes per day in 1960 to seven hours and four minutes in 1992." Because commercials and various forms of film and TV permeated this generation's upbringing at an age before Xers could decipher differences, they do not distrust advertising or marketing. Baby Boomers were raised on a much more individualistic level toward upward mobility, over community, as their yuppy roles were acquired later in life. Generation Xers were also the first generation to benefit from educational programming while in grade school.

In the 1990s, a wave of successful Indiewood movies (independent films dealing with representations of emerging subcultures) addressing Generation X caught the attention of Hollywood studios, with

*Reality Bites* (1994) its commercial culmination. The film begins with its protagonist, Lelaina Pierce (Winona Ryder), and the denunciation of her parents' generation (the Baby Boomers/counterculture of the 1960s turned yuppy) as the core of her college valedictorian graduation speech:

> And they wonder why those of us in our twenties refuse to work an eighty-hour week. Just so we can afford to buy their BMWs… why we aren't interested in the counterculture that they invented, as if we did not see them disembowel their revolution for a pair of running shoes… But the question remains, what are we going to do now? How can we repair all the damage we inherited? Fellow graduates, the answer is simple. The answer is… the answer is… I don't know.

Through this critique of the counterculture as "just fashion," these jabs directly reference Baby Boomers.

American Generation Xers first came of age in the 1980s, a decade marked by Reaganism, the AIDS crisis, the War on Drugs, the rise and fall of Wall Street, and end of the Cold War. Network TV was dominated by middle-class family sitcoms, with Bill Cosby and Roseanne its biggest stars, and night-time soaps about American affluence, from *Dallas* (1978–1991, Columbia Broadcasting Company [CBS]) to *Dynasty* (1981–1989, American Broadcasting Company [ABC]). The advertising boom expanded to new areas of expanded research and development marketing and public relations. Deregulation turned into conglomeration. Reagan's failed trickle-down economics showed greater wealth disparity in the nation.

Like early music programming that captured teen Baby Boomer culture, new niche cable programming like Music Television (MTV) and Black Entertainment Television (BET) catered to Gen-X teens up to predominantly urban-based youth in their 30s of their time. The shift to emphasize teen-targeted programming changed with the popularity of the sitcom *Saved by the Bell* and the soap *Beverly Hills 90210*, and cult-following series with less commercial success such as *My So-Called*

*Life* and *Freaks and Geeks* foreshadowed the type of niche-casting prevalent in post-network television. First, the 1970s sparked a shift in Nielsen ratings—demographics based on target audiences emerged as a precursor to niche- and narrowcasting programming in cable TV. Archival material and trade-press articles indicated that CBS wanted to push toward the 18–34 demographic and engage with liberal feminist consumers. The success of the progressive *All in the Family* certainly helped the rise of the *Mary Tyler Moore Show*, but it was also considered sufficiently traditional, and also innovative, to lead to varying opinions on its status as a new and relevant TV series.

Genre hybridity, like teen-crime drama, became the norm for American television in the late 20th century. Michael Newman refers to the hybridity of episodic and serial components present in contemporary programming, among other things, as primetime serials (PTSs), a style of genre since MTM Productions in the 1980s such as *Hill Street Blues*. He writes that the most distinguishing factor of a PTS is the associated investment in character through the character-arc device.[4] Genre hybridity and niche-casting that began to develop in the 1980s were both a reaction to the sociopolitical attitude of the time and the onset of specialized cable programming. Twenty-four-hour entertainment was introduced as part of cable, and combated daytime and primetime network slots. By 1977, Nickelodeon had already premiered, and the children's channel was one of the first unquestionable successes of branding and transmedia. In 1989, the Entertainment and Sports Programming Network (ESPN) was launched and did the same for athletes and the sports industry more generally—that is, both became iconic and were then able to be used as marketing tools. The Cable News Network (CNN), instituted in 1980 by soon-to-be media mogul Ted Turner, premiered in 1980 and challenged the traditional 6–10 PM news slot with a constant flow of real-time current events.

MTV promised to provide a constant flow of music entertainment, like the radio but with a visual aspect, and it debuted in 1981 with its first video premiere, "Video Killed the Radio Star" by The Buggles. Instead of disc jockeys (DJs), hosts were called "video jockeys" (VJs). Subsequent programming like *Miami Vice* (1984–1990) was heavily influenced by the mini-movies that videos provided and incorporated long shots such as a car driving down the road to current hits such as Phil Collins' "In the Air Tonight." The series yielded new inventions to classic police conventions.

The animated MTV teen series *Beavis and Butthead* (1993–1997) and its spinoff, *Daria* (1997–2002), would become symbols of Gen-X counterculture. Daria's dry wit, precocious nature, and weariness over high school popularity made her a highlight for teen girls who defied social norms. Even as an animated character, her black-rimmed glasses and skeptical eyes, Doc Marten Boots, and her long brown hair and bangs became an iconic costume. Postmodernism and pastiche were the norm, where Madonna sang "Like a Virgin" on a Venice gondola and emulated Marilyn Monroe in her 1983 "Material Girl" video, while former Motown kid and disco artist, Michael Jackson, became the King of Pop and introduced his own cinematic style into his videos (e.g., "Thriller" and "Beat it"). Jackson's "Thriller" (1983) remains the best-selling album of all time. The 1980s was a decade of stars, from film and TV to pop music and politics. Celebrity culture increased with tabloid magazines and series from *Entertainment Tonight* (1981–present, CBS) to *Lifestyles of the Rich and Famous* (1984–1994, ABC). Furthermore, MTV allowed radio stars to be seen and heard beyond the airwaves, cultivating a space for musicians to become recognizable icons similar to TV and film actors.

Despite MTV's cutting-edge image catered to youth, the channel also encountered the same issues concerning race and music programming that *American Bandstand* did, its broadcast predecessor. The program was initially focused on "rock" programming, which was predominantly white and generally did not include black artists until the prevalence of Jackson: his chart-selling albums and high production music videos made him the ideal MTV star. Madonna also signaled a new agency for women as stars rather than being viewed as objects of desire in rock videos or background "eye candy." To some extent, Michael Jackson paved the way for the proliferation of R&B and, later, for hip-hop artists to cross over.[5] Non-white women as pop and R&B stars also began to proliferate the airwaves and MTV screens, with the introduction of Michael's sister, Janet, 1980s sensation Paula Abdul, Mariah Carey, and one of the highest-selling and most awarded artists of all time, Whitney Houston. These artists would pave the way for future pop stars such as Britney Spears, Beyoncé, Lady Gaga, and Ariana Grande. Mexican-American Selena Quintanilla, known as the "Queen of Tejano," also helped mark a crossover for Latina artists. Collaborations between rock and hip hop, such as Aerosmith and Run DMC's "Walk This Way" (1986), also helped crossovers. The success of gangster rap, from artists such as NWA to Public Enemy, further shifted hip hop into mainstream culture. The gendered dynamics of music were still prevalent, however—that is, the virgin/whore dichotomy and understanding that "sex sells." Women rappers such as Missy Elliot and Lil' Kim faced particular struggles in a male-dominated field but also initiated entry points for future crossover stars Cardi B, Nicki Minaj, and Meg Thee Stallion.

Grunge, the defining alternative rock genre for Gen Xers predominantly out of Seattle and surrounding the Pacific Northwest region, went mainstream with Nirvana and Pearl Jam, as well as with Soundgarden, Mudhoney, and Alice in Chains. The suicide of Nirvana frontman, Kurt Cobain, in 1994 marked a seminal landmark for the genre—and the generation. His death, and subsequent cover on *Rolling Stone* magazine, was featured in *My So-Called Life*, and suicide prevention increased across the country.

Dissent in the 1980s turned into action in the 1990s. Cult-status teen programming in the 1990s, such as *My So-Called Life* (1994–1995, ABC) and *Freaks and Geeks* (1999–2000, NBC), each lasted only one season before the rise of premium cable mandates.[6] *Twin Peaks*, *My So-Called Life*, and *Freaks and Geeks* remain the most critically acclaimed teen-oriented series of the 1990s, which also coincide with low ratings and cancellation after one or two seasons. In many ways, these series are considered "ahead of their time" in that they appealed to niche, narrowcasting audiences with the industrial practices of network TV. *My So-Called Life* made history when it became the first series to yield an online fan-led campaign to drop cancellation. ABC received thousands of letters from fans, but it was ultimately axed due to low ratings and Claire Danes' reluctance to sign on for another season.[7] In 1995, ratings were a high priority and critical acclaim, including Danes' Golden Globe for acting at the age of 15, could not suffice. The series catapulted the film careers of both Danes and Jared Leto. In the post-network era, programs that gain praise from esteemed critics and receive prestigious awards are far more likely to stay on, rather than get cancelled, despite undesirable ratings. As Henry Jenkins writes, "for years, fan groups seeking to rally support for endangered series have argued that networks should be focused more on the quality of audience engagement with the series and less on the quantity of viewers."[8] The next chapter, Chapter 3, will reveal how fandom and fan culture is a part of Millennial generational identity, along with Jenkins' notions of participatory culture and convergence in the digital era.

Arthouse *auteur* David Lynch's foray into television, *Twin Peaks* (1990–1991, ABC), marked the beginning of quality TV discourses based on film industry proximity. At the center of his small-screen debut was a story of a murdered teen cheerleader and a postmodern take on 1950s teen culture, from jukeboxes in diners to jocks in letterman jackets.

*Saved by the Bell* (1989–1993, National Broadcasting Company [NBC]) reflected the respectability politics and upper-middle-class lifestyle of the Reagan Era. The series concurrently ended the same year Bill Clinton became the first democratic US President since Jimmy Carter's administration from 1977 to 1981. In 1996, he became the first democratic nominee since Franklin D. Roosevelt in 1936 to win a second term. Just as John F. Kennedy was the TV president, Clinton's appearance on the cable program during his 1992 campaign trail made him the MTV candidate.

The end of the grunge wave marked a new era of pop. Britain's *The Spice Girls* became a global success. Former *Mickey Mouse Club* musketeers Britney Spears and Christina Aguilera, as well as NSYNC's Justin Timberlake and J. C. Chasez dominated the pop charts. Additionally, rap and R&B increasingly crossed over into pop, as shown by Brandy Norwood and Will Smith and their involvement as teen musicians and TV actors. While Baby Boomer teen TV began the incorporation of fictional teen TV programming (often short-lived) focusing on outsiders and subcultures, Gen X shifted to outsiders as protagonists with series such as *My So-Called Life* and *Freaks and Geeks*. These series mirrored what was to come in cable programming beginning in the late 1990s on FX and Home Box Office (HBO), which catered to Gen-X adults.

Many teen TV series begin with an outsider moving to a new town and high school. At first, he or she is a disruptor, but then they eventually assimilate. Archetypes of the outsider, jock, nerd, cheerleader, rebel, and so on are established early in each series. As with most series in the network era, least offensive programming (LOP) was a mandate. Thus, teen series adhered to suburban Midwestern family values. It was not until the late 1990s and early 2000s with the television series *The O.C.* and the rise of the United Paramount Network (UPN) and Warner Brothers (WB, which would later merge into the CW) that youth subcultures and alternative lifestyles were seen on the small screen. Issues of class, social issues, and politics normally constituted a situation to be solved by the end of each episode in an almost after-school-special-like manner that emphasized moralizing and "talking down" to teens.

In *Saved by the Bell*, ethnically ambiguous army brat A. C. Slater disrupts popular kid Zach Morris' attempt to win cheerleader Kelly Kapowski's love. Following their tumultuous love triangle, the two eventually become best friends. Slater, a macho jock figure, is coupled with Zach's childhood best friend and resident brainiac Jessie Spano. Jessie resents Slater's machismo, but their attraction is based on the opposites-attract premise and their arguments provide comedic relief.

Zach and Kelly's on-again/off-again relationship evolves throughout the series. Zach lacks Slater's muscles and Jessie's brains, but he is the most clever and mischievous of his friends. His now iconic oversized cellular white telephone is emblematic of his socioeconomic status and social dominance in the high-school hierarchy. Each episode largely revolves around a scheme that goes horribly wrong but is solved before the comedy's 30-minute mark end. Zach is visibly wealthy, blonde, and good-looking: the typical all-American high schooler. In contrast, Kelly comes from a large family and, out of necessity, works at *The Max*, the local hangout. She is the only character who requires a part-time job.

*Saved by the Bell* sparingly deals with social issues. In Season 2, Episode 9, "Jessie's Song," the overachiever takes up a band called "Hot Sundae" with Kelly and Lisa. She becomes addicted to caffeine pills while trying to balance her studies and extracurricular music career. The episode culminates into one of the most famous scenes, commemorated today in dozens of GIFs. Zach confronts Jesse about her behavior and she reaches for more pills. Zach attempts to take them away from her while holding Jessie, and she begins to sing Donna Summer's "I'm So Excited" to prove herself, which ends in her screeching "I'm so excited, I'm so scared." In a rare moment for teen TV, Season 2, Episode 1, "The Prom," Kelly cancels her prom date with Zach when she takes back her dress to help support her family. In the end, Zach buys her a dress and the two solidify their relationship. In a much later episode, Season 4, Episode 10, "Drinking and Driving," the gang throws a toga party at Lisa's house while her mother is away. Drunk-driving leads the gang to crash Mrs. Turtle's car. While they attempt to make the money to pay for damages they are caught in the act and lectured on the perils of underage drinking and, most importantly, the consequences of drinking and driving. Grown-up morals and ethics always prevail in teen sitcoms like *Saved by the Bell*, while divorce plots do complicate things. For the vast majority, issues in the series dealt with popularity, competition, and schemes. Samuel "Screech" Powers and Lisa Turtle were minor characters often on the outside of the major couples' storylines. Screech serves as the series' nerd figure, who is primarily present for comedic relief. The nerd figure in teen TV and popular culture has certainly evolved since then. Finally, Lisa Turtle, originally imagined as a "Jewish American princess," is played by African American Lark Voorhies.

Producer Aaron Spelling's established success from the 1970s to 1980s on the ABC network (*Charlie's Angels* [1976–1981, ABC], *The Love Boat* [1977–1986, ABC], *Hart to Hart* [1979–1984, ABC], and *Dynasty* [1981–1989, ABC]) shifted to his teen primetime soap *Beverly Hills 90210* (1990–2000, Fox).[9] In addition to cable, the 'big three' broadcast bottleneck was further threatened by the newest network, Fox (1986–present), a branch of Rupert Murdoch's expanding media conglomeration, Fox Corporation. Todd Gitlin argues that 1980s network TV proved the socially conscious 1970s programming a brief detour from the standard formulas of LPO.[10] Spelling's producing prowess led the teen TV genre to evolve into a primetime drama slot. *Beverly Hills 90210* featured the relocation of a typical suburban couple and their teenage twins, Brenda and Brandon Walsh, from Minnesota to one of the wealthiest neighborhoods in America, Beverly Hills. The parents' Midwestern values and emphasis on curfews, keeping up grades, and general manners were quickly disrupted. At Beverly Hills High teenagers grew up fast in the absence of famous and rich parents. Discussions on drinking, drugs, and sex from the outset of the series are at the forefront. While Brenda is eager to begin her new life by meeting cute Californian boys and going to glamorous parties, Brandon attempts to protect his sister while also avoiding the pressure to drink. Brenda makes the brashest choices with regard to drinking and boys, and we see how she learns from her mistakes. Brandon, however, loses control when he gets drunk and is arrested for drunk-driving (Season 1, Episode 11, "B.Y.O.B"). By the end of the episode, the James Dean figure, Dylan, who has a troubled past and less affluence than the rest of the gang, takes Brandon to his regular Alcoholics Anonymous (AA) meeting. In this network primetime soap, teens are punished and learn from their mistakes, even if gratuitous sex and drinking are shown.

Throughout the series, Brenda and Brandon must consolidate their Midwestern background with their new Californian lifestyles, with their parents serving as moral and ethical pillars. In fact, lost members of the gang often come to Cindy and Jim Walsh for guidance, help and advice, as their own parents are aloof and absent. This upholds the Midwestern family values to which most primetime watchers would likely adhere, although facets of life in Los Angeles are certainly glamorized. *Beverly Hills 90210* became the gold standard for teen TV success. UPN and WB would soon focus their primetime lineup on teen programming such as strongholds *Buffy the Vampire Slayer* (1997–2003, WB/UPN) and *Dawson's Creek* (1998–2003), both catering to a niche teen subculture.[11]

The multichannel post-network era also saw convergence between film and television due to conglomeration synergies and overall deals.

With the shrinking of the "indie" and mid-budget movie in the late 1990s and early 2000s, more film practitioners went to cable television and then streaming. Creator-writer-producers of the 1980s and 1990s who went against the supply and demand and only cultivated small followings over mass audiences were faced with early cancellation, such as Mark Frost and David Lynch's *Twin Peaks*, Paul Fieg and Judd Apatow's *Freaks and Geeks*, and Winnie Holzman's *My So-Called Life*. Even these series based on subcultures leaning toward niche audiences included primarily white characters, whereas the creators of *Frank's Place*, Tim Reid and Hugh Wilson, were overly ambitious in their goals concerning the series' racial, regional, and cultural specificity, genre and style bending away from a traditional sitcom.

The beloved cult classic *Freaks and Geeks* (1999–2000, NBC) never found the audience and subsequent ratings to sustain a second season. The series centers around Lindsey Weir (Linda Cardellini). An early episode, "Beers and Weirs," initially pokes fun at a sober student improv group (the geeks), while later also pokes fun at the freaks who think (or pretend) they got drunk off a non-alcoholic keg of beer. Like *My So-Called Life* (1994–1995, ABC) before it, it was a network teen show about high school outcasts and subcultures. The portrayal of Rayanne Graff's addiction is one of the most nuanced, non-moralistic looks at teen substance abuse problems.

Both shows about female protagonists who venture outside strait-laced identities and experiment with drugs and alcohol represent some of the earliest signs of change. Ahead of their time, and before narrowcasting and multi-platform cable programming, these series signaled a new wave of programming to follow. *Buffy the Vampire Slayer* is considered as occupying a league of its own due to its hybridization of cult science-fiction quality and the teen narrative.[12] The WB/UPN dominated late 1990s programming with *Dawson's Creek* (1998–2003).[13] The shift from black-dominated comedies on UPN to white middle-class teens also ushered in an unfortunate gap in black-centered programming for years. *A Different World* (1987–1993, NBC), *The Fresh Prince of Bel-Air* (1990–1996, NBC), *Moesha* (1996–2001, UPN), *Sister, Sister* (1994–1999, ABC, WB), and *The Famous Jett Jackson*

(1998–2001, The Disney Channel) were the youthful counterparts to more adult-oriented series such as *Girlfriends* (2000–2008) to *Living Single* (1993–1998, Fox). Family-friendly series always spearheaded drugs and alcohol episodes as cautionary tales.

A family series such as *Growing Pains* (1985–1992, ABC) even incorporated a public service announcement (PSA) on the dangers of cocaine. When the Seaver family takes in Leonardo DiCaprio, they find out he emptied alcohol bottles because his abusive father was an alcoholic. In a rejuvenation of the cautionary tales of "fallen women" found in 19th- and 20th-century melodramas (and rehearsed in daytime and primetime soap operas), teen girls on TV who are not cautious about their sexual partners are often shown to pay the price for being subjected to relentless gossip, targeted by unsuitable partners because of their bad reputation and, in some cases, portrayed as driven from these experiences to become reckless and promiscuous—if self-hating on the inside. Just as *Rebel Without a Cause* (1955) is often a reference for teen-male narratives, *Splendor in the Grass* (1961) has been a clear influence on representations of teen female sexuality. Because teen shows deal in stereotypes, we see the mechanism especially clearly in these shows—that is, young women are defined in the stereotype by their availability to males as sexual partners (the tease, the bookworm, the good girl, the cheerleader). Sexually active teen girls usually come from families with problems, divorced parents, or working-class families. Note that for the male stereotypes the "jock," "regular joe," and "the brain," their loss of virginity is not as important, and emotional vulnerability is often not considered. When a virgin teen girl and a non-virgin teen male have sex, it is more about the vulnerability of the virgin and the power of the non-virgin. Teenagers who lose their virginity and believe themselves mature as a result are always shown as lacking in actual emotional maturity.

## *Beverly Hills 90210*

*Beverly Hills 90210* became one of the first teen series to discuss issues of sex, drugs, and alcohol as pervasive rather than isolated cases, and to actually show its teens as sexually active. In particular, this introduced the virginity-loss narrative as critical to the coming-of-age series. In Caroline Jones' analysis of three progressive teen series regarding gender (i.e., *Buffy*, *Veronica Mars* and *Gilmore Girls*) reveals the contradictions inherent in the idea of lost virginity that upholds the notions of "girl as victim" and "girl empowerment."[14] As she writes, "all of these series engage and challenge the dominant social ideologies about virginity yet continue to rely on them." We also see the influence of the *90210* virginity-loss narratives in future series such as *Gossip Girl*, when virgin Blair Waldorf (Leighton Meester) has sex for the first time with the lothario and villain, Chuck Bass (Ed Westwick), in the back of his limo in Season 1, Episode 7, "Victor/Victoria." In *The O.C.*, Season 1, Episode 19, "The Heartbreak," Seth (Adam Brody) and Summer (Rachel Bilson) lose their virginities to each other, but Seth later finds out Summer was also a virgin after he worries about his performance with his long-time crush. Other episodes discussed in this chapter include *Boy Meets World*: Season 5, Episode 22, "Prom-ises, Prom-ises" (Cory and Topanga, and Shawn and Angele contemplate having sex on prom night), *Veronica Mars*: Season 1, Episode 8, "Like a Virgin" (a purity test is circulated online and Veronica attempts to crack it), *Glee*: Season 3, Episode 5, "The First Time" (Kurt and Blaine, and Finn and Rachel contemplate whether or not they should have sex), and *Friday Night Lights*: Season 1, Episode 17, "I Think We Should Have Sex" (Julie tells Matt they should have sex).

Much like the virginity episodes, the party episodes deal with the push-pull tension between adolescents' childhood and adulthood and their betrayal of their parents by throwing a party while they are out of town. Later examples on cable programming of this occurrence often signal a rite of passage and transition into adulthood versus the previous media examples on network TV that use teen drug and alcohol use as a cautionary tale. Not only does dealing with exposure to alcohol and drugs in itself represent part of becoming an adult in American culture, but the use of mind-altering substances also reveals larger issues looming for the protagonists. From insecurities to mental health issues, adolescents who use drugs at parties often reveal hidden truths that become part of the serialized arc. The party episodes deal with the precipice of assuming greater responsibility, leaving home for the first time, and separating from the group of peers who have shaped the protagonists' fragile identities.

Gen X series showed teens who had sought out drugs and alcohol, and yes, had negative experiences. But these series did not hold the same moralistic and nationalistic values of previous teen shows that taught children a lesson from the parents' perspective. For the teen TV genre, experimentations with drugs, alcohol, and sex became seminal rites of passage and part of the transition into adulthood, or they foreshadowed issues that lead into young adulthood. This partly deals with narratives regarding parents' absence, from renting hotel rooms on prom night to throwing parties while mom and dad are out of town. Teen TV programming proves to be very careful in its representations of the type of loss of innocence that can have serious outcomes on the character's psyche. Whereas early family-centered network series and early teen-oriented TV focused on morally upright lessons and clear delineations of good versus bad choices, the post-network cable era showed new ambiguities and more complex lessons to learn. The family sitcom encouraged teens to conform to their parents' ideologies, while teen series shifted toward adapting to the rules of high school in order to survive the social landscape.

## *My So-Called Life*

The short-lived *My So-Called Life*, which was canceled due to low ratings after its first season, evokes a teen TV series that subverted the more traditional formulas and character types of the time, such as the sitcom nature of *Saved by the Bell* and teen soap *Beverly Hills 90210*. Before creating and showrunning the program, Winnie Holzman worked on *Thirtysomething*, a socially realistic attempt at the challenges of middle-class marriage and parenthood as Gen X approached their 30s. *Thirtysomething* creators and showrunners Ed Zwick and Marshall Herskovitz approached their series writer Holzman about developing a series that would share the same social realism when focusing on a teenage girl. Holzman was influenced by her background in poetry, as well as the type of television she grew up on and was inspired by—that is, series that dealt with culture and politics, such as *Mary Tyler Moore*, one of the first series to focus on a single career woman. After briefly considering the future *Clueless* star Alicia Silverstone, the team behind *My So-Called Life* hired a teenage Claire Danes. Under the law, minors were mandated to work fewer hours than their adult counterparts. This casting choice led the series to be more of a sprawling ensemble, including Angela's parents, friends, and their family lives within the series.

*My So-Called Life* both captures Gen-X cultural specificity and elements of universal teenage angst, heartbreak, rebellion, trouble with parents, and topical issues such as teenage addiction and homelessness. It was also one of the first series to feature an openly queer character, Rickie Vasquez (Wilson Cruz).[15] While series such as *Will & Grace* (1998–2006, NBC) and the coming out of future daytime host Ellen DeGeneres was featured in her eponymous series, non-heteronormative teen sexuality would be featured along with the coming-out narrative in millennial series. *My So-Called Life* essentially began what many millennial and Gen-Z series could later touch on outside broadcast television and, eventually, on network programming such as *Glee* (2009–2016, Fox). Same-sex marriage would not be legalized in the US until 2015 under the Barack Obama presidency, and Gen Z series began to reflect and represent issues of trans and non-binary teens.

Danes as Angela Chase in *Life* is the star, as the series follows her through her diary-like voiceover narrative, with a handful of episodes featuring the voiceover of other characters. The pilot begins with Angela and Rayanne (A. J. Langer) breaking the fourth wall, asking for spare change while they cannot help but laugh as they fabricate the reasons they need the money. As the girls giggle and run off, the title credits and theme song briefly flash and Angela's initial voiceover begins:

> So, I started hanging out with Rayanne Graff, just for fun, just 'cause it seemed like if I didn't I would… die or something. Things were getting to me. Just how people are. The way they always expect you to be a certain way. Even your best friend.

Angela is in the midst of a new friendship with Rayanne and Ricky, leaving her childhood best friend, Sharon Cherski (Devon Odessa), behind. These teen series begin with frustration with their expectations from family and established friends and lead to a forging of their own identity with new friends, tastes, and behaviors. This spans *My So-Called Life* to *Gossip Girl* to *Euphoria*. As Angela then half listens to Sharon's gossip while they walk down the school hallway, she also speaks about the complicated nature of dealing with "boys," who "have it so easy," while girls have to pretend they are not watching them while clearly being looked at.

Her disdain for peppy cheerleaders, the protagonists for previous teen series, is clear when she asks why they cannot just cheer "like… to themselves?" She then looks outside to see Rayanne and Ricky holding hands to skip school. Angela then poetically decries that "school is a battlefield… for your heart." The protagonist later dyes her hair bright red with the help of Rayanne, who told her new friend her hair was "holding her back." As Angela looks at herself in the mirror, her voiceover states she has to listen to her new friend because she acknowledges her hair is a symbol for her own life. Seemingly radical changes in appearance are often an early first step toward rebellion for teen characters. Angela's transformation is met with much dismay from her confused mother and Sharon. They both fear they are losing touch with Angela as a result of her new friendships and appearance, which serve as a foreshadowing of future conflicts in the series. The establishment of Angela's rebellion, along with Rayanne's addiction issues, Ricky as a homeless, gay teen stands in stark contrast to characters in past series such as *Saved by the Bell* and *Beverly Hills 90210* with respect to assimilation into normalcy and the desire to be popular. The jocks and cheerleaders—and popular kids as a whole—are no longer the central protagonists but the stock characters filling in the background. This marks the shift to early niche teen TV programming on network television.

While Angela adheres to a certain alternative Gen X grunge aesthetic and angsty mentality, the series' Nielsen TV ratings did not match the crossover success of *Nirvana* and *Pearl Jam* on the Billboard charts and airwaves. Although the series is remembered as distinctly Gen X, Holzman did not have this intention at the time. She credits the creative collaboration between cast and crew who added to the script, such as costume designer Patrick Norris, who went on to become a director. The script also took into account the interests of the teen cast itself as inspiration. The series was beloved by teens and adults alike, perhaps in part due to Holzman's take on the universality of the human spirit over generational specificity:

> There are different generations, but part of the truth about that show was that I was operating on an assumption, a belief, you could say, that things don't change that much on a deeper level from generation to generation. Because if I had to write about things in terms of generation, I would have been paralyzed. I was about to turn 40, and I would have not been equipped to do that.

Angela's parents, for example, who attended the same high school, were constantly reminded of their lives as teenagers. While her father was a "nerd," her mother was popular, and they were not a couple until they graduated. The aftermath of their high school experience still haunts them in various ways, as the series explores their insecurities and various traits, which were shaped by their adolescence. As Holzman states, the adult characters were "struggling with and being challenged by aspects of their own teen identity. And that's how I linked it all."

Network executives did not take into account the small yet strong cult fan base. The series was also the first to have an online campaign, "Operation Life Support," to save the series. This would foreshadow future grassroots fan communities uniting to attempt to save a series. Communication via physical fan mail was still common, with Holzman stating that viewers wrote about how the series gave them a sense of belonging. Holzman went on to write the playbook for the Broadway blockbuster *Wicked* and returned to television in 2018 as the showrunner of *Roadies*. Danes and Leto would become stars in their own right, which will be discussed in the next section.

## Gen Z Stardom: Claire Danes and Jared Leto

By the end of *My So-Called Life*, Holzman stated she knew Claire Danes was becoming a movie star. For her television debut in the short-lived series, she already received a Primetime Emmy nomination for Outstanding Lead Actress in a Drama Series, and a Golden Globe Award for Best Actress. The same year that *My So-Called Life* premiered, she made her film debut in *Little Women* (1994) alongside Gen Z heroine Winona Ryder, Kristen Dunst, and Susan Sarandon. She was also cast as Juliet opposite Leonardo DiCaprio in Baz Luhrman's *Romeo + Juliet* (1996). The film was a film festival, critical, and commercial box office success that writers continue to praise. This marked the shift from Danes' career into film acting. DiCaprio's star power would catapult the following year with the release of *Titanic*, which became the highest-grossing film at the time. It also launched him as a worldwide teen idol and led to one of his many Oscar nominations. Like Danes, DiCaprio began his work as a teen television actor (although as a supporting cast member) on *Growing Pains*. Even then, his performance as an orphan with an alcoholic parent placed him as a future star. While DiCaprio is one of the most highly paid and successful actors of his generation who continues to be a film star, his peers' careers are marked by transitions and more opportunities in television as they approach middle age.

Following her role as Juliet, Danes worked steadily in film, but her return to television rejuvenated her career. First, her titular role in the 2010 HBO film *Temple Grandin* led to her first Emmy Award and second Golden Globe. The following year, she was cast as the star of the Showtime CIA political thriller *Homeland* (2011–2020), for which she won numerous accolades and acting awards: her second Primetime Emmy, two additional Golden Globes, and a Television Critics Association Award.

As a teen and young adult, Danes' performances in *My So-Called Life*, *Little Women*, and *Romeo + Juliet* were marked by her emotional vulnerability and sensitivity, a balance of precociousness and youthful naivete, and naturalistic yet expressive acting style. At any given time, she could represent Gen X ambivalence and aloofness, and then suddenly break into visceral sobbing. Furthermore, for her role as CIA counterterrorism agent Carrie Matheson in *Homeland,* she exuded professional toughness and determination.

For his role as Jordan Catalano, Jared Leto became a teen idol for many Gen Z women and future fans of *My So-Called Life*. A scene in HBO's *Euphoria* even depicts protagonist Rue's younger sister watching the series on her laptop. The 17-year-old states that she hopes she won't fall for a boy like Catalano, to which she responds, "but he's so cute." Jordan was initially an elusive crush and tumultuous relationship for Angela. He had the grunge uniform that Cher's *Clueless* (1995) would later deride for its sloppiness and lack of effort: long, messy hair, flannel shirts, and baggy, ripped jeans. The camera often cut to his mysterious gazes, and his problems with literacy showed a sensitive and vulnerable side to the character. In the end, he was as shallow as a prototypical jock when he wrote a song about his car, "Red," that Angela mistook for a reference to his love for her and her amber hair. He remains immortalized for his role as Catalano, primarily through Gen X women. Upon the anticipated DVD release of the series, a 2007 *New York Times* article described the Jordan Catalano phenomenon:

> To a certain sort of woman who is somewhere between late youth and an unacknowledged middle age, the name Jordan Catalano isn't a television reference, it is a sense memory. You don't recall Jordan Catalano, you feel him, as you do the erotic miscalculations of your own adolescence.[16]

Leto's career shows how white male actors' careers are often not deterred by growing older, as ageism is more often directed toward women. He worked throughout the 1990s and 2000s in various supporting and leading roles. Leto retained a certain edgy, bad-boy persona on and off the stage, and gained much acclaim for his role as a heroin addict in *Requiem for a Dream* (2000). For his role as a transgender woman (which defied his type) alongside Matthew McConaughey in *Dallas Buyers Club* (2013), Leto won an Academy Award, Golden Globe and Screen Actors Guild Award for best-supporting actress.

## Gen Z Stardom and *Freaks and Geeks*

*Freaks and Geeks* also deals with the same type of rebellion of a "good girl gone bad," with central protagonist Lindsey Weir (Linda Cardellini) changing her expected identity following the death of her grandmother. Instead of dying her hair, she begins to wear her grandfather's oversized green army jacket over her clothes every day. A star student and prominent member of the math club, she begins to hang out with the school "freaks," who are known for skipping school, smoking pot, and listening to progressive rock. The series, which premiered in 1999 but is set in 1981, begins with a cliched scene of high school popularity. This is quickly followed by defiance of this image to establish that the series will not be your typical teen television program. The geeks, including Lindsey's younger brother Sam, are freshmen.

Shortly after the end of *Freaks and Geeks,* Apatow created *Undeclared* (2001–2003, Fox), which centered around college life and also starred alumni Seth Rogen and Jason Segel, who he would later collaborate with in the film industry. Busy Phillips also appeared in two episodes of *Undeclared*. However, the series would only last one season before cancellation. Beginning in 2005, Apatow went on to have a lucrative career as a film producer.

Apatow also went on to support the writer-actor and director-actor careers of *Freaks and Geeks* alumni Rogen and Segel, while James Franco reached stardom in his own right yet still frequently collaborated with his former castmates. Rogen co-starred in Apatow's *Knocked Up* (2007), and Apatow produced Rogen projects such as *Superbad* (2007) and *Pineapple Express* (2008), which co-starred Franco. Apatow also supported Jason Segel's project *Forgetting Sarah Marshall* (2008). These successful film collaborations propelled Rogen and Segel as commercially and critically acclaimed comedic writers and actors. Creator Paul Fieg's career also grew, and he and Apatow would work together on the Kristen Wiig star project *Bridesmaids* (2011). Following the success of the series, the film and television industry sought out new talent from women, and Apatow returned to television to produce Lena Dunham's *Girls* (2012–2017, HBO).

Linda Cardellini and Busy Phillips' careers did not initially thrive as much as their counterparts, which could further account for the difficulties women face in the industry. Yet, both found success in television later in their careers, in which their future roles would be influenced by their *Geeks* characters. Phillips retained the spirit of Kim Kelly and often played outspoken and confident women. She went on to be a recurring cast member in *Dawson's Creek* from 2001 to 2003 as Joey's extroverted college roommate, Audrey. This mirrored the Lindsey-Kim dynamic, even echoing a love triangle. Just as Lindsey was initially intimidated by Kim, Joey found Audrey too much of a party girl. In both cases, Phillips' characters helped the shyer starring roles come out of their shell, which led to lasting friendships. Later, she was cast in the prominent primetime medical drama *ER* from 2006 to 2007. After playing supporting roles in films, she again gained recognition for her performance in *Cougar Town* (2009–2015, ABC). In her 2018 memoir, *This Will Only Hurt a Little*, Phillips' advocacy for sexual abuse victims heightened alongside the height of the #MeToo and #TimesUp movements. She revealed James Franco assaulted her on the set of *Freaks and Geeks*, which constituted one of many supported accusations against the actor. Phillips also briefly hosted a late-night talk show, *Busy Tonight* (2018–2019, E!). Her goal of inclusion for women in the late-night talk show genre was laid out in her memoir, yet its short-lived nature on the cable program reveals the persistent challenges of women's place in the genre and platform.

Like her former co-star Phillips, Cardellini also went on to play in *ER* (from 2003 to 2009). She played Velma, a nod to her nerd-girl role as Lindsey Weir for discerning fans, in the film reboot of *Scooby Doo* (2000) and its 2004 sequel. While poorly received by critics, the teen mystery franchise's success at the box office showed its enduring appeal. The expansion of niche-casting on cable and streaming platforms opened new opportunities for Cardellini. Her guest appearance in *Mad Men* led to an Emmy nomination, and she co-starred in two prominent Netflix original dramas, *Bloodline* (2015–2017) and *Dead to Me* (2019–present). Both series play on Cardellini's characters' proclivity toward naïveté and introverted roles, but in the context of crime.

*The New York Times'* columnist Carl Wilson laments the nostalgia of the 1990s and Generation X. He sums up his generation by two defining characteristics: "our dislike of nostalgia and our irritation whenever our barely formed narratives were appropriated and marketed back at us."[17] In a feature from the following year, fellow *New York Times* writer and Gen Xer A. O. Scott (also the newspaper's leading film critic) addresses the notion of a "Generation X midlife crisis" with an expected sardonic approach. He jabs at Baby Boomer editors' distaste of using the word ironic, a landmark term of Gen X. As Scott writes:

> We grew up in the shadow of the Baby Boomers, who still manage, in their dotage, to commandeer disproportionate attention. Every time they hit a life-cycle milestone it's worth 10 magazine covers. When they retire, the Social Security system will go under! When they die, narcissism will be so much lonelier.[18]

## *Dawson's Creek*, the Rise and Fall of the WB, and Narrowcasting in the Post-network Era

*Dawson's Creek* (1998–2003) became one of WB's first teen soap successes, often lauded as "quality teen TV" based on the heightened vocabularies of its main characters, adult-like content, and class consciousness. Unlike its network predecessor *Beverly Hills 90210* (1990–2000, Fox), it returned to a less glamorous location but also did not hold a moral, Midwestern center through its parent figures, who were all as flawed as their children. Set in a small, predominantly white New England fishing town and quaint tourist destination, Dawson was the only child of an upper-middle-class family, and an enthused cinephile, who actively worshipped the films of Steven Spielberg. His best friend Joey Potter (Katie Holmes) was the precocious brunette abandoned by her parents and raised by her older sister and partner, who ran the town bed and breakfast. Pacey (Joshua Jackson) was Dawson's other best friend and served as the bad-boy, blue-collar heartthrob. New student Jen (Michelle Williams) was introduced, followed by siblings Andie (Meredith Monroe) and Jack (Kerr Smith). Jen was forced to move to the sleepy town with her grandmother after she was ignored by her New York City parents and acted out via drug and alcohol use and hypersexuality. Much like the original plot of *Riverdale*, which premiered nearly ten years later (2017–, CW), Betty and Joey were the book-smart, virginal-girl next-door archetypes, Jen and Veronica were the street-smart, sexually active new girls from the city, Dawson and Archie were the impressionable and relatable protagonists, and Pacey and Jughead were the blue-collar outcasts.

Jack eventually comes out in the series, and a kiss with a classmate launched the first male gay kiss on primetime television. His sister Andie dated Pacey but is most remembered for her mental health problems coupled with her ambition to get into Harvard. In Season 4, Episode 6, "Great Xpectations," she steals an ecstasy pill from Jen to celebrate her acceptance into the ivy-league institution, leading to a psychotic break that ultimately sends her to a psychiatric ward rather than university. *Dawson's Creek* was also one of the first series to provide a narrative transition into the college years and continued to attract audiences while Dawson struggled at film school in California, Jen stayed close to home at an affordable institution, and the love triangle with Pacey continued when Dawson returned to the East Coast.

The writers of the series also incorporated popular film and music of the time, while also employing cross-promotions in its popular soundtracks by Warner Brothers artists. *Dawson's Creek* became one of the first series to highlight songs featured in a given episode at the end of the program, promoting the series' accompanying CD soundtrack.

Many of the series' teen stars, such as Katie Holmes, Michelle Williams, and Joshua Jackson, gained success after the series' end, while the titular star James Van Der Beek's career was less lucrative. While Holmes continued to act, she is perhaps most well-known (and reached her celebrity status) for her infamous marriage to Tom Cruise during the height of his commitment to Scientology, which was rumored to be a contributing factor to their divorce. Michelle Williams became an indie film starlet and was nominated several times for an

Academy Award as Best Supporting Actress (i.e., for *Brokeback Mountain* [2005] and *Manchester by the Sea* [2016]) and Best Actress (i.e., for *Blue Valentine* [2010] and *My Week with Marilyn* [2011]). Joshua Jackson was already a child film star when he started on *Dawson's Creek*, known for his appearances in the popular *Mighty Ducks* series and as the central protagonist in the J. J. Abrams-led science fiction series *Fringe* (2008–2013). Busy Phillips joined the cast during the college years after the cancellation of *Freaks and Geeks* on NBC. Although both series featured non-traditional, smart, and outcast-like characters, *Creek's* soap tactics via its love triangles, along with its sex appeal with more freedom on the WB, contributed to its success over the idiosyncratic cult hit *Freaks and Geeks*, which is today considered more of a "quality" series and early example of narrowcasting. *Dawson's Creek*, on the other hand, is considered more dated and remembered for its soap quality, music, and stars. In the post-network era, a popular CW teen series like *Riverdale* chose to defy the Archie-comics love-triangle trope, while *Dawson's Creek* embraced it in several iterations: from Jen, Dawson, and Joey, to Joey, Jack, and Dawson, to its most long-running, Dawson, Joey, and Pacey.

The Joey-Dawson-Pacey love triangle is the series' most long-running and most famous, serving as the final cliffhanger for the series finale. This manifests through a ten-year time jump in which Joey picks Pacey over Dawson, and the two watch Dawson's teen soap series, which he created based on his real life and in which his proxy character gets the girl. This parallel hints to the series' auteurist nature of creator and showrunner Kevin Williamson, a marketing scheme that would soon benefit Joshua Schwartz in one of the last major network teen series, *The O.C.* (2003–2007, Fox), and Fox's return to dominate the genre after WB's height in the late 1990s and early 2000s. *Dawson's Creek* lasted almost as long as its network WB, which first aired in 1998 and ended in 2004 upon its merge with UPN to create the current youth-driven network The CW. The shift in WB and UPN to focus on white teen audiences and related programming saw a decline in black-centered series, from *Moesha* (1996–2001, UPN) to *The Jamie Foxx Show* (1996–2001, WB), while budding showrunner Mara Brok Akil's *Girlfriends* (starring

Tracee Ellis Ross) transitioned from UPN from 2000–2006 to the CW in 2006–2008, making it one the longest-running live-action sitcoms on network television during its time. This was preceded by the likes of *Cheers* (1982–1993) and *Ozzie and Harriet* (1952–1966) and was followed by *Two and a Half Men* (2003–2015) and *It's Always Sunny in Philadelphia* (2005–present). After her success as a showrunner for BET after the demise of UPN, Akil and her husband Salam Akil received an overall deal with WB, marking her return to the CW with the DC superhero adaptation of *Black Lightning* (2018–, CW). This is part of television's recent turn to include more diversity on and offscreen. CW continues to be the leader of successful primetime teen series, while ABC Family sitcoms such as *Fresh Off the Boat* (2015–present) centers around a Chinese-American family, and Black-ish (2014–present) includes central teen protagonists. The latter even led to ABC Family's *Grown-ish* (2018–present), a spinoff mirroring *The Cosby Show* and *A Different World* about the eldest daughter, Zooey's, transition into college life.

With the demise of *90210* and *Dawson's Creek* in the early 2000s, *The O.C.* (2003–2007, Fox) and *Veronica Mars* (2004–2007, UPN/CW) signaled a new era of teen TV. In the pilot episode of *The O.C.*, outsider and James Dean-inspired Ryan Atwood accompanies nerd indie-boy Seth Cohen (Adam Brody) to a typical Harbor High School party. Ryan drinks alcohol and gets into a fight, which is not new for him. It does appear to be new territory for Seth, the outsider at his own high school. Although the two face a hangover and lecture from Cohen's parents the next day, the after-school-special moralistic lesson is less present than in previous teen series. Marissa Cooper (Mischa Barton) later has to confront her substance abuse issues when she is caught shoplifting. Amidst the struggles of the SATs and college, Seth starts to rely on marijuana as an escape from his life, which he eventually stops. In latter Millennial and Gen X series like *Gossip Girl*, *Friday Night Lights*, *Veronica Mars*, *Riverdale*, and *13 Reasons Why* drinking and taking drugs is ubiquitous with the teen experience. Perhaps US TV took a cue from Canadian series *Degrassi* or the UK's *Skins*, which is discussed further in the following chapters.

## *Degrassi*

Through its various spinoffs and reboots, *Degrassi* spanned decades since the late 1970s, representing all four core generations. New installments were developed based on new generations at *Degrassi High*, and the strongest thread can be seen through Spike, the former teenage mother, of *Degrassi High*, of *Next Generation's* Emma. The series balanced keeping the same narrative rites of passage for each new cast but provided new outcomes and issues, with shifts in the identities and issues relevant to North American teens.

Due to the public-service-television nature of *Degrassi*, along with the commitment of its creators, showrunners, and producers to relay significant issues for teens, the Canadian series depicted unprecedented topics for the teen TV genre. In an interview with co-creator, Linda Schuyler, she states that the series had a "double mandate" to inform and educate, as they knew it would be a new resource for classrooms as a "discussion starter." While some after-school specials were precedents for *Degrassi*, Schuyler believed they had failed to address the actual problems kids face in their lives, which she had witnessed as a junior high school teacher. This gap in teen media is what inspired her to conceive of socially relevant content for the age group. Schuyler aimed to treat young people and their lives with respect and not allow adults to fill the position of ultimate authority and problem solver for resolution and closure. This adolescent independence stands in contrast to previous family programming and budding teen TV that placed parents and adults as the gatekeepers of right and wrong. Schuyler even emphasized that the natural inclusion of adult figures in the teens' lives would still be told from their perspective.

Schuyler's strive for authenticity is reflected both on and offscreen, where she hired expert writers on the topics and age-appropriate actors for both the teenage and adult roles. Teen TV has been criticized for hiring actors in their twenties, sometimes approaching their thirties, who portray its protagonists. Furthermore, parent roles can also face scrutiny when they are too close in age to their onscreen children. Representation of sexuality was also important for Schuyler, as she cites the series evolved from first including a gay brother, to out gay and bi roles in *Degrassi: Next Generation*, to trans and non-binary characters in its most recent installation, *Degrassi: Next Class*. With this dedication to authenticity came workshops and the introduction of expert consultants and new writers who could provide the perspectives necessary to reflect onscreen inclusion. This understanding that the offscreen representation in the writer's room that leads to higher-up positions in the television hierarchy (producers, directors, executive producers, showrunners, creators) is important to properly portray onscreen characters and their arcs is what US academics, TV critics, and industry professionals have pushed for from media industries. While this type of thoughtfulness and attempt at equality is ingrained in *Degrassi*, it remains a rarity in US television, despite incremental change since the rise of streaming platforms that is unstable. With Canada's proximity to the US, Schuyler mentioned that some topics such as school shootings were intentionally relevant to her home country's response rather than a result of its own violence.

Schuyler produced and directed several short after-school specials for the Canadian Broadcasting Channel (CBC) before the first iteration of the franchise series, *The Kids of Degrassi Street* (1979–1986). These were *Ida Makes a Movie* (1979), *Cookie Goes to the Hospital* (1980), *Irene Moves In* (1981), and *Noel Buys a Suit* (1981). Throughout the franchise Schuyler, along with her partner and fellow former junior high school teacher, Kit Hood, created and developed the various iterations of the series, while Yan Moore served as the longest-running head writer. The program was also distributed in the UK (BBC), the US (Showtime and Disney Channel), Australia (Nickelodeon Kids and ABC TV), Ireland (RTÉ One and RTÉ Two), South Africa (M-Net), India (Star Plus), Gibraltar (GBC-TV), Namibia (NBC), Zambia (ZNBC), Malaysia (RTM 1), and Kuwait (KTV 2). In 1988, the *Los Angeles Times* designated *Degrassi* as a children's program, "but it is one that portrays the problems of adolescents with a frankness that might startle even the adult audiences of its competition." *Degrassi* tackled teen issues that most US programs avoided: abortion, alcoholism, AIDS, body image, bullying, death, cheating, date rape, depression, divorce, domestic violence, drug abuse, eating disorders, the environment, gang violence, gay rights and homophobia, mental health, self-harm, suicide, virginity loss and, later, school shootings, disabled rights, and transphobia (among others). The pop culture blog *Vulture* recounted 239 topical issues the series tackled in its 12 seasons.

Its second installment, *Degrassi Junior High* (1987–1989, CBC), was lauded by TV critics and educational boards for approaching major and minor adolescent issues (e.g., pregnancy and puberty to a prescription for glasses) in teens' own languages. It was lauded for not exploiting adolescence but treating it with unprecedented thoughtfulness.

*Degrassi High* won best children's show for the International Emmy Awards in 1987, the grand prize at the TV Banff Festival in 1988, and was endorsed by the National Education Association and the American Association of School Administrators.

While the first two *Degrassi* series were not directly linked as predecessors or spinoffs, *Degrassi Junior High* and *Degrassi High* (1989–1991) marked a clear continuation of the same characters and storylines. In a narrative involving teenage abortion, the US distribution on PBS censored anti-abortion protests. The N network, as Schuyler stated, has also censored abortion episodes since 2005.

Treatment of abortion, particularly teen abortion, remains sparse and taboo on US television. The longevity of the series also allowed for an audience age range of 12–35 years. The original late 1970s and 1980s installments of *Degrassi* targeted younger Baby Boomers and their families, while Gen X teens and their Baby Boomer parents could watch *Degrassi Junior High* and *Degrassi High*. The child conceived by *Degrassi Junior High*'s Shane McKay and Christine "Spike" Nelson, Emma Nelson, became one of the lead characters in *Degrassi: The Next Generation*. *Next Generation* lasted for 14 seasons, originally aired on CTV from 2001 to 2009, and was followed by *Much Music* from 2010 to 2013 and MTV Canada from 2013 to 2015. The series became the most-watched drama on Canadian television during its first season. Thus, thirty-something Gen Xers could watch the series with nostalgia and interest for future installments and/or together with their Millennial children. It was distributed on Teen Nick in the US and in over 140 countries. In 2012, *Degrassi* also became the longest-running program in Canadian history. In January 2016, *Degrassi* entered the streaming era with the sequel, *Degrassi: The Next Class*, which would stream on Netflix in the US.

## Stardom and *Moesha*: Brandy Norwood

Teen series before the streaming era were already rare, but those that centered on non-white protagonists were even rarer. While black teens were featured on family network sitcoms, they would not reappear until a series like *Black-ish* (2014–, ABC) and its *A Different World*-inspired college spinoff, *Grown-ish* (2018–, Freeform). *Moesha* stands out for its rare status as a black cast sitcom and teen TV series, and for its impact on both Gen X and Millennial viewers. The series also sheds light on the scarcity of black cast series following the demise of the UPN network. Born in 1979, Brandy Norwood's music and acting career would appeal to younger Gen Xers and rising Millennials, and for the micro-generation of "Xennials." As a product of the MTV generation and R&B and pop crossover, her music videos and guest appearances would also be featured on Black Entertainment Television (BET). Millennials would be especially familiar with the heavy rotation of her 1998 duet with Monica, "The Boy is Mine," which also won a Grammy Award for Best R&B Performance by a Duo or Group with Vocal.

Norwood tapped into the music industry before its digital downfall with her new jack swing brand of R&B, which signaled the rise of online illegal downloading services such as Napster in the late 1990s. Her self-titled 1994 debut album, released at the age of 14, reached 20 on the Billboard charts and gained quadruple platinum status.[19]

*Moesha* became UPN's most popular show and her performance gained Norwood an NAACP Award for Outstanding Youth Actor/Actress in 1997.

Alfred L. Martin Jr., a media scholar of blackness, sexuality, genre, and industry, places *Moesha* in the genre of black-cast sitcom and family sitcom with teen star, before the teen genre that it also influenced. As he states, "*Moesha* was a Black-cast teen show that dealt with teen issues, including homosexuality, because series creator Ralph Farquhar imagined the series as a bit edgier."[20]

*Moesha* also incorporated Norwood's musical talent, from Norwood recording the series theme song showing single-camera performances in contrast to the three-camera sitcom style to which it adhered.

The teen dramas on the CW that followed *Moesha* would switch to single camera.

Furthermore, deferring *Moesha* from CBS to UPN showed how a black-centered teen series made network leaders uncertain of its "mainstream" appeal. As Martin states:

> This conundrum returns to the casting-contingent terms of Moesha's pickup at CBS. Brandy was largely unknown to the white executives at CBS because she was understood as a black singer, not a "universal" black singer in the vein of Whitney Houston or Janet Jackson.[21]

After Whitney Houston, Norwood became the second black woman to be featured on the cover of *Seventeen* magazine. Martin states that this marked her crossover to both mainstream youth and television culture. Norwood and Houston would later co-star in the 1997 live-action musical remake of *Cinderella* (ABC, Disney Channel). Pitching *Moesha* with Norwood as the star was also based on past black R&B-turned-TV stars such as *Will Smith* (Fresh Prince of Bel-Air, 1990–1996) and Queen Latifah (*Living Single*, 1993–1998, Fox) and "demonstrated how success in the music industry could translate these elements of black culture into mainstream sitcom success."[22]

Martin also astutely argues that *Moesha* was a precedent for UPN's future teen series, many of which would cross over to the CW in 2006. As he writes:

> After two seasons on the air (and establishing itself as a hit for the network), *Moesha* had transcended its status as "only" a Black-cast sitcom, thus, UPN used the show to build its white-cast teen programming, including series like *Clueless*

(ABC, 1996–1997, UPN, 1997–1998) and *Veronica Mars* (UPN, 2004–2006, The CW, 2006–2007, Hulu, 2019). Signaling the differences in the imaginations of Black versus white teen audiences, *Veronica Mars* would frequently engage with gay storylines throughout its three-season run on UPN.

Although *Moesha* continued to be a ratings success, it was cancelled in 2001 after its sixth and final season. Critical media and race scholar Philana Payton notes that *Moesha* was one of several black-centered series that included teen issues, but that the demise of the UPN network marked a drought in black programming:

> *Moesha* was definitely special, but it didn't feel like a rare occurrence for us because there were many options as opposed to what happened following the UPN/WB merge and into the 2000s Black TV drought. This was something that was noticeable, essentially UPN was the station with the most Black television shows and, after the merge, they cancelled them all with no comparable replacements.[23]

Payton also remarks on the generational specificity for Millennial black audiences:

> For me, and other Black folks of our generation, there was a range of television shows centered on blackness, and several specifically with Black teens as the focus.

*Moesha*'s demise mirrors the ultimate end of the UPN. As Martin writes, "Nevertheless, Norwood's successes were largely confined to black audiences, [who where] a demographic UPN executives were reticent to target." Furthermore, as he quotes from his interview with series creator, Ralph Farquhar, he goes on to state the following:

> It is a cold fact of the television advertising business that programs that attract a largely minority audience command

lower advertising rates, from a smaller pool of advertisers, than shows with broader appeal.[24]

Black series on UPN would be largely replaced on the WB network by white-cast teen TV series. The television landscape continued to lack black cast series, which were more commonly found via BET, such as *Girlfriends* (2000–2006 [UPN] and 2006–2008 [CW]) spinoff, *The Game* (2011–2015), which originally aired on the CW from 2006 to 2009. *Girlfriends* and *The Game* were both created by showrunner Mara Brok Akil, who also later conceived the former teen film star Gabrielle Union series *Being Mary Jane* (2013–2019). In 2018, Akil returned to the CW as a producer for her collaborator and husband, Salam Akil, on the *Black Lightning* (2018–) project, which is an adaptation of DC Comics first black superhero story. Originally planned for Fox, its switch to the CW shows how the network has now become known for taking greater risks than traditional networks, as well as the rare status CW carries over from its UPN and WB predecessors. Smith and Latifah's acting and recording continued to thrive after their sitcom series, and their status as NBC and Fox stars (in contrast to UPN) can be attributed to Norwood's initial post-*Moesha* career slump. For Issa Rae, creator and star of HBO's *Insecure* (2016–), *Moesha* was her most recent precedent for a series about a "regular black girl."[25] The series inspired her to pursue television, and she used the script formats as models for her own.

With *Insecure*, Rae became the first black woman to create and star in an HBO original series. Before her, Wanda Sykes was the first black woman to do so on primetime TV with her series *Wanda at Large*, which lasted two seasons (2003, Fox). For Rae, whose series is not about the burdens of being black but is intended to be about what is both universal and unique about average young black life, this scarcity in representation is simply a sad notion: "Isn't it sad that it's revolutionary? It's so basic... but we don't get to do that. We don't get to just have a show about regular black people being basic."[26]

Despite a decline in album sales in the 2000s, Norwood remains one of the best-selling women solo artists of all time, culminating in over

40 million records worldwide. She has also won two Grammy Awards and several Billboard Music Awards.[27]

Norwood's career resurged in the 2010s. In 2015, she made her Broadway debut. She returned to acting on television with BET's *The Game* in 2012, which also originated in UPN. *Moesha*, along with early seasons of *The Game*, *Sister, Sister*, and other UPN series, finally became available to stream online in 2020.[28]

## Winnie Holzman, Creator and Showrunner of *My So-Called Life*

### Interview

*Stefania Marghitu:* I'm interested in what your early interests were with youth culture. Medium wise, you were interested in poetry, then musical theatre, and then you started working in television. Where did your interest in writing about youth come from?

*Winnie Holzman:* I grew up watching television. I was certainly interested in poetry at an early age and started writing it at an early age. But I was always watching TV and I was certainly influenced by shows like *The Mary Tyler Moore Show*, and other shows that were making an impact when I was growing up. *Mary Tyler Moore* was about culture and politics and the news.

How did I first start writing about teens? I was writing for this show called *Thirtysomething* and the men who created that show, Ed Zwick and Marshall Herskovitz, came to me about developing another show. They were interested in me creating it. And that's where it started. They [Zwick and Herskovitz] had had an idea years before this for a show about a teen boy, and that led to them suggesting that I create a show about a teen girl. And I've said this before in interviews, but I don't think I would have come up with the idea if I was left with my own devices. I wasn't thinking about teenagers or my own teen years at the time. However, when they suggested this idea, I wanted to try it. It just shows the power of a positive collaboration. I really trusted them, and I still do.

And the more I started writing, with them encouraging me, the more it came together. And this is a process over many months, it was a conversation.

SM: And my understanding is you went to some local high schools for research as well, that influenced writing the diary of Angela Chase [that became the voiceover in *My So-Called Life*]?

WH: Yeah, I started writing a diary, at Ed Zwick's suggestion. It was fairly short. I did it as a jumping off/ starting point, which was helpful. And as for the research, it was really about putting myself back in that space, picking up on things like language and posture. I did a very small amount of research, to be clear. I did three days, four days tops, worth of research at high schools. They were all in Los Angeles. I went to public schools and a private school a distant friend from college worked at. But I'm talking about maybe two days at each school, but not even full days. So I don't want this to be "Oh she created a documentary."

SM: I'm curious as to the intent of *My So-Called Life* and if there was an intention to show the specific generation, there have been articles about this generation between Generation X and Millennials that the series encapsulates—known as Xennials or the Jordan Catalano generation. So I was curious about the development process—choosing Angela Chase to be into grunge. Did you work with music supervisors, costume designers to capture that specific moment in time? I'm thinking of the episode with Kurt Cobain's death and Catalano's band.

WH: We worked with a very creative group of people, and everything kind of came from the script. We had this costume designer Patrick Norris who has since become a director, and he was really incredible with what he did with the costumes. He would read the script and get excited about ideas. Even the kids (actors) themselves had influence. And everyone was talking to each other.

In terms of Kurt Cobain, that's just stuff that was happening. I was just trying to be aware of what was going on around music. When you talk about Xiennials, I don't really think about stuff like that. I don't think about people in that way. I'm not into categorizing people by generation.

There are different generations, but part of the truth about that show was that I was operating on an assumption, a belief, you could say, that things don't change that much, on a deeper level, from generation to generation. Because if I had to write about things in terms of generation, I would have been paralyzed. I was about to turn 40, and I would have not been equipped to do that.

SM: That's very insightful, that for you it was about the universal. For example, in contrast Paul Feig didn't want to do a teen show about contemporary teens in the late 1990s, so *Freaks and Geeks* was set in the early 1980s when he was a teen.

WH: And, of course, I took things from my own history, and my friends' histories. But I was also trying to be awake to the times for the show. And it was also about being around a great group of young, creative actors, and we observed them and were influenced by them.

SM: And it also brings to mind something as poignant as Angela reading the *Diary of Anne Frank,* which is something generations of teens have read for decades. And Angela herself being able to relate to it. I also love the

|       | Chase parents trying to understand their daughter, and think back to when they were young. So you see them questioning what it was like for them and trying to figure out the pieces of the puzzle of adolescence. |
| ----- | ----- |
| WH:   | And I also felt that I was trying to show, as I said, that who we are in high school, we are either always running from that or trying to embrace that somehow. I saw all the adults in the show as struggling with and being challenged by aspects of their own teen identity. And that's how I linked it all. That was a principal of mine and what I was doing. |
| SM:   | Could you speak to the choice of making the show an hour-long drama over the more popular 30-minute comedy-oriented sitcoms of the time? |
| WH:   | When I first wrote the pilot, it was as a 30-minute show. And I didn't think it would work for us or accomplish what we wanted. It was probably a lot to do with the fact that I was used to writing an hour-long show, as I'd just been writing on *Thirtysomething*. |
| SM:   | So many fans have several parts of the show they look back at and remember so fondly. What are some of your most distinctive favorite parts of My So-Called Life when you look back at it? |
| WH:   | Everything about it. The fact that we made an interesting show. The people I was working with. And the fact that people took a lot from it and it gave them a feeling of belonging. That's a wonderful feeling for me. And certain of us from the show keep in touch, and we are all just deeply proud. That's the best way I can describe it. |
| SM:   | It's also great to know the show had so much physical fan mail but that it also became the first series to have an online campaign, "Operation Life Support" to save the show from cancellation, right on the cusp of a digital era. In terms of that physical mail, my understanding is you received quite a lot, especially after. |

WH: It got cancelled. Yeah, we did. You know you make a pilot and it was a very long time before it got picked up and aired. It was clear from the beginning, from the crew reaction, that it would connect to people. So it didn't come as a shock that there were a lot of reactions. All of it was gratifying. That's what you want, or what I want- to make something people can connect to. And make something that is genuine. That was our goal.

SM: Is the emphasis on family something that continues for you? I've read your latest show *Roadies* being described as a family, or even the school as a family in *Wicked*, or a micro-community or alternative family, something that continues to interest you and your work? But for me it's also about how you position difference, and how its treated in social hierarchies. How does that influence your writing? For me your work embraces difference rather than isolate it. And showing subcultures, loners, etc. Is that something you think about in your intention?

WH: Well yeah, all of the language that you just used I would never use because it's all pretty academic. [Laughs] It's just not how I talk. But yes of course I think about stuff like that. I think many people feel isolated, and alone. People who "fit in" and don't fit in feel that way. People being lonely, in general, I think about. And people's need to be accepted, or belong somewhere. Yes, that's something I give a lot of thought too. I think it's part of being human. What I'm interested in is how people appear to be so different and deep down we are all so connected, and how to reveal that.

SM: Was there a shift in the show's popularity once it started also airing on MTV?

WH: More people saw it, that's all. And it started being shown in Canada and other parts of the world. It just got exposure. I mean Claire [Danes] was already a movie star by then.

## Notes

1 Sherry B. Ortner, "Generation X: Anthropology in a Media-Saturated World," *Cultural Anthropology* 13, no. 3 (August 1998): 414–440.
2 Douglas Coupland, *Generation X: Tales for an Accelerated Culture* (London: St. Martin's Press, 1991).
3 Jonathon I. Oake, "*Reality Bites* and Generation X as Spectator," *The Velvet Light Trap* 53 (2003): 83–97.
4 Michael Newman, "From Beats to Arcs: Towards a Poetic of Television Narrative," *The Velvet Light Trap*, no. 58 (Fall 2006): 16–28.
5 For more on MTV, see Rob Tannenbaum, *I Want My MTV: The Uncensored Story of the Music Video Revolution* (New York: Dutton Penguin, 2011).
6 For more on *My So-Called Life*, see: Michelle Byers and David Layery, eds., *Dear Angela: Remembering My So-Called Life* (Lanham, MD: Rowman & Littlefield, 2007).
7 http://mentalfloss.com/article/56115/19-things-you-might-not-know-about-my-so-called-life
8 Henry Jenkins, *Convergence Culture: Where Old and New Media Collide* (New York: New York University Press, 2008).63.
9 For more on Beverly Hills 90210, see E. Graham McKinley, *Beverly Hills 90210: Television, Gender and Identity* (Philadelphia, PA: Temple University Press, 1997).
10 Todd Gitlin, *Inside Prime Time* (Berkeley, CA and Los Angeles, CA: University of Los Angeles Press 1983).
11 Glyn Davis and Kay Dickinson, eds., *Teen TV: Genre, Consumption and Identity* (London: British Film Institute, 2004), Sharon Marie Ross and Louisa Stein, eds., *Teen Television: Essays on Programming and Fandom* (Jefferson, NC: McFarland, 2008).
12 For more on *Buffy The Vampire Slayer*, see: Elana Levine and Lisa Parks, eds. *Undead TV: Essays on Buffy the Vampire Slayer* (Durham, NC: Duke University Press, 2007); Rhonda W. Wilcox and David Lavery, eds., *Fighting the Forces: What's at Stake in Buffy the Vampire Slayer?* (Lanham, MD: Rowman and Littlefield, 2002), and Roz Kaveney, ed., *Reading the Vampire Slayer: The Unofficial Critical Companion to Buffy and Angel* (London: I.B. Tauris, 2001).
13 For more on *Dawson's Creek*, see: Lori Bindig, *Dawson's Creek: A Critical Understanding* (Lanham, MD: Lexington Books, 2007).
14 Caroline E. Jones, "Unpleasant Consequences: First Sex in Buffy the Vampire Slayer, Veronica Mars, and Gilmore Girls," *Jeunesse: Young People, Texts, Cultures* 5, no. 1 (Summer 2013), The Centre for Research in Young People's Texts and Cultures, University of Winnipeg.
15 Wilson Cruz would later be featured in the Netflix series *13 Reasons Why* (2017–2020).
16 Ginia Bellafante, "A Teenager in Love (So-Called)," *The New York Times*, October 28, 2007, accessed September 9, 2017, https://www.nytimes.com/2007/10/28/arts/television/28bell.html
17 Carl Wilson, "The Gen-X Nostalgia Boom: My So-Called Adulthood," *The New York Times*, August 4, 2011, accessed August 1, 2017, http://www.nytimes.com/2011/08/07/magazine/the-gen-x-nostalgia-boom.html?pagewanted=all/.

18 A.O. Scott, "Gen X Has a Midlife Crisis," *The New York Times*, May 7, 2010, accessed August 7, 2017, http://www.nytimes.com/2010/05/09/weekinreview/09aoscott.html?pagewanted=all.
19 https://www.allmusic.com/artist/brandy-mn0000608945
20 Alfred L. Martin Jr., *The Generic Closet: Black Gayness and the Black-Cast Sitcom* (Bloomington: Indiana University Press, 2021).
21 Ibid.
22 Ibid.
23 Stefania Marghitu, personal communication, May 17, 2017.
24 Martin Jr. *Generic Closet*.
25 *NPR*, "Issa Rae Turns Basic Into Revolutionary With 'Insecure,'" *NPR*, October 7, 2016, accessed September 3, 2017, https://www.npr.org/2016/10/07/496984892/issa-rae-is-first-black-woman-to-create-star-in-premium-cable-show
26 Ibid.
27 IMDB – Brandy Norwood Awards, IMDB, accessed September 3, 2017, https://m.imdb.com/name/nm0005275/awards
28 *CBS News*, "'Moesha,' 'Sister, Sister' and 5 Other Classic Black Sitcoms are Coming to Netflix," *CBS News*, July 30, 2020, accessed July 30, 2020, https://www.cbsnews.com/video/moesha-sister-sister-and-5-other-classic-black-sitcoms-are-coming-to-netflix/

# 3

# MILLENNIAL TEEN TV

Millennials, born between 1981 and 1996, would be the last generation that did not have access to the Internet from birth, although they are often defined by their relationship to online exposure and digital behavior starting in their childhood and teen years. Thus, Hulu's *Pen 15* (2019–) depicts the anxiety and excitement of its protagonist's first log in to AOL Instant Messenger. More generally, the generation's attitude toward and inextricable connection with the Internet would be subsequently coupled with the repercussions of growing up online and with mobile technology. Millennials remember receiving their first cell phone, panicking about Y2K, watching the World Trade Center collapse on a school television, and logging in to Facebook once they established their university email account. Along these lines, Louisa E Stein's *Millennial Fandom* explores how the generation's comfort with and subsequent dependency on digital technologies is a running theme of discourses that either "celebrate millennial technological skill put to good use or . . . condemn [millennials'] technology-induced] social isolation and ethical depravity."[1]

Millennial teen TV ranges from *Degrassi: The Next Generation* (2001–2015, CTV/Much Music/MTV Canada) and Josh Schwartz's *The O.C.* (2003–2007, Fox,) and *Gossip Girl* (2007–2012, CW), through *Mean Girls* and Young Adult novel adaptations, to MTV's shift from music videos to reality TV programming, with MTV's *Real World* (1992–) and subsequent reboots, spinoffs, and imitations having given rise to the popularity of youth reality TV. Millennials witnessed the end of the network era, and the rise of the multi-channel era. While they are known for their digital savvy, they can still remember life before the Internet and smartphones. Millennials lived through two Bush presidencies, the Clinton and Obama eras, and then the rise of Trump in their twenties and thirties. Millennials born in the early 1980s often align with elements of Gen Z, a "micro-generation" sometimes referred to as "Xennials" but also often nicknamed "The Oregon Trail Generation," after the early video game; this micro-generation preceded the rise of "Mainstream Tech" and the "Catalano Generation," whose name is taken from *My So-Called Life*'s lead heartthrob.[2] Indeed, the availability of syndicated programming, DVDs, and streaming platforms gave millennials unprecedented access to a wide variety of media. Millennials continued to gain more access to education, delaying marriage and parenthood like Gen Xers before them.[3] US teen TV programming in this era also had an expansive global reach, particularly on burgeoning UK networks.[4] Millennial teen TV would highlight the issues of race, ethnicity, class, sexuality, and gender identity that would become priorities for the generation's first wave of elected politicians: from Alexandria Ocasio-Cortez to Pete Buttigieg.

Stein provides a useful framework for understanding millennial representation in teen TV in relation to convergence and participatory culture.[5] She states:

> The tensions that emerge in the millennial media landscape between increased corporate consolidation and more democratized opportunities for digital authorship affect our understandings of the ideological work of millennial media and the possibilities of audience engagement and authorship.[6]

Further, Stein emphasizes how teen TV is an intrinsically transmedia genre, and also notes the proliferation of paratexts in the digital era. Stein exemplifies this point by juxtaposing *Glee*'s progressive and conservative messages. *Glee* (2009–2015, Fox) initially depicts a harsh high school hierarchy in a midwestern town, with the football players and cheerleaders as bullies at the top, and everyone else at their mercy. These borders are broken down with the inclusion of the All American Finn, bad boy Puck, and cheerleader Quinn in the Glee Club, along with various outsiders. Further, the story arcs of Santana, a Latinx cheerleader and reformed mean girl, and blonde bimbo Britney, reveal both characters to be bisexual.

Early seasons of *Glee* show the once-popular characters' reluctance to relinquish their social cachet; this relinquishment leads to their experiencing the kinds of punishments they once administered. Eventually, they choose the fulfillment they receive from both singing and dancing in the Glee club, along with the relationships and sense of community and belonging that the space provides. The eventual unity of the Glee students affords a utopian image of diversity that also breaks down high school hierarchies. While Finn and Quinn, the initial ideal cheerleader-jock couple, are white, Santana, a tertiary character, is Latinx. Finn's new relationship with a precocious, scholastically ambitious, and Glee-driven Rachel further breaks down the high school hierarchies. Rachel is also perceived as not traditionally beautiful, in contrast to Quinn, although her choice in fashion and styling contribute to her image as a "nerd girl."

The verbally precocious protagonists of *Dawson's Creek* reflect the Xennials who came of age before mainstream technology, but enjoyed greater access to media than Gen Xers. Meanwhile, characters like Seth Cohen of *The O.C.* and the eponymous protagonist of *Veronica Mars* reflect millennials' pop-culture literacy and digital know-how. US millennials are more ethnically and racially diverse than past generations, and LGBTQIA+ and the push for immigrants' rights represented prominent civil rights milestones. Series such as *My So-Called Life*, *Moesha*, *Dawson's Creek*, and *Veronica Mars* began to embrace greater inclusivity with respect to race and sexuality, while *Glee* became a mainstream teen series with queer protagonists, signaling that, as Raffi Sarkissian writes, "Gay teens had arrived on TV" and that teen TV was finally ready to portray them as complex characters not solely defined by their othered sexuality. Sarkissian expands:

> Most LGBT characters are reduced in narrative conceptualization to the trope of "coming out of the closet," precluding the development of a fully realized and layered character, whose purpose in the narrative (while not exclusively) is to play the foil to the heterosexual characters. Due to the relative multitude of LGBT characters in *Glee*, however, they present a spectrum of relations to "coming out of the closet," none of which make it out to be an individual problem or one presented exclusively from the heterosexual characters' point of view. Instead, they are presented as complex, intricately related to larger plot lines and falling in line with broad themes of identity exploration that all the characters experience.[7]

While Josh Schwartz will be the central showrunner discussed in this chapter, *Glee* showrunner Ryan Murphy's influence on television in general and teen TV, in particular, as well as on LGBTQIA+ representation, has also been significant. Before the success of *Nip Tuck* (2003–2010, FX), Murphy, in *Popular* (1999–2001, WB), was less free to include gay teen characters, and instead used tertiary adult roles, along with queer references and intertextuality. The short-lived series was a takedown of social hierarchies in high school, as told through two dueling stepsisters: a popular cheerleader and a rebel. Murphy is perhaps best known, however, for his series of anthologies, *American Horror Story* (2011–, FX), *American Crime Story* (2016–, FX as a producer), and *Feud* (2017–, FX). *Pose* (2018–, FX) would later bring acclaim as well as criticism for its portrayal of the New York ball culture of *Paris is Burning* (1989). It brought this culture into the mainstream, and included more gay and transgender characters, actors, writers, producers, and directors. Murphy's college-set *Scream Queens* (2015–2016) was a hybrid take on the teen horror genre, and after his move from FX to Netflix, *The Politician* (2019–, Netflix) featured an ambitious closeted teen protagonist living in the privileged bubble of Santa Barbara, California, determined to hide his sexuality in order to gain success in the political world.

## *Mean Girls* and Reality Teen Moms

Starting in the 1940s, when panics over juvenile delinquency began to take root, the teen villain tended to be a charismatic but violent gang member or hot rodder. He embodied an often vaguely psychopathic desire for revenge against adults or "squares," and a lust for high stakes thrills such as drag racing or joyriding—just to find a victim to harass. Since the popularity of *Mean Girls* in 2004, among other factors such as YA adaptations, and the overall orientation of network television shifted toward female audiences, mean girls became the overwhelming favorite for kicking up narrative action and becoming the female characters "you love to hate," similar to J.R. Ewing on *Dallas*. Shows exploited the affordances of the villainess, who brutally excludes others from her clique, basks in her popularity, and uses social media and other electronic means to control the social space of the high school. Thus mean girls have been a running theme, as well as the engine of narrative conflict, on teen television since the 2000s, nearly displacing male villainy. The *O.C.*, *Gossip Girl*, *Veronica Mars*, and *Pretty Little Liars* all reflect this trend.

The trend was reinforced in parental advice literature with Rosalind Wiseman's 2002 self-help book *Queen Bees and Wannabes: Helping Your Daughter Survive Cliques, Gossip, Boyfriends, and the New Realities of Girl World*. It reached its apogee, however, in the 2004 box office hit *Mean Girls*. The film grossed $129 million worldwide and continues to have a cult following on online forums, from Twitter to Tumblr. Discussing *Mean Girls*' hold on pop culture, Priya Elan writes:

> For the high-school genre, Fey's hilarious script was unusually astute and provocative. Replicating teen doublespeak with brilliant authenticity, the dialogue was full of zingers, accounting for its continued life online. Not only has it

spawned a huge number of memes and gifs, phrases like "fetch" and "word vomit" have fallen into common parlance. Its cyber-life has afforded the film a special cachet.[8]

This same period saw a meteoric rise in book sales for Young Adult titles targeting teen girls. (Boys, always a tough sell for books, have been completely lost to video games, which tend to eat up their entire budget of disposable income, not to mention their leisure time.) With the success of *Mean Girls* in the box office and *The O.C.* on Fox, as well as *Laguna Beach* and *The Hills*—both reality format programs highly dependent on villainess characters—cable programming continued to target youth audiences from ABC Family to The CW. It thereby tapped into the preexisting fan base of Young Adult novel readers, who were apt to follow their new TV adaptations.

Teen pregnancy is often used as a narrative device, one that involves the repercussions of unprotected sex and "fallen women" stereotypes. It serves as a cautionary tale and lesson to audiences, while also affording substantial drama and tension. Due to network television's Least Offensive Programming agenda, showing teen sex, and subsequent teen pregnancy, continued to be taboo until the late 1990s. Even then, teen pregnancy tales were used either for heightened drama or as moral exempla. Teenage pregnancy in film is a natural precursor to teen TV narratives. When teenage girls are confronted with teen pregnancy, the repercussions highlight the female characters' relationship to sociopolitical issues of the time, depending on their decisions regarding the pregnancy.

Teen films of the 1980s were dominated by the relatively innocent white suburbia envisioned in John Hughes's films, from *Sixteen Candles* to *The Breakfast Club* to *Ferris Bueller's Day Off*. Molly Ringwald became a star in such films; but her 1988 appearance in *For Keeps* focused on the harsh realities of teen parenthood. In a 2010 interview with popular feminist blog *Jezebel*, Ringwald noted her disappointment in the 1980s film, which in her view did not succeed in conveying the difficulties of being a teenage mom. As Ringwald put it, "Being a teenager and not finishing high school, I just think the reality of it is so much more difficult. And I would have liked to have shown that more."[9] Ringwald also commented on Bristol Palin, the daughter of the 2008 Republican Vice President Candidate Sarah Palin. Bristol Palin was at the time of the interview both a teen mom and an abstinence supporter. For her part, Ringwald suggested that the abstinence-only model is ultimately "unrealistic."

Ringwald later co-starred in *The Secret Life of the American Teenager* (2008–2013), playing the mother of a pregnant teen who becomes a mom in her own right (Shailene Woodley). The ABC family series attempts to show the realities of teen parenthood, from conception to the raising of the child. In 2007, the year before *Secret Life* first aired, *Juno*, an Academy-Award winning film centered on a pregnant teen, purportedly caused an unlikely wave of teen pregnancies in the US. *Time* magazine first coined the term the "Juno Effect" after 17 high school girls in a Massachusetts town simultaneously became pregnant.[10] The levity, tenderness, and happy ending of the film supposedly made pregnancy attractive and desirable for young girls. In a 2008 NPR interview, Jane Brown, a professor at the University of North Carolina, argued that the "Juno Effect" was a reality. Even as schools and parents failed to communicate with teens about safe sex and the perils of pregnancy, media images, like those conveyed in *Juno*, had become educators on the matter. Brown's Teen Media Project studied early teenage girls, finding that those with "'heavier sexual media diets' were more than twice as likely to become sexually active by the age of 16" than girls who did not have such "diets."[11] Further, Brown stated that glamorized images of unwed mothers exacerbated the problem:

> This is unusual and rare that we would have movies like *Juno* or *Knocked Up*, or that we would now be glamorizing celebrities who are pregnant and we don't even know who the fathers are . . . For [girls], looking to see who's got a baby bump is really compelling somehow.[12]

Whether or not the "Juno Effect" was real, US audiences were captivated by film and TV representations of teen moms during this time. The series premiere of *The Secret Life of The American Teenager* was the most highly rated show for the network, with 2.8 million viewers. Following each episode, ABC Family aired a PSA (Public Service Announcement) message from the National Campaign to Prevent Teen & Unplanned Pregnancy.[13] While *Secret Life* was a ratings success, critical reviews were varied. Ken Tucker of *Entertainment Weekly* called it a didactic TV series-version of an after school special.[14] In a *Variety* interview, series creator Brenda Hampton stated her distaste for the PSA, primarily because "The PSA sounds like an apology for the fact that we're dealing with teenage sex. I don't think we should apologize for that."[15] Hampton also asserted that her writing was not influenced by the group's message. Meanwhile, MTV established a reality series franchise on the tails of the "Juno Effect" with *16 and Pregnant* (2009–2014), followed by three spinoffs: *Teen Mom* (2009–2012; 2015-present), *Teen Mom 2* (2011-present), and *Teen Mom 3* (2013).

Television plots surrounding abortion and teen mothers are historically ambivalent when it comes to political and social stances, with a few exceptions. The first TV narrative focusing on an abortion was Norman Lear's *Maude*, in a two-part arc entitled "Maude's Dilemma." The middle-aged protagonist—already a grandmother—decided to have an abortion due to her age and desire to not have any more children. The titular protagonist (played by Beatrice Arnold) is known for being straightforward and unapologetically progressive. Ahead of its time, this episode aired in 1972, a year before the Roe V. Wade Supreme Court case. However, abortion had already been legalized in New York State, where the show is set, in 1970. Franchise showrunner Shonda Rhimes, a fierce, very public supporter of Planned Parenthood, has likewise included abortions in her widely popular series *Grey's Anatomy* and its spinoff *Private Practice*.

Teen TV teen moms, even those who do proceed to have an abortion, historically have a safety net to fall back on. To date, one of the only primetime television abortion narratives centering on a teen character is Jason Katims's *Friday Night Lights*. In *The O.C.*, Ryan is in limbo, as he thinks he has impregnated his hometown sweetheart. She and Ryan both hail from a neighborhood not unlike East Los Angeles, and the show dwells on the difficulties of teenage parenthood for both the mother and the father. After lying to Ryan about her abortion, Teresa ultimately keeps the baby.

Katims's *Friday Night Lights* and *Parenthood* show the potential repercussions of female teens' decision to terminate their pregnancies. In *Lights*, a lower-class Becky decides to not follow the same path of her own mother, who was a teen mom herself. The repercussions of the abortion are shown in the backlash of the small town's conservative Christian community against Tami Taylor (Connie Britton), who ethically points out all of Becky's options. However, both the town and Becky's boyfriend's Christian mother use Taylor as a scapegoat for Becky's decision to have an abortion. In *Parenthood*, which faced fewer ratings troubles than *Lights*, centers on an upper-middle-class family in Berkeley, California. The abortion in this instance is pursued by a tertiary character who is ready to embark on college at an elite university. The financial strain in *Parenthood* is less prevalent, although the issue of choice is stressed, with Planned Parenthood being a visible presence in the episode. In Season 1 of The *O.C.*, Ryan's former girlfriend, Teresa, one of the few non-white teen characters, seeks him out in his new home while fleeing from domestic abuse from her boyfriend. As they rekindle their relationship, Teresa becomes pregnant, and lies to Ryan about terminating her pregnancy. Teresa is a vestige of his former life who would prevent him from living out his new, affluent white existence. She essentially disappears from the series until Ryan eventually learns he has a son who has been raised by a single mother, just like he was.

## *The O.C.*

Josh Schwartz is one of the most prominent teen TV content creators of the early 21st century, due to the success of *The O.C.* and *Gossip Girl*. In creating these shows, Schwartz drew on his background as an East Coast Jewish teenager from Rhode Island who moved to Los Angeles for college at the University of Southern California. His time in an affluent fraternity and his outsider status informed the premise of

*The O.C.*, especially the story of one of the central characters, Seth Cohen (played by Adam Brody).

*The O.C.* was the first instance of Josh Schwartz's teen programming; he developed the show at the age of 27, and then followed the series with *Gossip Girl*. *The O.C.* became *90210*'s natural successor as a highly rated teen-oriented network series. Both *The O.C.* and *Gossip Girl* continue the dynamic of outsider disruption/assimilation pioneered in *Beverly Hills 90210*, in Southern California and Manhattan, respectively. But while *90210* captured a mainstream version of Gen X (including its subcultures), *The O.C.* attempted to show a new millennial sensibility. Instead of focusing on an outsider assimilating into a new life, two outsiders become stepbrothers and unsuspecting best friends. Class and social differences are more at the forefront of *The O.C.*, with class commentary and critique being more evident. The series is based on creator and showrunner Josh Schwartz's experience as a nerdy, East Coast Jew who was transplanted to the University of Southern California's film school and the surrounding archetypal surfer culture. The series' nerd hero, Seth Cohen, the first indie rock performer to be a mainstream character, is modeled after Schwartz. Seth is the son of a Kristen Cohen, blonde, affluent WASP mother who works for her mogul father's dubious real estate empire. She fell in love with an East Coast Jewish kid, Sandy Cohen, while the two were attending the University of California at Berkeley. Sandy is a bleeding heart liberal who works as a public defender, while Kristen's salary supports their affluent suburban lifestyle.

The Cohens only child, Seth, is precocious, likes punk and indie rock, comic books, video games, and skateboarding. Although these elements of "nerd culture" are now assimilated into the mainstream, they were previously markers of anti-social outcasts. Seth would have likely remained a social outcast throughout high school if it had not been for Ryan Atwood, a troubled teen who was arrested for stealing cars. Sandy, his public defender, notices that Ryan's high test and aptitude scores don't match his lackluster grades and criminal behavior, and attempts to reach out. A James Dean figure with a white tank top and black leather jacket, Ryan recoils from the idea of bonding with anyone. When Sandy drops Ryan off at his home in Chino, California, he discovers that his mother has abandoned their home. The pilot then deals with Ryan's introduction to Orange County: he bonds with Seth over their outsider status, flirts with girls, gets drunk, and ends up in a fight. When Seth is accosted by buff, blonde water polo players at a beach bonfire, Ryan comes to his rescue. In the fight, Ryan asks, "Do you know what I like about rich kids? Nothing!" before he punches one of the players. The physical attack from Luke to Ryan is then met with a "Welcome to the O.C., bitch!" with the central conflicts of the series' first season becoming crystallized. Teen TV often gives rise to new trends in adult primetime, and MTV's *The Real OC: Laguna Beach*, a response to *The O.C.*, led to a series of spinoffs and franchises. Just as *The Real Housewives* franchise lacked the wit and satire of the original *Desperate Housewives*, *Laguna Beach* was largely a reality TV soap opera focused on dating, female competition, and consumerism.

*The O.C.* became one of the first mainstream US teen TV series to center on outsiders banding together against the popular kids, rather than assimilating so as to be more like them. However, it remained largely white and heteronormative, despite upsetting the status quo. Filmmaker Rachel Summers recalls how she admired the series for its countercultural energies, but noted that it also was a lesson in whiteness and capitalism. While the pilot episode sensationalized the party scene of Orange County, subsequent episodes focused on character and plot development involving the teens characters—Seth, Ryan, Marissa, and Summer—as well as adult characters such as Sandy and Kristen Cohen and Julie and Jimmy Cooper.

As Summers puts it, "The OC explored a class of sickeningly wealthy white people that I was taught to aspire to from my mediocre lower middle class existence."[16] In many ways, the series frequently satirized and mocked an affluent suburban neighborhood filled with consumerism, plastic surgery, parental infidelity, and addiction problems. The central teen characters were precocious, but not overtly mature like the characters in *Gossip Girl*. The adult characters, meanwhile, struggled with moral flaws and problems of their own. Summers points to issues ranging from "Jimmy's money laundering and embezzlement, to

Caleb forging ecological surveys so he could expand his McMansion empire on top of indigenous lands forcing black and brown people further out of this Newport Beach bubble," whereby non-white characters largely serve "as domestic workers and as plot point affairs."[17]

In Season 1 of *The O.C.*, Seth and Ryan are outsiders for drastically different reasons. Although Seth was born and raised in the OC, his parents met as Gen X hippies at Berkeley. His father Sandy is originally from the Bronx, grew up poor, identified as Jewish, and is a public defender. He loathes living in Newport Beach because of what he sees as its vapid culture, and the greed of the corporations and residents located there. Seth shares his father's anti-OC mentality, not least because he was constantly bullied by his water polo peers. His interests are not the same as his peers, either. He skateboards and sails, and likes comic books, video games, and punk and indie rock. Kirsten, Seth's mom, is a native of Newport who has returned to her hometown after college to support her wealthy father's real estate development company. Her loyalty to her widowed dad is what uprooted the Cohens from Berkeley. Further, Kirsten is comfortable as the breadwinner, while Sandy pursues his passion as a "bleeding heart liberal" in the role of a public defender. Throughout the series, Sandy and Kirsten argue over this imbalance and their different ideals. Sandy even accuses Kirsten of enjoying having the money in the family, whereas Sandy's job means they have not "sold out" and are unlike their greedy and shallow neighbors. This reversal of expected gender roles in a marriage, and the dissection of the complexities of married life, remains fairly unprecedented in television, especially teen TV. As Summers puts it,

> Sandy Cohen will always be the soul of the show, watching him teeter back and forth on his anti-capitalist ideals, selling out, buying in, attempting to fight the man, but also knowing it would be mutually assured destruction [if he were to win out].[18]

Kirsten is also initially wary of bringing Ryan, a juvenile delinquent, into their family. Sandy, by contrast, sees himself in Ryan, and states he is a better influence on Seth than a trust-fund peer would be. Kirsten is won over by Ryan in Season 1, and they adopt him. Seth, meanwhile, is also unique. For example, he embraces his mother's Christianity and his father's Judaism, as shown through his invention of the super holiday "Chrismukkah."

In *The O.C.*, outsider boys and insider girls join together, outside of the hierarchy of their clichéd school tropes. They mature and come of age as they bond, no longer influenced by teen peer pressure. This dynamic mirrors Jim and Judy coming together at the end of *Rebel Without A Cause*. Marissa and Summer are in the upper echelons of the social hierarchy at Harbor School, but this does not last.

*The O.C.* presents different archetypes to millennials and Southern California, and subverts precedents set by shows such as *90210* and *Saved By The Bell*. *The O.C.* begins with Ryan meeting with public defender Sandy Cohen after he is arrested for stealing a car with his older brother Trey. Sandy brings Ryan to their lavish Newport Beach home when his mother abandons him, with Newport Beach standing in stark contrast to Ryan's hometown of Chino. A brooding, muscular, and blond Ryan instantly experiences a mutual attraction with the popular, beautiful, and troubled girl next door, Marissa Cooper. Ryan's jeans and leather jacket provide an updated version of James Dean's character in *Reb*el. Marissa soon invites him to a charity fashion show. After bonding with Ryan over video games, Seth, the outsider loner, confesses his unrequited love for Summer Roberts, Marissa's best friend. He clearly has no friends and holds his peers in contempt, but is convinced to attend the fashion show to see Summer.

After the fashion show, which establishes for viewers the lifestyle of Newport Beach, Ryan is invited to an after-party, and once again Seth attends because of Summer. As they enter the beach house, the teens snort cocaine, smoke marijuana out of enlarged bongs, and drink copious amounts of alcohol. Marissa's boyfriend Luke is clearly cheating on her, while she shows early signs of alcoholism. When the water polo players begin to bully and beat up Seth, Ryan comes to his rescue. Luke fights back, telling the outsider, "Welcome to the O.C, bitch!" Ryan, fighting back, in turn shows his disdain for the polo players when he asks, "Do you know what I like about rich kids? Nothing."

Marissa is a secret rebel, and she confesses her angsty tendencies to Seth and Ryan in Season 1, Episode 2, "The Model Home." She mirrors Natalie Wood's Judy, in *Rebel*, in her proclivity for trouble and her vulnerability to peer pressure. When she tells the boys she likes punk music, Seth sarcastically retorts that Avril Lavigne, the teen pop singer who commodified punk music on the Billboard charts, is not punk. She then rattles off a list of 1970s punk bands from The Cramps to The Clash. A befuddled Seth then states he must kill himself because he listens to the same music as her. Ryan, who "likes everything" and isn't as particular about music, is surprised and intrigued by Marissa's taste. She coyly responds, "I'm angry."

In Season 1, Episode 7 of "The Escape," while Seth, Summer, Ryan, and Marissa are on a road trip to Tijuana, their budding romances bloom. When Summer expresses concern about the appearance of her hair, Seth mentions his "Jewfro." Summer's shock is likely reflective of the casual anti-Semitism that creator Schwartz, after whom Seth is modeled, faced as an outsider in the seemingly homogenous environment of the University of Southern California's film school. And the showrunner's subsequent success story was aspirational to fans of the series who could relate, and who for those who aimed to create teen TV from their perspective.

Summer expresses her distaste for Seth's preference for indie rock music, which she describes as "one guitar with a whole lot of complaining." Seth quickly retorts by mentioning his favorite band, which was popularized on the series: "Don't insult Death Cab [for Cutie]." Although he initially mentions punk, contemporary indie rock is Seth's defining genre.

Before the new school year starts, Marissa's social status drops when her peers find out that her boyfriend cheated on her; her father bilked dozens of local families as their financial advisor, through a series of bad investments; and her drug addiction leads to a near-fatal overdose. Her mother Julie, who is an archetypical gold digger who marries for money, divorces her father Jimmy, and her younger sister is sent away to boarding school. Summer, who still wants to hold on to the status that comes with popularity, encourages Marissa before the first day of sophomore year, noting that she "owns the school" as social chair. Yet Marissa is no longer interested in high school popularity. Rather, she chooses her new romance with Ryan over her status at school. When Anna, a new student who shares the same interests as Seth, becomes the first girl to show romantic feelings toward him, Summer realizes she is jealous, which launches a new love triangle.

Eventually, with her best friend Marissa becoming an outsider, and Summer herself falling in love with Seth, Summer is also changed. Even Luke, the shallow polo player who betrays Marissa and serves as an antagonist to Seth and Ryan, is welcomed into their group when he is faced with the news that his dad is gay. Although Luke was previously the most popular boy in school, he is the least interesting addition to the group due to his limited intellect. By contrast, Summer's individualism and intelligence shines as she separates herself from her former self. However, Luke is essentially a loyal friend.

Essentially, the central characters in *The O.C.* are mature and the new "cool kids" because they opt out of the homogeneity and shallow social hierarchies of their high school lives. The series also attracted teen boys and young men by including the teen boys' point of view. This encouraged male viewers to look through the characters' eyes, before their adult lives began and they became disillusioned with life after the confines of high school conformity.

Subsequent series like *Veronica Mars* also depicted a protagonist in Southern California who was outcast from the popular crowd, partly due to her father's conduct and her lower-class status, but above all because of her understanding of the high school social hierarchy as inane. Instead of assimilating to the worlds of their parents or peers and entering the fold of homogeneity as consumer-citizens, the millennial teens featured on *Veronica* and other shows came of age as mature teens with wise-beyond-their-years perspectives on high school. This is the lesson imparted by the shows to their target audiences, who are intelligent individuals who do not necessarily "fit in" vis-à-vis social norms or expectations. These outsider teens, who are seen as more special than the status quo, find each other, and belong together. This is thus a direct lineage connecting these programs with Gen X shows about outsiders who do not belong, and do not want to, such as *My So-Called Life*, *Daria*, and *Freaks and Geeks*. Like the earlier shows, too, these cult shows for millennials did not initially succeed on a mass scale but eventually found their niche audience. *The O.C.* was able to thrive on network TV due to the new millennial viewership, and by maintaining teen drama generic conventions such as love triangles, albeit with updated characters and novel narrative turns. The early aughts also began to incorporate subcultures like indie rock, comic book culture, and general nerd culture into "geek chic," as the pattern of commodification continued on commercial programming.

## Indie Rock and *The O.C.*

*The O.C.* presented indie rock as anthem music for teens who identified with Seth Cohen, and sequences and montages with up-and-coming artists, as well as musicians' cameos as live performers as part of the fictional "Bait Shop" lineup, helped catalyze these artists' careers. It also provided a mature element to the teen series—something for both precocious teen music fans and older audiences to appreciate. What is more, the quintessential Southern California beachside Bait Shop venue where Seth worked could be traced back directly to *90210*'s retro diner "Peach Pit," as well as *Never Too Young*'s Malibu beachside concert venue, The High Dive.

In Season 2, the Bait Shop also brought in Seth's co-worker Alex, played by Olivia Wilde, a future film star and director of the successful 2019 teen film *Booksmart*. Alex was an independent young adult whom Seth swooned over, but the mature, effortlessly cool, and bisexual Alex was ultimately not interested in Seth. During a breakup period between Marissa and Ryan, Alex and Marissa briefly fell in love, and Marissa moved in with Alex. This subplot constituted a pioneering gay-love storyline for a central protagonist on teen TV. Marissa, who still struggled with adult tasks such as cooking, cleaning, and doing laundry, found her new life difficult. Further, while Alex was deeply invested in the relationship, Marissa ultimately broke her heart. Marissa's relationship with Alex seemed to represent a rebellious "phase," rather than a marker of fluid sexuality. Furthermore, aside from experiencing shock from her mother, Marissa did not face homophobia. Summer did not judge her, and Seth and Ryan merely ogled at their former girlfriends embracing each other. The relationship was, in this sense, subjected to the straight male gaze, but it did at least feature non-heteronormative characters. One scene with Alex and Marissa included Rilo Kiley's indie hit "Portion for Foxes." As the *O.C. Weekly Review* reported, the band added a new level of "indie cred" to Los Angeles:

> We used to think that LA had nothing to offer us musically. We spent our days wishing we had been born in D.C. Or Chicago. Or even some small town in the Pacific Northwest. That is, until Rilo Kiley came along. With their soft guitars, nearly naked production, and Jenny Lewis' bitter and ironic—she sings ironically! Really, she does!—vocals, the band became LA's best kept secret with their 2001 release, *Take Offs and Landings*.[19]

Kiley shared the same record label (Saddle Creek Records) with one of Seth's favorite bands, Bright Eyes. The 2001 album elevated the band and their Los Angeles native identity, especially with frontwoman Jenny Lewis's background as a child actress in films such as *Troop Beverly Hills* (1989, co-starring Shelley Long). Lewis eventually went solo and became one of the few women to feature prominently in the indie rock/emo era. She also provided her voice to a side project of Seth's favorite band, Death Cab for Cutie, called The Postal Service. In Seth's Season 1 gift "starter pack," he includes albums from Death Cab for Cutie, Bright Eyes, and The Shins. All three acts would gain crossover success, boosted by the show, and be remembered as major indie rock artists of the early 2000s. The Portland-based Shins gained further popularity when they were heavily featured on the indie soundtrack for the Zach Braff and Natalie Portman film *Garden State* (2004), released a year after *The O.C.* premiered. Lewis' singer-songwriter career made her a bigger indie darling and LA icon, just as Bright Eyes' Conor Oberst continued to thrive as a solo artist.

Indie rock of the early 2000s became synonymous with *The O.C.*'s "mixtape" soundtracks. Print journalism, including music criticism, was in a state of great decline. While online music was more available and indie rock more visible through various blogs and review sites during this time, its limited accessibility (in contrast to the accessibility offered by platforms like Spotify today) showed the importance of enlisting music supervisors and using soundtracks to build the image of a series. *The O.C.* music supervisor, Alexandra Patsavas, helped propel indie music's acceptance, and continued to work on *Gossip Girl*, Shonda Rhimes' hit medical drama *Grey's Anatomy,* and the Young Adult novel box office adaptation of the *Twilight* trilogy that, launching the careers of Robert Pattinson and Kristen Stewart, made the vampire love story relevant for a generation of teens. Patsavas helped cultivate the tastes of this generation, propelling a genre and its artists to crossover success. As Summers recounts in one episode, the series is synonymous with her adolescence and view of Southern California, as is reinforced by the bright and hopeful theme song, Phantom Planet's "California":

> The 24 episodes of the first season will always be perfect for me even if the show wasn't intended for me as a viewer. "We've been on the run driving in the sun looking out for number one" were the lyrics I listened to as I drove down the 405 for the first time. I arrived in California and I was transported back to my teen ritual super fandom.[20]

## *Gossip Girl*

*Gossip Girl* is one of the earliest successful Young Adult novel franchises adapted to the small screen in the post-network era, with *The Vampire Diaries* (2009, 2017, CW) and *Pretty Little Liars* (2010–2017, ABC/Freeform) soon following. Schwartz developed and executive produced *Gossip Girl*, alongside with *O.C.* alumna Stephanie Savage. They adapted Cecily von Ziegesar's young adult novels (published between 2002 and 2011) to create the *Gossip Girl* (2007–2012) series for the fledgling CW Network. As Schwartz remarked, "I was very skeptical ... I don't want to do 'The O.C. NYC.' But I thought the books were smart. The characters are worldly in a way that Orange County kids aren't."[21] As Stein notes, "The teens of *Gossip Girl* deal with the social problems of high school, but they also drink in martini bars, have sex in New York City taxicabs, and even run their own burlesque clubs."[22] While *The O.C.* was Schwartz's original creation (with several influences and references), the adaptation of a popular YA novel series, which involved a sexually mature and salacious teen lifestyle, tapped into an established fanbase. When the watchdog group the Parents Television Council (PTC) reprimanded the series, claiming it reflected a hedonistic lifestyle that was taking hold in the US at the time, the group's censure reflected how the series rarely resorted to moral or ethical lessons like its predecessors, and represent its characters' actions as morally ambiguous.[23] Instead of backing down, however, The CW chose to use this "bad publicity" as a marketing tool to entice viewers, with a newfound "OMFG" campaign that touched on the taboo topics that the PTC criticized, mirroring tabloid headlines. As Stein states:

> *Gossip Girl* became a visible representation of all that was supposedly wrong with millennial culture at the turn of the century—including most especially sexual knowingness and sexual activity—whether this was the fault of millennial themselves, the industries and media producers who sought to take advantage of them, or both.[24]

As a millennial series, *Gossip Girl* dealt with digital cultures more directly than its predecessor, which had reflected the rise of cell phone communication before social media became ubiquitous for teens. The storyline of the later series centers on an eponymous blog dedicated to exposing an affluent group of Upper East Side preparatory school students in New York City. Narrated with a voiceover provided by former teen star Kristen Bell (*Veronica Mars*), each episode would typically begin with a greeting to "Upper East Siders" and a sign-off of "You know you love me, XOXO Gossip Girl." The episodes revolve around the scandalized actions and reactions of its central characters' secrets, which are unveiled through blog post updates received on cell phones and personal computers. Thus, these characters are constantly engaged with social media. Set (and released) during the rise of Hollywood celebrity gossip blogs, *Gossip Girl* features posts that are the catalyst for the plot, taking the form of secrets unveiled. The characters often negotiate with the anonymous blogger in an effort to keep their secrets, while attempts to reveal *Gossip Girl*'s own identity become a frequent plot point.

While *Gossip Girl* was not a ratings success when it originally aired, the series thrived in its afterlife on streaming platforms both in the US and abroad. As Stein asserts, digital discourses also helped heighten the series' popularity, which was ahead of the television industry's understanding of young viewers. She cites a *New York* magazine article titled "The Genius of Gossip Girl" with the tagline: "How a wunderkind producer, seven tabloid ready stars, an army of bloggers, and a nation of texting teenagers are changing the way we watch television."[25] Schwartz's position as a powerful, highly connected showrunner who could tap into the millennial interest in teen series, highlight the potential for stardom of all of the program's major characters, and prominently feature cross-generational online and mobile technology contributed to the show's success. Essentially, participatory culture became more visible in the digital era, and was no longer seen as a purely subcultural phenomenon that could not cross over to the mainstream. Executives were bewildered by the new digital viewership of the series. Flaws in traditional Nielsen ratings were exposed when *Gossip Girl* was ranked 100, but achieved a ranking of 14 in the "power content ratings," which combined "Nielsen ratings, traffic online and buzz."[26]

Onscreen millennial teens also possessed digital-savviness within the series. The titular character is an anonymous online character, with a network of informers, who taunts and torments the rich protagonists. (At the end of the final season, Gossip Girl's identity is revealed.) When the series begins, Dan Humphrey (Penn Badgley) is positioned as a Nick Carraway-like (from the *Great Gatsby*) insider-outsider at the private school. Unlike her peers, Dan is not initially immersed in the role of an Upper East Sider outside of his high school. The Williamsburg, Brooklyn, resident, rather, comes across as a "nerdy" outsider, akin to *The O.C.'s* Seth Cohen. While Seth's personality, not location, sets him apart, both factors hinder Dan's potential popularity. While he is certainly wealthier than the average American teenager, his outsider status only emphasizes how wealthy and affluent the central characters are. His counterparts all come from generations of inherited wealth. Although Williamsburg would indeed become the hub of hipster gentrification in Brooklyn, its up-and-coming status stood in sharp contrast to the preppy elitism of Dan's peers.

Blair Waldorf (Leighton Meester), the series "Queen Bee," is one of Dan's frequent antagonists. She views her "mean girl" persona as necessary to retain her popularity and social standing, and her ultimate goal is to attend Yale University. Blair's academic rival is Nelly Yuki, a rigorous student who is also an outsider for several reasons: her Asian ethnicity becomes the basis for a stereotyped nerd character who is less social, fashionable, and attractive than her peers. Her large glasses are her signature style. Indeed, Nelly is an example of Kristen Warner's "plastic representation," which involves non-white characters who are included for the sake of diversity. These characters are not as fully developed as other characters, and their portrayal often adheres to racist and sexist stereotypes. Nelly's intelligence, however, gives rise to a kind of social cunning, which prevents her from being constantly defeated by Blair and gains her admission to Yale. This slight subversion of the norm, however, only heightens the relevance of the nerdy and determined Asian stereotype.

As Nelly's role suggests, Blair is constantly challenged by outsiders who threaten her superiority. She lives in a penthouse with her fashion designer mother and maid/unlikely sidekick Dorota. Blair is a brunette who dresses in the classic preppy and feminine upscale style, and her main influences are Hollywood starlet Audrey Hepburn and iconic designer Coco Chanel. Blair's best friend or mortal enemy, depending on the drama of the moment, is Serena Van der Woodsen (Blake Lively). Whereas Blair is a classic traditionalist, Serena's style is trendier, and her personality and social attitudes are more open. The series begins with her return to New York, after escaping the city when she betrays her best friend by having sex with Blair's boyfriend, Nate Archibald (Chace Crawford), who was a virgin at the time. Whereas Serena has had several sexual partners at this stage, Blair is determined to lose her virginity to, and ultimately marry, Nate, once again revealing her traditional and conservative tendencies. When Gossip Girl reveals Serena and Nate's act of deception, the first major friction and rivalry between the two characters begin. Serena is alienated, allowing Dan, who has silently pined for her, to begin a relationship with her. Meanwhile, Nate pines over Serena, despite her regrets about their liaison; he is also ambivalent about continuing his relationship with Blair. Nate and Blair evoke the ideal Upper East Side couple. Nate appears to have the most established generational wealth, hailing from a typical WASP (White Anglo Saxon Protestant) background. His father's poor and immoral financial choices, however, lead his family into bankruptcy, providing a riches to rags story that parallels the 2008 financial crisis.

Nate's best friend, Chuck Bass (Ed Westwick), initially comes across as the most egregiously wealthy, pompous, and elitist character. He is the heaviest drinker and drug user of the core characters. The show also implies that he is not beyond sexually abusing teenage girls. Chuck is also the most isolated from a sense of family: his mother purportedly died from childbirth, and his father is cold and distant. Chuck does not care about school and is generally unkind, particularly to Dan, the ultimate outsider.

Just as adult shows of this post-network-TV era emphasize anti-heroes, or fatally flawed and morally ambiguous protagonists, *Gossip Girl*'s teen soap tendencies blur the lines between "good" and "bad." No character is immune from lying or cheating. Chuck's storyline, in particular, plays out as that of the "poor little rich boy." His childhood and relationship with his father reveal why he is so caustic and hides under his wealth and abusive behavior. When Chuck takes Blair's virginity, the series shifts, as his love for her salvages his character. Their tumultuous relationship reveals someone who is unable to commit, but who can overcome his limitations in the name of true love. Chuck is known for his presumptuous catch phrase, "I'm Chuck Bass."

The series struck a chord with adult audiences because of its maturity, and also because it aired during a period of flux for prime-time entertainment. A *New York* magazine cover story titled "'Gossip Girl': The Most Important Show of Our Time" listed the "gloriously implausible—and uncomfortably plausible" elements of the series pilot, from Lively's authenticity as a high schooler to the show's self-reflexivity to its emphasis on romance. As the writer put it, "Teenage sex is awkward, no matter how much money you wrap it in."[27] Indeed, *Gossip Girl* marked a return to *90210*'s unlikely mature teen-adults, thereby enticing a twenty- to thirty-something demographic, which was the CW's ideal target audience.

By the end of the series, most of the central characters have been (heteronormatively) romantically involved with one another. Important side characters in the form of younger siblings include Eric, Serena's brother who is gay and has drug addiction issues, as well as Jenny (Taylor Momsen), Dan's sister who "breaks bad" and turns into a rebellious teenager. For their part, Serena and Nate fall frequently in and out of lust, and sometimes fall in love with new characters. Dan's father, Rufus, is a former 1990s alternative rock star, who is wealthy due to the residuals from his music. He was once romantically involved with Serena's mother, Lilly, until she left him to marry her first husband for wealth, even though she loved Rufus. They are reunited when their children begin dating, marry, but then divorce. In the series finale, Rufus is in a relationship with one of the most well-known women in 1990s alt-rock, Lisa Loeb, who appears as herself in the episode. Loeb is one of many musical guest stars, mostly incorporated via Rufus' background, to appear in the series. Schwartz initiated this practice in *The O.C.*, though ultimately the music of *Gossip Girl* would not be as well-known as its fashion.

In moving from *The O.C.* to *Gossip Girl*, viewers move from a wealthy Southern California suburb to the epicenter of Manhattan's wealthiest adolescents. Sex, drugs, and alcohol are pervasive and readily available in both settings. In *The O.C.*, Ryan clearly comes from a troubled family life: his father has left, his mother is an absent alcoholic, and his brother encourages him to steal cars with him. The specificity of his hometown of Chino is unclear, although as a whole it is meant to be much less affluent than Newport Beach. Judging from Summer's response to Ryan's revelation of his hometown—"Chino—ew!"—the audience understands that Newport Beach residents would look down on the location.

By contrast, Dan, who is meant to be the outsider through his Brooklyn location and lower-income family, does not have a troubled home life in *Gossip Girl*. His father is a former rock star who runs a local gallery. His parents' divorce later in the series, but this is not uncommon among his peers. Accordingly, we see Dan's residence in Williamsburg as a way to reveal the heightened wealth and affluence of Blair, Serena, Chuck, and Nate in the Upper East Side of Manhattan.

The influence of fashion on *Gossip Girl* mirrors the influence of music on *The O.C.* Although fashion and teen culture are synonymous for many girls, *Gossip Girl* heightened the role of fashion in TV and popular culture prior to the emphasis on fashion via digital cultures. The competition series *Project Runway* (2004–, Bravo/Lifetime/Hulu) helped bring high fashion into suburban homes, but *Gossip Girl* showed fashion in the context of teen agency, like the 1995 film *Clueless* had before. *Gossip Girl*'s costume designer Eric Damon, who previously worked on the fashion-heavy *Sex and the City* (1998–2004), has noted that designers' interest in the show increased as its popularity rose. Blake Lively's immersion into the fashion world was also crucial, as the actress soon began collaborating with designers like Karl Lagerfeild. Soon, designers asked to be featured on *Gossip Girl*, and Blair, Serena, Jenny, and Chuck particularly had specific fashion identities. Whereas the teen boys of *Clueless* primarily dressed in the slacker style that the protagonist Cher (Alicia Silverstone) loathed, *Gossip Girl* elevated teen boys' and men's fashion. This practice marked a transition period, also influenced by series like *Mad Men*, in which classically tailored pieces and fashion forwardness became more acceptable for straight men. Damon credits Ed Westwick, who played Chuck, for his willingness to be dressed in innovative ways. He also attributes this willingness to Westwick's past experiences as a theatre actor and his European background. This transition showed that even young men could wear well-fitted pants and shirts, eschewing the baggy-jeans norm that had been dominant before then.

## *Veronica Mars* and Suicide

A pivotal suicide occurs in each of the three seasons of *Veronica Mars* (2004–2006, UPN; 2006–2007, The CW). The central storyline in the first season revolves around the attempt by Veronica (Kristen Bell, who later provides the voiceover for *Gossip Girl*) to find the killer of her best friend, Lilly (*Mean Girls'* Amanda Seyfried). After Lilly's death, Veronica's sheriff father Keith Mars (Enrico Colantoni) is ousted from his position for accusing Lilly's influential father of killing her. As a result, the once-popular precocious teen becomes an outcast at her affluent high school. Her boyfriend Duncan (Teddy Dunn), Lilly's brother, suddenly breaks up with her with no explanation. Further, Lilly's ex-boyfriend Logan (Jason Dohring), along with the rest of the "in" crowd at the fictional Neptune High, perpetually taunt her, and ensure that she is alienated from her former circle. Like Joey Potter of *Dawson's Creek*, Seth Cohen of *The O.C.*, and Rory Gilmore and Lane Kim of *Gilmore Girls*, Veronica is mature and knowing beyond her years, and frequently inserts literary and pop culture references.

Veronica begins her fledgling private investigator career in order to find Lilly's killer. She also attempts to uncover who raped her, and subsequently took her virginity, after Veronica was drugged at a party. The series incorporates Veronica's voiceover narration, consistently using flashbacks to the period before Lilly's murder and after her rape. The PI makes progress on the case in each episode, while also taking on smaller jobs partly to earn extra money, but also because the work is her passion and calling. The series heavily criticizes the wealthy Hollywood-based residents of the fictional Southern California town of Neptune, as Veronica reveals their lying, cheating, and hypocrisy in the cases she takes on. The petite white teen detective shows solidarity with and helps the Mexican-American community of her town, while also befriending Eli "Weevil" Navarro, the head of a Latino biker gang who was secretly romantically involved with Lilly. Veronica's closest friend is Wallace Fennel, a new kid at school. Because he is Black and not rich, he is originally seen as an outcast. Later, when he becomes popular due to his role as the star basketball player, he remains close with Veronica. Her other close friend is Cindy "Mac" McKenzie, a middle-class computer genius who embodies the "female nerd" archetype. Wallace and Mac frequently assist Veronica in her cases.

*Veronica* succeeds in showing the diverse racial and socioeconomic community of a fictional Southern California town, while also including principal minority characters. Although a series like *The O.C.* also criticized the rich and famous of Southern California, especially through the class-conscious critiques of characters like Sandy and Seth Cohen and Ryan Atwood, it ultimately whitewashed a predominantly Latino region. Likewise, in dealing with crime and punishment, *Veronica Mars* also shows the injustice and inequality in how blue-collar versus white-collar crime is handled. As Sue Turnbull asserts, the first two seasons of the series, dominated by the characters' experiences in high school, "manages a remarkable balance between the focus of the individual and the recognition of larger social patterns."[28] *Veronica Mars* thus remains one of the few US teen series to tackle social issues as they relate to the intersections of race, class, and gender.

In Episode 12 of Season 1, "Clash of the Tritons," viewers see the destruction of Logan Echolls's movie star parents' marriage. Aaron and Lynn Echolls are played by the actual married celebrity couple Harry Hamlin and Lisa Renner. Lynn exposes Aaron's affairs, and the situation becomes a tabloid free-for-all. When she threatens to divorce him, he assures her that she would subsequently be left penniless. Lynn storms off to her luxury red corvette, and digs for her pills in her designer bag. In the episode's final scene, we see an aerial shot of the same car on a bridge, accompanied by a voiceover from a police scan reporting a suicide. In the following episode, "Lord of the Bling," a grieving Logan chastises his father's agent for discussing business at the funeral. Aaron then fires him and quits his acting career. Logan's family is one of the many wealthy families of Neptune that *Veronica Mars* uses to critique class relationships as well as the effects that absent, morally compromised parents can have on their adolescent children.

Logan remains troubled throughout the series; he is frightened of intimacy and monogamy, and takes to sex, drugs, and alcohol as an escape.

Logan is initially convinced that his mother did not commit suicide because no body was found. He tells his best friend Duncan that she escaped her old life. At the end of the episode, Logan asks Veronica to search for his missing mother. In the next several episodes, the two work together on the case. In Episode 15, "Ruskie Business," Veronica learns that Lynn's credit card is in use at the Neptune Hotel. They soon discover that Logan's estranged sister Trina (played by former *Buffy the Vampire* star Alyson Hannigan) charged the card for her own stay. Logan then breaks down sobbing in the hotel lobby, falling into Veronica's arms. This working relationship eventually leads to an on-again, off-again romance between the two. By the end of the episode, Logan accepts that his mother committed suicide upon learning that she amended her will shortly before her death, leaving her entire estate to him. His newfound wealth and orphan-like identity further contributes to his dysfunctional adolescence.

In the Season 2 finale, "Leave It to Beaver," Veronica discovers, after unearthing a series of tapes, that Logan's father Aaron is Lilly's real killer. Their affair was the secret Lilly previously boasted about in flashbacks. When Aaron realizes that Veronica knows about his culpability for the murder, he tries to kill her, but he saves her in the end, risking his own life. With a dead mother, absent sister, and murderer father, Logan spirals even lower, while his relationship with Veronica is further complicated and strained.

While Season 1 focuses on the aftermath of Lilly's and Lynn's deaths, Season 2 involves a mass murder perpetrated via a faulty school bus, killing students, a teacher, and a bus driver from Neptune High. Throughout the season, Veronica investigates the mass murder while also working on other cases. In a midseason arc, Veronica helps clear Logan of the murder of local biker gang member Felix Toombs. In the Season 2 finale, Veronica graduates from Neptune High, and uncovers that Cassidy "Beaver" Casablancas committed the school bus crash killings. Earlier in the season, she had discovered that two of the murdered students were the victims of sexual abuse by a wealthy local little league coach (played by Steve Guttenberg). When his former teammates plan to expose their abuser, Cassidy fears the shame and affront to his masculinity that coming forward will cause, and vows to silence his teammates. Veronica also learns that Cassidy is her rapist, which positions the troubled and bullied youth as the perpetrator of the several crimes.

When Veronica confronts Cassidy on the hotel rooftop at her school's graduation party, he informs her that he has installed a bomb on the coach's private plane, which is en route, and which is also transporting Veronica's father, who investigated the sexual abuse allegations. She sees the plane explode in the distance and begins to sob uncontrollably. Cassidy then attacks Veronica with a taser gun, and tells her to fake her own suicide by jumping off the building, or he will shoot her dead. He plans to frame Aaron Echolls, now a free man staying at the same hotel, for her death. When Logan arrives after receiving Veronica's text, Cassidy shoots toward him, and then the two fight on the roof. Veronica grabs the gun, wanting to shoot Cassidy for raping her, and for killing her father and the bus crash victims. Logan convinces her to drop the gun, and Cassidy then jumps to his own death. Later, Veronica's father returns home: it turns out that he did not board the plane with Woody, the sexually abusive coach. For a brief moment, Veronica and Logan were both simultaneously orphans and high school graduates. Meanwhile, Duncan has arranged a hitman to kill Aaron in his hotel suite, after he sleeps with Cassidy's stepmother. Logan now truly is an orphan.

Cassidy's suicide, and the issue of teen suicide in general, is not directly addressed in Season 3, as Veronica begins her college career. Logan initially told "Beaver" not to jump, to which he replied that his name is "Cassidy." This exchange highlights how the character, who is short of stature, has been subject to bullying and taunting from his peers. He asks Logan why he should not jump, and Logan is left speechless. The fate of Cassidy, who is the victim of sexual abuse, a rapist, and a mass murderer, is an example of one of the two possibilities associated with the Bildungsroman trope of suicide. The Bildungsroman suicide is caused by rejection in love, and a subsequent refusal to enter the adult world that beckons. The other possibility associated with this trope, that of rapprochement, is denied to Cassidy, due to his crime. Cassidy's first sexual encounter was molestation, and his refusal to confront or heal ultimately ruins his chance of recovering. It is unclear whether Cassidy is gay or not, but he presumably used his relationship with Mac to hide his psychological problems, not his sexuality. Further, he commits suicide on the night of Veronica's graduation, while he is still enrolled in high school. By contrast with the series heroine, who is constantly challenged yet achieves rapprochement at every obstacle, Cassidy could not step forward publicly as a victim of sexual abuse. Nor can he deal with the scrutiny of further being a known rapist and serial murderer. He chooses to reject the adult world and harsh consequences of his actions, leading to his suicide.

In Season 3, Veronica enrolls at a nearby university, Hearst College, after her absent alcoholic mother takes her tuition money and leaves town again in the Season 2 finale. As with the college seasons of *Saved By The Bell* and *90210*, the central characters attend a local university to extend the high school structure of the series, rather than creating a new setting. Wallace and Mac join Veronica at Hearst. Her relationship with Logan turns into a love triangle with the addition a new romantic interest—namely, Stosh "Piz" Piznarski (Chris Lowell). Piz also serves as a middle-class contrast to Neptune High and Logan, and his radio show serves as a narrative tool used to capture the "mood" of the college, according to series creator Rob Thomas.[29]

Veronica continues to solve cases on the Hearst campus while studying criminology. The main story arc in the series' only college-based (and final) season involves identifying a serial rapist on campus, with these crimes having already been mentioned in Season 2. For Veronica, who is a victim of rape, the case is particularly important, and the plot sheds light on sexual abuse issues at universities. The secondary crime involves Hearst College dean Cyrus O'Dell (Ed Begley, Jr.), who reportedly committed suicide. His widow asks Veronica's father, Keith Mars, to investigate a possible cover-up for his murder, but, as usual, Veronica ultimately cracks the case. In "Papa's Cabin," she pieces together that Professor Hank Landry's Teaching Assistant, Tim, killed O'Dell by emulating a paper that Veronica wrote for Landry's class entitled "How To Get Away with the Perfect Murder." Tim kills the administrator after he bugs Landry's phone, and finds out that his mentor did not support him for a permanent job at the university. He fakes the dean's suicide, sloppily, to enact revenge on Landry, who was sleeping with the dean's wife, and who would therefore be an obvious suspect. The TA is then able to take over the professor's class and accomplish his goal of permanent employment. Tim offers to help Veronica clear Landry's name, but she eventually discovers that he has also bugged her phone and lifted ideas from her essay. Tim is arrested, and Veronica becomes Landry's new TA.

Veronica's vocation for criminal investigations was clear since the series pilot, and college allows her to take one step closer to legitimating her career. Later in the season, Veronica passes the Private Investigator license exam, and takes an internship with the FBI. Her new relationship with Piz is left unresolved in the series finale.

## *Skins*

*Skins* (2007–2013, E4), like *Degrassi* before it, was committed to an ensemble cast that represented the multifaceted identity of its respective nation. The father-son creator and showrunner partnership between Bryan Elsley, a TV veteran, and his millennial son, Jamie Brittain, has contributed to an inter-generational understanding of the teen genre since the show began production. The series was fueled by Brittain, who was 22 at the start of the series, to push beyond the limits of past teen series and probe the issues of his generation. Brittain challenged his father to do a show that revealed "that being a teenager, by definition, means behaving badly, having sex, flirting with drink and drugs," and that departed from typical teen series' portrayal of this behavior, which the series either hide or punish by death. Elsley and Brittain also enlisted a team of relatively inexperienced writers, whose average age was 22, to further contribute to the authenticity of the series. It also became the first teen series to be run on BBC America. Elsley states the teenagers' perspectives of adults was also critical:

Our philosophy is that teenagers think grown-ups behave in very strange and warped ways . . . What we wanted to do was give a slightly exaggerated version of that perspective, with the parents behaving disgracefully, swearing all the time, being in terrible relationships and being appalling parents. We wanted to reflect that perspective.[30]

*Skins* received both critical acclaim for rejuvenating a genre, and criticism for its exaggerated emphasis on bad teen behavior. The series would go on to win numerous awards, including the Rose d'Or for Best Drama series in 2008 and the BAFTA Phillips Audience Award in 2009. Also, mirroring *Degrassi*, the series is split into biennial "cohorts" of teens who attend the same Bristol high school. The first two seasons involve the original cohort, starring Nicholas Hoult (*About a Boy*, The *X-Men* franchise, *Mad Max: Fury Road, The Favourite*) as Tony. Each episode, however, is told from the perspective of one character. The following seasons center around Tony's sister, Effy (Kaya Scodelario), and her group of friends. Cassie (Hannah Murray) has a vivid personality, but she also deals with issues such as anorexia, drug abuse, low self-esteem, and suicidal thoughts. She is ignored by her parents, who are consumed by their newborn baby. As Murray notes, Hannah is not solely defined by her problems: "I think she's a very clever girl, and she's also kind of silly and dreamy and quite fun at the same time as being a very tragic character."[31]

Jal (Larissa Wilson) is a talented young clarinet player, and a proto-feminist who chastises Tony's treatment of his girlfriend Michelle. She also faces abandonment, as she is eventually homeless and moves in with Chris. *Skins* launched the career of Dev Patel, who would go on to star in *Slumdog Millionaire* (2008). For his role in *Lion* (2016), he was nominated for an Academy Award for Best Supporting Actor, becoming just the second actor of Indian descent to be nominated in the Oscar acting category. In *Skins*, Patel plays Anwar, whose exuberant personality is coupled with a modern, loose approach to his Muslim heritage, in contrast to his devoted immigrant parents. For example, he does not let his religion interfere with any sexual opportunity. Anwar fears his family will chastise his friend Maxxie because of his homosexuality, but his father maintains an open, faith-based attitude and seeks to someday be enlightened by God in the topic. In the second cohort, one of the teens is an immigrant from the Democratic Republic of Congo, Thomas (Merveille Lukeba). Portraying the intersection of adolescence and immigrant experiences remains all too rare in the genre.

*Skins* still utilized soap and sitcom elements of teen TV, but the show did not attempt to talk down to viewers about social issues, or let the characters be defined by their sexuality, race, ethnicity, class, or mental health issues. In this way, the series set a new standard for authentic, nuanced portrayals of teens. The Thai teen series *Hormones* (2013–2015), set in a Bangkok high school, was inspired by *Skins*, and faced fierce criticism and even calls for censorship. The director believed this response was due to "adults closing their eyes to reality." Sex education was integral to the series, addressing Thailand's high teenage pregnancy rates.[32]

As Susan Berridge asserts, academic and journalistic discourses of "authenticity" surrounding a series like *Skins* often oversimplify the issues involved. Further, Berridge argues that, "despite its [*Skins'*] emphasis on teenage nihilism, a closer examination reveals that it is underpinned by a more conservative sexual politics."[33] This judgment mirrors Stein's argument about *Glee*, where she finds a progressive vision that is juxtaposed by conservativism. Berridge also discusses the specific national context for *Skins*, which is a product of Channel 4's youth-centered E4 programming, which challenges the traditionally educational nature of children's public service broadcasting in the UK. As Faye Woods states, "as a publicly-owned, commercially-funded public service broadcaster, Channel 4 has a heterogeneous brand identity related to its hybrid form."[34] Channel 4 in some ways mirrors newer networks like Fox, UPN, and the CW in the US, given that it emerged in 1982 as a "young" platform in contrast to the BBC, and aimed to cater to diverse social groups and address cultural shifts in the UK.[35] What is more, Channel 4 showcased the youth-centered programming from these US networks as part of its brand identity. Berridge discusses the scrutiny that Channel 4 received in the 1990s for seemingly abandoning its public service mandate in favor of taking cues from a US teen series that was particularly influential in the UK, *Dawson's Creek*. Woods, too, notes that series like *Skins* were influenced by their US precedents, combining "aspirational glamour with elements of British surreal comedy."[36] Woods's astute observations foreshadow the global and glocal teen programming for Gen Z, such as Noway's *Skam*, and Netflix originals such as Spain's *Elite*.

By the 2000s, Channel 4 and its digital platform E4 continued to commission other WB and CW teen series, while niche casting its own original content toward teen audiences—in a manner that critics continued to describe as antithetical to public service broadcasting. Berridge stresses that the father-son authorship behind the series complicates attempts to ascribe to the show the kind of "authenticity" associated with a desire to "do something for the kids."[37] As she notes, the series "claimed to be free from a moralising adult agenda," as indicated by interviews with the creators and cast of the series.[38] Nonetheless, for Berridge, *Skins* adheres to conservative sexual politics akin to a US teen series. She also remarks that the series is predominantly white with white protagonists, despite tertiary non-white characters; in this respect, the show mirrors *Glee*'s way of registering diversity: through its supporting cast rather than leading stars. Berridge also addresses *Skins*' emphasis on monogamy and gendered ideas of teenage sexuality, specifically in connection with the concept of virginity. Teenage girls who lose their virginity in the series have more at stake than their male counterparts, as is shown through Jal's trajectory: her pregnancy is presented as her problem, not her partner's. Further, narratives about teenage boys losing their virginity, like those centering on Anwar and Sid, include few negative consequences. Berridge thus argues that *Skins* "replicates the traditional notion that heterosexual intercourse is a woman's responsibility and perpetuates the stereotype of male sexuality as something that men cannot control."[39] In making this point, she draws on previous analyses of US series like *My So-Called Life*, which portray the loss of one's virginity as emotionally charged and potentially harmful for teen girls. This thematic continuity further indicates the crossover influence of Gen X programming on millennial teen TV. As Woods states:

> Lury's argument that British youth television encourages a viewpoint that oscillates between cynicism and enchantment is fundamental to understanding the tone and ideals presented by T4. Her discussion of "yoof's" Generation X can be extended to T4's Generation Y audience, as we find a continuation and cultural pervasiveness of "yoof's" "uneasy *play* between investment and alienation, between an outsider's distaste and detachment and the insider's investment and knowledge."[40]

Berridge argues that, ultimately, the contradictory construction of teenage sexuality leads to an obfuscation of sexual victimization:

> This interplay between, on the one hand, the series' construction of the teenager as highly independent and rebellious and teenage life as free from moral lessons to be learned, and, on the other, the conservative ideology at its centre, has key implications for narratives involving sexual violence and teenage sexual vulnerability.[41]

Woods describes this thematic emphasis as an extension of Gen X sensibilities:

Whilst this "play" may have been "uneasy" in 1980s "yoof" TV, I suggest that due to the cultural pervasiveness of irony, together with the simultaneously strong hold melodrama has on youth-targeted media, Lury's investment and detachment has now been normalised and is present in both US and UK youth-focused television.[42]

This juxtaposition of perceived sexual progressiveness and traditional conventions of gendered stereotyping also extends to the next "cohort" on *Skins*, which includes Effy Stonem, Tony's sister. As Berridge points out, Effy's sexual maturity and wild behavior are established early on, in her role as a peripheral character:

> The overall ethos of *Skins* further complicates straightforward ideological readings of sexual violence in the programme. The nihilistic sensibility that underpins the series' teenage characters–a sensibility that can be traced back to the history of youth programming that the programme emerges from as well as its position on E4–obscures the seriousness of the sexual violence committed upon them. Thus Maxxie quickly excuses Dale's behaviour in favour of kissing him, while Effy is obscured altogether following her drugging. This makes it difficult to take seriously these representations of sexual violence, or to discern any clear, didactic stance on this abuse. The eschewal of didacticism reflects Elsey's assertion that "lecturing [young people] is hopeless."[43]

Although *Skins*, in popular discourse, is treated as a more authentic and edgy show than its UK and US counterparts, Berridge argues that the characters' nihilism and apathy do a disservice to progressive, non-traditional attitudes toward sexuality and sexual violence. In contrast, *Degrassi* portrays a wide spectrum of sexual orientations, and though its characters embody certain apathetic and blasé tendencies, the show's public service mandate also creates a more earnest drive to address issues of oppression. *Degrassi* achieves this balance of authenticity, self-awareness, and progressiveness through decades of serialized storytelling, and serialization within its own various "generations." The multiple generations in *Degrassi* mirror the various cohorts of *Skins*; but as Berridge notes, *because* Skins gives each character his or her own episode, the show lacks narrative continuity as well as ideological accountability when it comes to non-straight teen boy characters becoming the victims of violence.

## Millennial Stardom and *Degrassi*: Aubrey Drake Graham

Aubrey Drake Graham, born in 1986, represents the outspokenness of millennials with respect to their multicultural identity, as well as the phenomenon of pervasive crossover stardom from teen TV to music. Graham is half African American and half Ashkenazi Jewish Canadian, from his father's and his mother's side, respectively. At 15, he was cast as the wealthy and popular basketball player Jimmy Brooks in *Degrassi: The Next Generation* (2001–2015), which gave him global exposure due to the series' transnational distribution success. Graham appeared in 100 episodes of the long-lasting and highly popular series. Jimmy dates several girls in the series, and he is shown losing his virginity with his long-time girlfriend Ashley. The best-known story arc in *Degrassi* concerning Jimmy revolves around the series' infamous school shooter tragedy, which leaves Jimmy paralyzed from the waist down and in a wheelchair for the remainder of the series. The series chronicles Jimmy's experiences with physical disability and his social frustrations. While his father encourages him to pursue wheelchair basketball, a new love interest helps him explore his musical talent.

Millennial teen TV tends to defy dichotomous jock and outsider stereotypes, and Jimmy's transition from basketball player to musician can be attributed to this disruption of narrative norms. His performance also represents a rare mainstreaming of disabled adolescents in teen TV, as opposed to stigmatizing disability, not including disabled teens in the cast, or only featuring them as tertiary characters. Jimmy also remained popular and continued to have several girlfriends after he became paralyzed. His physical therapy sessions restore Jimmy's sexual functioning, a source of positive reinforcement for the teenager. He is also shown in several interracial relationships throughout the series.

Six years later, after his *Degrassi* debut, at the age of 21, Graham left the series to pursue his music career full-time, under the name Drake. After the independent release of two mixtapes, he was signed onto Lil Wayne's record label, Young Money. Wayne would serve as Drake's mentor, producer, and collaborator early on in his career. His 2010 debut studio album, *Thank Me Later*, reached number one on the Billboard 100 in the first week of its release. The album went platinum in the US, Gold in the UK and double platinum in Canada. Drake's musical style combined rapping and singing, included synthetic beats influenced by electronic and pop music, and featured transparent introspection about fame and heartbreak. Instead of rapping about violence and drug dealing, he was known for singing about first lusts and loves, and rapping about his celebrity status, new lavish lifestyle, and changing relationships.[44] In true Internet fashion, Drake's acting past was unearthed, and "wheelchair Drake" was transformed from an early mixtape lyric to a dance, to a meme.

Drake's Jewish identity is also a distinct part of his image. He attended a Jewish day school and celebrated his Bar Mitzvah, which he would later satirize when he hosted *Saturday Night Live* in 2014. He is vocal about his Judaism and the prejudices he faces as a Black Jew, and he has been open about the religious holidays he and his family celebrate. The rapper even held a Bar Mitzvah themed 31st birthday party. At the beginning of his music success, he was called the biggest Jewish rapper since the Beastie Boys. He would go on to become one of the biggest-selling rappers, and recording artist of all time.[45] *Forbes* magazine estimates Graham's 2019 net worth at $150 million, which made him the fifth wealthiest hip hop star of the year.[46]

Many rappers, including Drake, show pride for their hometown in their music and other creative endeavors, but it is noteworthy that Drake helped popularize the "Toronto Sound." He is an ardent fan of the city's basketball team, The Raptors, and is frequently shown onscreen during their games. He popularized "The 6," as the city's nickname, which derives both from a shortening of its area code (416) and from its six distinct areas: Old Toronto, Scarborough, East York, North York, Etobicoke, and York. He mentions his city countlessly in his lyrics. Drake's fourth studio release, *Views,* considered his ultimate hometown homage, includes a (photoshopped) cover of the rapper on top of the city's tallest building and landmark, the CN Tower. The album is further influenced by dancehall, Afrobeat, West Indian and West African music, and trap, among other styles. As a massive mainstream artist, he is a controversial figure in local underground communities.

Toronto Rapper Mo-G, who created the "Ginobili Dance," has criticized Drake for not compensating him for popularizing the move. Fellow Toronto artists generally recognize Drake's role in bringing attention to the city's hip-hop and R&B scene, but musicians and journalists alike have stated the Toronto sound has evolved and expanded over the years.[47]

In the context of the #MeToo and #TimesUp era, Drake has faced several supported charges of sexual assault, and engaged in dubious communications with underage teen stars such as Millie Bobby Brown (of Netflix's *Stranger Things*) and musician Billie Eilish.[48] In 2018, he settled a sexual assault lawsuit.[49] In 2019, even naysayers and apologists were confronted with video evidence of the rapper kissing an underage girl onstage during a concert. The footage included audio in which Drake stated he was not deterred by her status as a minor.[50]

---

**Drake's lyrical *Degrassi* references:**

"The Presentation," *Comeback Season* (mixtape), 2007
"Ransom," *So Far Gone* (mixtape), 2009
"You Know, You Know," B-side, *Thank Me Later,* 2010
"Worst Behavior," *Nothing Was the Same*, 2013
"If You're Reading This It's Too Late,"
*If You're Reading This It's Too Late*, 2015

---

Emerging genres and subcultures have grown with the demand for more inclusive representation beyond white, heteronormative, middle-class characters, for explicit treatment of issues involving mental health, sexuality, and gender identity, and for heightened political awareness and activity. As a result, later Gen Z teen TV shows on streaming services and other niche platforms would continue to cater to fans who valued outsiders and iconoclasts. Further, stereotypes did not need to dominate the formula. Athlete or cheerleader characters did not have to be unintelligent, and ambitious students did not have to be unattractive or socially awkward.

## Eric Daman, *Gossip Girl* Costume Designer Interview

*Stefania Marghitu:* Can you talk about your initial experiences working in costume design?

*Eric Daman:* My first endeavor in costume design was through the indie film world, with *The Adventures of Sebastian Cole*. It was Adrian Grenier's breakout role. And I was coming out of the [fashion] editorial world. I was working with reality-based imagery, doing something All-American, as part of the Terry Richardson and Harmony Korine's *Kids* world. It was fashion that wasn't just about being as glamorous as you can be.

My friend at the time was hitting a wall in his career and not getting callbacks from the big magazines. And in doing editorial he was being told, "you have to use this Prada jacket," which was restricting creatively. Then the two of us were approached to do *The Adventures of Sebastian Cole*. It was really great for me to see how you can create character and tone and emotion, and art, through a wardrobe. And what clothing meant to the actor and the viewer, and how it really helped build a scene. Especially the trans element, there's an extra layer of costume design, creating a male and female persona. Creating an arc around that and what it meant. It was a kaleidoscope, and a dream to be a part of. And learning it on the fly was incredible. I loved this idea of using clothing to build emotion and character and help build a film.

It was really my first education in the film world, and I didn't formally pursue costume design before; I studied French Literature at the University of Sorbonne.

*SM:* How did your French Literature studies at the Sorbonne influence work as a costume designer?

*ED:* All the analytical stuff I had to do at the Sorbonne, like breaking down paragraph by paragraph, all those

SM: So your fashion education was through practice?

Yes. Fashion was more of something I loved and had a knack for. Growing up as a kid in nowhere Michigan, there was no Internet. I had to drive an hour plus to get Interview magazine. MTV was also so inspiring; I was just wide-eyed at the time. I was so inspired by Cindi Lauper and Boy George and Madonna, and pushing boundaries. It really influenced my design decisions as I progress. Who knew, 30 years later, I would be doing *The Carrie Diaries* and see all these copies of *Interview*? And *Sebastian Cole* was my first education in costume design.

SM: And you moved to New York after shooting that upstate?

ED: Yes, shortly after that I ran into Patricia Fields (*Sex and the City* Costume Designer), who I knew from Paris. We were friendly, and kept in touch and we were both part of that Downtown nightlife scene. And I told her I just finished designing my first film, and she asked if I was interested in coming on as an assistant costume designer for *Sex and the City*. Knowing my background in editorial with a downtown edge, she said they also wanted that look for the show. So she asked if I wanted to meet Sarah Jessica Parker and see how I felt about it.

And at first I didn't know if it was right for me. I had a great indie film experience. And the first season of *Sex and the City* was very different in terms of fashion. It was all little black dresses, so you thought that was

|       |                                                                                                                                                                                                                                                                                                                                                                                                                                                                                                                                                                                    |
|-------|---------------------------------------------------------------------------------------------------------------------------------------------------------------------------------------------------------------------------------------------------------------------------------------------------------------------------------------------------------------------------------------------------------------------------------------------------------------------------------------------------------------------------|
|       | all New York women wore. First seasons are all about making producers happy, and not going to far out creatively. Especially then, now you can push boundaries a lot more. I was this cool hip, downtown kid and I didn't want to sell out! But I talked to my friend who produced *Sebastian Cole* and she said I had to meet with them. She was more part of the entertainment industry and understood what it could mean for me. |
| SM:   | How was your first interaction with Fields and Parker?                                                                                                                                                                                                                                                                                                                                                                                                                                                                    |
| ED:   | We met and just had this wonderful meeting. It was very exciting, and the pulse and creativity Patricia and Sarah Jessica had together was really inspiring for me. So I joined them as Patricia's assistant designer on Seasons One, Two, Three and Four. And it was an incredible ride. It was the best 101 in costume design, that was my full-blown experience, you can't buy that kind of education. |
| SM:   | It's interesting because now the indie world and premium TV world is much more interconnected. With the likes of Jill Soloway and Lena Dunham and Jane Campion. In Sebastian Cole even I saw the parallels between the trans characters in *Transparent*, that transition from a father to a mother. The costume design both focused on this matronly, earth mother look. |
| ED:   | (Laughs) Yeah, we must have done something right, because it still holds up. But yeah, it has really evolved and changed. And not knowing what TV is anymore. At first, we had to work around waist up or even neck up shots. Full body shots were not the norm. |
| SM:   | Can you speak to that a little bit more and how it impacted your costume designing for TV? |
| ED:   | Right, most of the camera shots in television were shoulders up, and reaction shots of faces. Patricia and Sarah Jessica knew that very well, and used it to their advantage to highlight signature accessories. Think the Carrie necklace or the oversized flower, and how to |

|       | |
|-------|-|
| SM:   | use sequins and different necklines and cuts. It was about catching the light and using it to make a statement in that quarter frame from the shoulders. We were always designing from head to toe, but we had to emphasize that area. And Patricia and Sarah Jessica really know how material transforms to camera. I learned how important it was, and also the need to have things tailored, shaving a quarter inch or trimming a hemline. |

SM: Was there a transition for *Sex and the City*? You mentioned Season One wasn't as fashion forward. Was there a turning point where the fashion became integral?

ED: I think Season Two was more expanding the editorial boundaries, and pushing the producers comfort zones. And then it exploded and all the press came with it. So by Season Three, the match had been lit. And in that season we started doing more head to toe shots, more pullouts. The Louboutoins needed to be seen, and the full pullbacks of all four women.

And oddly enough, I feel like it was almost the exact same for *Gossip Girl*. It happened during this hiatus for Season Two during the Writer's Strike 2008. And especially at first for *Gossip Girl*, because it was network television, they only wanted quarter frame shots and reaction shots. That's something I definitely carried my knowledge over from *Sex and the City*, using accessories, headbands, and signature pieces. For Blair Waldorf, I knew however it was going to be cropped, they were not going to get rid of that headband!

SM: I remember the CW would put up a lot of stills on their *Gossip Girl* web page that really mirrored editorial fashion shoots. And this was before you could really watch it online and screenshot so you would take a photo of the screen maybe, but you could look at those stills for quality versions to recall the best outfits in a given episode. That became such a huge mainstay and attraction for the viewers. The CW was very smart and aware of that. They made the most of the fashion and that property. We would do publicity shots, but you could use from the set.

And that was really what Stephanie Savage (*Gossip Girl* Co-Creator and Executive Producer) wanted for the show. She wanted it to be a living editorial straight form *W* or *Vogue* magazines. That effort was really set from the beginning for production design and myself. And when I first met with Stephanie, we both had layouts of what we imagined from the show, and from day one, we had essentially the same identical vision.

SM: And that must have been the influence from the *Gossip Girl* original book series too. You mentioned how Sarah Jessica Parker was so involved in designing the Carrie character, but as an adaptation I imagine you had to work heavily with the original source material and honoring that.

ED: Definitely. There was such a built-in fanbase for *Gossip Girl* because of the book. The characters were so well drawn. There were so many identity pieces, brand shout outs and brand shout outs. Living in Manhattan is like living editorial. The city itself, in both *SATC* and *Gossip Girl*, was a huge influence.

SM: You mentioned your friend earlier who worked in editorial and found it creatively restrictive when the push for what kind of brand and product to use was there. I know *Sex and the City* later on was critiqued for its commercialism rather than expression. Did you ever feel that pressure when working in TV, and with product placements?

ED: In *Gossip Girl*, we had some product placements. Stephanie Savage was very smart about which ones we incorporated, so that it felt germane and seamless within the show. We had something with Victoria's Secret early on, so there was a party, and the way the script was laid out, it became part of the DNA of the show so it wouldn't be this commercial entity. If something felt out of place, Stephanie wouldn't go through with it.

With the fashion it really changed. At the beginning with Season One I couldn't get any showroom samples from higher fashion houses. And the budget was pretty minute for what expectations were in how we wanted the show to look. Once it hit, and the network pushed that publicity with the cast, it took off. It was about Blake wearing a Coach purse and that brand identity. Also at this time, Anna Wintour was really pushing to put celebrities on the cover of *Vogue*. I don't know how she and Blake encountered each other, but they met and got very friendly. Blake was brought into this world, and then she was having lunch with Karl Lagerfield, and running around with Christian Louboutin and getting shoes named after her. That was all part of Blake's trajectory. Her first fitting was like a wide-eyed princess playing dress up. Leighton, on the other hand, already had this avant-garde, downtown signature style. She was all about transforming into Blair.

So once one big brand says yes to you, everyone falls in line. Once Chanel said they'll give us bag, it followed. And we would have to use the bags on multiple characters, and it was very specific in terms of laws and rules governing all that. And some brands would come back and say, "We only want our stuff on Blake, or Leighton." And we had to do it like that, or we couldn't do it at all. I think there were some minor losses of brands because of that, but that means they weren't supposed to be on the show, it didn't work out.

| | |
|---|---|
| SM: | And, of course, with premium cable, product placement isn't needed in the same way as network. Could you speak to that dynamic on the early seasons of *Sex and the City* in contrast to that? It feels like, you know, the classic case in The Sopranos where they had Coca Cola and Pepsi products, but the mobsters drank coke and the feds drank the opposite. |
| ED: | There's a much bigger freedom in that, because of that. And product placement is great, because it means you can go to Paris, and get financing to make the show even better. Stephanie was really smart about using the product placement and the money that came in from it. She did that in a way I don't know a lot of producers have done. She was such a visionary. |
| SM: | A lot of discussion surrounding TV that is quality is usually its association or likeliness to film, and that comes through stating it looks cinematic through cinematography. But I think what is overlooked is how the costume design and production design contribute to that as well. |

At the same time, I think the character of Blair held this kind of intellect, and neurosis, that a lot of smart girls and women were attracted to. Particularly for film fans, the Blair Audrey Hepburn dreams were really psychological and emblematic of her mindset in a nuanced way. Even if Serena/Blake were the It Girls, there was something about Blair that struck a chord for a lot of viewers. Or it opened people up to Blair's sophisticated taste, in the same way teens who watched *The O.C.* learned about indie music through Seth Cohen, or identified with him because they already had the same taste.

What was the intent behind those Hepburn recreations? Were they originally in the book and adapted for screen?

ED: I think in the books, Blair loves Audrey Hepburn. And that love of her, and old world glamour, and Tiffany's, helped pave the way for the fantasy sequences. That was a Stephanie Savage invention. And they were always so fun to do. You would try to recreate these classic outfits with contemporary clothes, while trying to stay true to the look of it, while staying true to our DNA. Those were really great moments. And it added something extra special to the show and Blair's depth.

SM: And I think there's a lot to be said about the highbrow fashion world coming into network TV and everyday, suburban teens' world. There's also the contrast between the larger than life Blair and Serena characters and the contrast with Jenny. Although she only lived in Brooklyn, which was not as affluent as it is now, she kind of symbolized the normal girl contrast who made her own clothes, or went thrift shopping, to establish her look. And it sounds like that mirrors your own upbringing too.

ED: Yeah, Williamsburg really wasn't what it is now, ten years ago. I always bring it back to Molly Ringwald making her own prom dress in *Pretty in Pink*. So Jenny could make her own clothes and still be a part of this world. And she knows how to make something fantastic and one of a kind. And seeing that she used her wiles and talent to do that. And she made her own dress line later on, and I was the designer behind it. Because of the schedule with serial television, it's very hard to do original pieces because of the limited time with turnaround.

And with Blair's mom, Eleanor Waldorf's line, we used a friend of mine, Abigal Lorick's own line. It was the ideal thing we wanted to do for Eleanor, and we added a few other pieces to make it good for television. So it was great to include these other things in

| | |
|---|---|
| SM: | the show that were fashion DNA. And to bring New York designers, and the city into the foreground of the show. And creating the characters visually based on the book, that really went back to my French Lit college background again. |
| SM: | When you were designing the outfits of a character, and they were in conflict, or in harmony, did you use that to express it? |
| ED: | Definitely. If Blair and Serena were in conflict, we made Blair even more buttoned up. And then showing the closeness between Blair and Chuck, I would put in little Easter eggs. If Blair were in mint green, Chuck would wear a mint green pocket square. I used color similarities to pull it in together. From a design point of view, it was really great to convey that emotion and closeness without hitting you over the head with it. Because I'm not sure most viewers noticed it. |
| SM: | I think their fashion sense added a lot to the precociousness and wordliness of the characters. I think of it a lot in contrast to *The O.C.* They seemed precocious then for mentioning pop culture and music, which was central to the show. But with *Gossip Girl*, it wasn't a suburb anymore. It was in the city. |
| ED: | And it's true to growing up in the city, a 13-year-old in New York is like a 30-year-old in the Midwest. Very different. Very elevated. And fast paced, and fascinating. The tween age is where it really gets dodgy. There's also a lot of danger and sophistication that is around you all the time. They really nailed that with the dialogue and the characters, and how they acted much older than their age. I think that was also an attraction. |

This was really during the dawn of digital media. There was no Instagram, people weren't on Twitter. They were on Facebook. Texting was a thing but not like it is now. And there was really this hunger for that generation to feel more sophisticated. I mean I wanted to be 21 when I was 14. And to see someone your age act so mature on national television made it more real. And we see this generation and teens now much more elevated than ten years ago, much less 20 years ago.

Like, I'm a fan of *Chopped Jr.* and *Project Runway Jr.*, and you see a ten-year-old knowing how to make cucumber foam and know everything about silk.

I do feel like we hit the zeitgeist at this moment. And in a way filled up the slot of *Sex and the City* for fashion on TV. In our demographic we had a lot of teens and tweens watching, but oddly enough, we had thirty and forty-somethings obsessed with *Gossip Girl*. The college students that were watching *Sex and the City* were now mothers watching *Gossip Girl*, because of the fashion and drama. There was also this strange straight man obsession with the show, which I never realized until we went out and met the fans.

SM: And with that being said, the men's fashion the show was so influential. With teen media, you usually think of fashion for the girls, and music or something else for the guys. It was that way in *Clueless*, and in *The O.C.* What you all did with Chuck Bass really ushered in a new level of fashion for the straight male consumer. It really opened the floodgates.

ED: Yeah, at the time it was all about mean just wearing jeans and t-shirts. And then when they dressed up it was Ed Hardy shirts and bootcut jeans, this sort of metrosexual hideousness. And I had to explain that men are peacocks, they want to stand out and look good. I just could not tolerate it for another minute.

And there's nothing better than a man in a beautiful suit. There's a power about it. Throughout the ages, men have dressed in a way that is dapper and dandy and show-offish.

|  | I think Chuck Bass was a big breakthrough stylistically. And a lot of that we owe to Ed Westick, who is a Brit. He comes from a theater background, and understood, at an early age, costume and bespoke clothing. He took it to his character's advantage and his advantage for his fans. And that was great for me to just keep pushing this straight billionaire bachelor playboy on lost weekends, doing high end pub crawls, and swigging $150 a glass whiskey, all while wearing a pink ascot. And guys could watch him and identify, or want to identify with him, and go out and try to look like that. Not that there was a surge of ascots immediately, but there was one for bow ties and pocket squares because of Chuck Bass. |
|---|---|

*SM:* Bringing that fashion world for teens was really huge. We talked about it for Jenny, but breaking through to men is even huger.

*ED:* Much bigger.

*SM:* And it does go back to Classic Hollywood like you mentioned. It was also around the same time as *Mad Men*, but that's a period piece. Even if Jon Hamm because this GQ figure of sophistication as a contemporary figure, it was more about *Mad Men* themed party or costumes, not everyday contemporary editorial looks as we saw with Chuck.

*SM:* And the show ended around the peak recession, so it was interesting to see more suburban or everyday brands or stores start to collaborate with higher end designers. I think *Gossip Girl* showed there was a market for that interest in high fashion looks, at more affordable prices. The show was airing during this time that teenagers and young adults became more involved active participants in fashion. That Jenny generation. You had Tavi Gevinson for *Rookie* Magazine, and *Nylon*, and young fashion bloggers and vloggers

| | |
|---|---|
| | who became influencers. And the recession played a huge part in the cross section between high and low brow fashion. Seeing Target work with high end designers. Did you experience that? |
| ED: | Exactly, there was a big coup on Target's end to start those high-end collaborations. As high end as they want to be, they want to reach a mainstream audience. You know, there's still Vera Wang for Kohl's, and they are doing their thing while also still getting to have a mass distribution. |

When we started Gossip Girl, we discussed that high low compromise. We didn't want to alienate those watching who didn't have Balenciaga bags and Tory Burch flats. And I think during Season 2, into Season 3, Charlotte Russe brought me on as their Creative Director. Then I worked with Payless. It was this constant dialogue I had that I wanted to push forward.

I wanted to let women and girls know they could have this look without having to have all that money. I wanted to inspire confidence, and it's still one of my mantras that confidence is our best accessory. And confidence is free.

And just in the digital era, the availability to know and understand fashion is so much bigger now than it ever was.

| | |
|---|---|
| SM: | You must have started shooting the *Sex and the City* teen prequel, *The Carrie Diaries*, for the CW right after *Gossip Girl* ended. And even if it was meant to be set in the 1980s during Carrie's adolescence, the costuming wasn't period. It was 1980s inspired clothing, but in the style of what kids would want to wear now. |
| ED: | Yes. We did the pilot for *The Carrie Diaries* while we were doing the finale for *Gossip Girl*. It was crazy. |

And we called that "aspirational authenticity." I think Stephanie Savage actually came up with that.

And it provokes giggles, but it's exactly what we wanted to do. Luckily for us the 1980s were all over the runways at that time. There was a lot of neon and stuff that worked to our advantage, as far as being able to use contemporary available fashion. And, of course, it was not the Carrie Bradshaw we know and love, it was this adolescent Carrie getting her footing in New York while still living in the Connecticut suburbs. So all the colors and the prints going on really lent itself to what we were doing.

And I feel really bad we didn't get another season. It was a shame.

SM: Luckily everything is coming back. So if there was that fanbase, which I think there was and still is, there's hope.

## Notes

1 Louisa Ellen Stein, *Millennial Fandom: Television Audiences in the Transmedia Age* (Iowa City: University of Iowa Press, 2015), 7.
2 Melissa Kempf Taylor, "Xennials: A Microgeneration in the Workplace," *Industrial and Commercial Training* 50, no. 3 (2018): 136–147.
3 Kristen Bialik and Richard Fry, "Millennial Life: How Young Adulthood Today Compares with Prior Generations," Pew Research Center, February 14, 2019, https://www.pewsocialtrends.org/essay/millennial-life-how-young-adulthood-today-compares-with-prior-generations/
4 Faye Woods, "Teen TV Meets T4: Assimilating *The O.C.* into British Youth Television," *Critical Studies in Television* 8, no. 1 (Spring 2013): 14–35.
5 Stein, *Millennial Fandom*.
6 Stein, *Millenial Fandom*, 22.
7 Raffi Sarkissian, "Queering TV Conventions: LGBT Teen Narratives on *Glee*," in *Queer Youth and Media Cultures*, ed. Christopher Pullen (London: Palgrave Macmillan, 2014), 148.
8 Priya Elan, "Why Tina Fey's *Mean Girls* is a Movie Classic," *The Guardian*, January 29, 2013, https://www.theguardian.com/film/shortcuts/2013/jan/29/tina-feys-mean-girls-movie-classic
9 Irin Camron, "Molly Ringwald On Teen Pregnancy, Brisol Palin, and *For Keeps*," *Jezebel*, April 28, 2010, http://jezebel.com/5526331/molly-ringwald-on-teen-pregnancy-bristol-palin-and-for-keeps

10. Mike Pesca, "In Cluster of Teen Pregnancies, 'Juno' Comes to Life," National Public Radio, June 26, 2008, http://www.npr.org/templates/story/story.php?storyId=91906103
11. Ibid.
12. Ibid.
13. John Dempsey, "ABC Family Scores with 'Teenager'," *Variety*, August 15, 2008, http://variety.com/2008/tv/features/abc-family-scores-with-teenager-1117990639/
14. Ibid.
15. Ibid.
16. Personal communication, August 10, 2019.
17. Ibid.
18. Ibid.
19. OC Weekly Staff, "Rilo Kiley – *The Execution of All Things*," *The OC Weekly*, October 24, 2002, https://www.ocweekly.com/rilo-kiley-6384981/
20. Personal communication, August 23, 2019.
21. Suzanne C. Ryan, "OCcupational Hazard: Every Whiz Kid Has to Grow up, a Lesson 'O.C.' Creator Josh Schwartz is Learning as the Once Hot Show Struggles," *The Boston Globe*, October 29, 2006, http://archive.boston.com/news/globe/living/articles/2006/10/29/occupational_hazard/
22. Stein, *Millennial Fandom*, 87.
23. Ibid.
24. Ibid.
25. Stein, *Millennial Fandom*, 85.
26. Ibid.
27. "'Gossip Girl': The Most Important Show of Our Time," *New York*, September 10, 2007, https://nymag.com/intelligencer/2007/09/gossip_girl_the_most_important_1.html
28. Rhonda V. Wilcox and Sue Turnbull, "Introduction: Canonical Veronica: *Veronica Mars* and Vintage Television," in *Investigating Veronica Mars: Essays on the Teen Detective*, eds. Rhonda V. Wilcox and Sue Turnbull (Jefferson, NC: McFarland and Company, 2011), 1.
29. Jeff Jensen, "The 'Veronica Mars' Creator on His Recent Job Hunt," *Entertainment Weekly*, October 24, 2006, http://ew.com/article/2006/10/24/veronica-mars-creator-his-recent-job-hunt/
30. Margy Rochlin, "A Show Written for the Young by the Young," *The New York Times*, August 15, 2008, https://www.nytimes.com/2008/08/17/arts/television/17roch.html
31. Neil Wilkes, "'Skins' Star Hannah Murray," January 1, 2007, https://www.digitalspy.com/tv/a41979/skins-star-hannah-murray
32. Kate Hodal, "Thailand's Answer to Skins Shocks Some, Thrills Others," *The Guardian*, August 19, 2013, https://www.theguardian.com/tv-and-radio/2013/aug/19/hormones-thailand-school-tv-drama-sex-drugs
33. Susan Berridge, "'Doing it for the Kids'? The Discursive Construction of the Teenager and Teenage Sexuality in *Skins*," *Journal of British Cinema and Television* 10, no. 4 (2013): 787.

34 Faye Woods, "Teen TV Meets T4," 15.
35 Berridge, *Skins*, 789.
36 Woods, "Assimilating The O.C.," 18.
37 Berridge, *Skins*, 793.
38 Ibid.
39 Berridge, *Skins*, 795.
40 Woods, "Assimilating The O.C.," 21.
41 Berridge, *Skins*, 796.
42 Woods, "Assimilating The O.C.," 21.
43 Berridge, *Skins*, 799.
44 Andy Kellman, "Drake Biography," All Music, accessed September 3, 2017, https://www.allmusic.com/artist/drake-mn0001035294
45 Maya Mirsky, "Rapper Drake Has His Own Brand of Jewishness," *Jewish Telegraphic Agency*, October 10, 2018, https://www.jta.org/2018/10/10/united-states/rapper-drake-brand-jewishness/amp
46 Zack O'Malley Greenberg, "Drake's Net Worth: $150 Million In 2019," *Forbes*, June 14, 2019, https://www.forbes.com/sites/zackomalleygreenburg/2019/06/14/drake-net-worth-150-million-in-2019/#54a7cae01774
47 Lidia Abraha, "The Complexity of Toronto's Sound and the Waning Relevance of Drake," *Unaffiliated Press*, February 1, 2018, https://www.unaffiliatedpress.ca/article/2018/1/29/the-complexity-of-torontos-sound-and-the-waning-relevance-of-drake
48 Allie Jones, "What's up with Drake Texting Teens?" *Vice*, December 20, 2019, https://www.vice.com/en_us/article/k7eq5y/whats-up-with-drake-texting-teens
49 Tom Skinner, "Drake Reportedly Settles Lawsuit against Woman Who Accused Him of Sexual Assault, Made False Pregnancy Claims," *NME*, December 2, 2018, https://www.nme.com/news/music/drake-settles-lawsuit-sexual-assault-pregnancy2415696-2415696?amp
50 Bethy Squires, "Video Emerges of Drake Kissing Underage Girl on Stage," *Vulture*, January 5, 2019, https://www.vulture.com/2019/01/video-emerges-of-drake-kissing-underage-girl-on-stage.html

# 4

# GEN Z TEEN TV

This chapter surveys new directions for teen programming catered toward Gen Z, while outlining the challenges marketers face in holding teen viewers' attention in a media-saturated, smartphone-driven world. Gen Z identity is still evolving. According to the Pew Research Center, the Gen Z demographic begins with those born in 1997, as the oldest Millennials in 2019 approached 40. By 2019, the first cohort of Gen Z began to graduate from university. While the lines are still blurred between Millennials and Gen Zs, historical events such as September 11 and Barack Obama's 2008 presidential election stand out as key markers.[1] Gen Z is also surpassing Millennials as the most ethnically and racially diverse and highly educated generation to date.[2] Trans rights and climate change, as well as the #BlackLivesMatter and #MeToo movements, are key political elements of Gen Z, particularly through the lens of online activism. Preliminary reports differentiate between the two generations but place Gen Z as a continuation of the diversity and socially conscious nature of their predecessors. They are more likely to be based in cities, and less likely to be foreign-born. Factors such as the COVID-19 pandemic, 2020 US presidential election, and immigration reform, for example, will likely be significant benchmarks for Gen Z teens. The discussion of Asian-American and non-immigrant Hispanic teens is significant to note here for Gen Z as well:

> More broadly, the post-Millennial generation is being shaped by changing immigration patterns. Immigration flows into

the U.S. peaked in 2005, when the leading edge of the post-Millennial generation was age 8 or younger. The onset of the Great Recession and the large decline in employment led to fewer immigrants coming to the United States, including immigrant children. As a result, the post-Millennial generation has fewer foreign-born youth among its ranks than the Millennial generation did in 2002 and a significantly higher number who were born in the U.S. to immigrant parents, though this may change depending on future immigration flows.[3]

First, this chapter examines the Hulu program *East Los High*, and how its novel origins and funding led to it being one of the few teen series to focus on Latinas and safe sex education through nonprofit funding production practices. Further, its classification as what Laurie Ouelette refers to as a "do-good" turn, in the same vein as ABC programming of the 1980s and 1990s, with its *Afterschool Specials* as the only clear predecessor in US programming. This is followed by an interview with Kathleen Bedoya and other contributors to the project who sought out TV production as a means of incorporating more effective public health messages for teens into a widely accessible medium. Second, the chapter examines the hybrid teen TV crime series as a dominant pairing, following supernatural, sci-fi, and adventure fusions. The chapter concludes with the potential of representations of mental health, sexuality, sex identity, abuse, addiction, and more through HBO's first teen series, *Euphoria*, as well as the rising popularity of non-US or English-speaking programming in an increasingly globalized, and glocalized, streaming era.

## *East Los High*

American teen television, like most US programming, was historically created with a commercial incentive rather than a public service initiative. It rarely uses non-commercial funding for productions. This section will first briefly map out some slightly alternative methods in the history of teen TV to this norm, but argue that Hulu's *East Los High* is the exception to the rule. In many ways, *East Los High*, whose first season was funded by the nonprofit organization the Population Media Center (PMC), shifted this production practice standard for American teen TV by straying from a primary commercial motivation.

This case study will examine the implications of the first season of the teen series funded by a nonprofit organization and subsequently distributed on Hulu—a streaming platform owned by media conglomerates that works with the traditional media industry rather than compete with them, such as Netflix or Amazon. The first part will map out the production and distribution practices surrounding *East Los High*, while the second will dissect the commercial and marketing strategies employed once the series became co-owned by Hulu in its second season. While the former stands out as an anomaly in the television industry, the latter is one of the most traditional implementations in the medium's history: integrated product placement based on a targeted demographic. Therefore, while the production signals democratization and a "do-good" turn in US television, it is further supplemented by one of the standards of media marketing in capitalist industry.

First, the primary resource interview of *East Los High* co-creator and co-showrunner Kathleen Bedoya (included here) will be drawn on for further information on the development, production, distribution, outreach and engagement, and reception of the series. When Bedoya first began working in television in the 1990s, she states the major networks did not have a "true financial and creative commitment … to reach the [Latino] audience in an innovative, authentic and resonating manner." However, Hulu allowed this opportunity decades later. Bedoya's interest in youth programming began when she worked on a telenovela for MTV Tr3s, when she embarked on research to "integrate messaging regarding sexual consent, STDS, HIV, domestic, violence, and contraception among other topics," to Mexican and Latin American Youth. As will be discussed in further detail, Bedoya, Carlos Portugal, and Katie Elmore Mota were first hired for the development of *East Los High* as a series that specifically targeted the high pregnancy rate of Latinas in the US. They decided to focus the fictional series in the Los Angeles neighborhood of Boyle Heights, due to its own high teen pregnancy statistics and dominant Latinx population and cultural heritage.

The two publications most relevant to the production of the series are Laurie Ouelette's "Citizen Brand: ABC and the Do Good Turn in US Television" and John McMurria's "Pay-for Culture: Television Activism in a Neoliberal Digital Age," both chapters in Sarah Banet-Weiser and Roopalo Mukherjee's 2012 edited collection, *Commodity Activism: Cultural Resistance in Neoliberal Times*. Ouelette argues that amid a deregulated, conglomerated media landscape, the ABC network began to display what she calls a "do-good turn" in commercial television, which:

> Operates as an informal partnership between a supportive (but minimally involved) public sector, commercial television networks, socially responsible advertisers, private charities and nonprofit organizations, and TV viewers, who are increasingly expected to use the resources coordinated by television (and it's tie-in websites) to modify their lifestyles, support causes, build communities, consume ethically and perform volunteerism.[4]

Ouelette further argues that this turn is part of a shift in corporate social responsibility and branding for ethical, community-building TV viewers/citizens. She states that essentially, "ABC enacts a model of good government that is in synchronicity with current political rationales and capitalized on the results."[5] Hulu, the distributor-turned-owner of *East Los High*, mirrored ABC's actions in 2006. If a socially conscious series funded by a nonprofit is also popular with a targeted demographic, this is considered good business with an added bonus and potential awards from civil rights and social organizations.

Additionally, because few series hold mass appeal anymore in a fragmented TV landscape, the drive toward specific audiences based on age, ethnicity, and political allegiances has increased in the digital post-network era. Jessica Kumai Scott, a Hulu creative executive, also stated in a phone interview that the target age for Hulu viewers is

14–25 years, a younger range than the majority of streaming platforms, network TV, and cable channels. Scott further explained that unlike networks and cable channels, Hulu is less concerned with a cohesive or unilateral "brand identity."[6]

Hulu was initially implemented as a platform for cord-cutters (which inherently implies a younger demographic who does not rely on traditional television) who wanted to watch network TV programs weekly but did not want to pay a cable bill or own a television. Hulu first acquired several series, then began development for original series. The company is adept to understanding the benefit of committed niche audiences. For example, when Fox cancelled *The Mindy Project* in 2015, Hulu picked it up based on its online fan bases that would subscribe just to watch the series. Similarly, Hulu acquired *Difficult People*, starring cult-like popular internet-based comedians Julie Klausner and Billy Eichner, when the series partnership with USA floundered. Klausner was known for her podcast and Eichner for his unconventional pop culture game show, and both had cultivated their personas, fanbases, and brands through Twitter. As dramas garnered more acclaim, the platform also invested in *Casual*, *The Path*, and the upcoming *The Handmaid's Tale*. Ultimately, catering to niche audiences with varied and diverse programming becomes a way to reach a wider audience as a whole.

While Hulu adapted the "do-good turn" in television with *East Los High*, the initial production of the series is a different case. This is where McMurria's conceptualization of television activism in a neoliberal digital age becomes useful. Again, because the initial season of *East Los High* was the first known US commercial TV series wholly funded by a nonprofit, it is a rare case study.

By the 1970s, US network television shifted from "least offensive programming" to attract a wide mass audience to niche and narrowcasting based on demographics. Likewise, the civil rights and second-wave feminist movements established some of its core goals, and US society became more accepting of feminism and non-racist rhetoric. Subsequently, as more women and racial minorities gained upward mobility, the television industry saw them as a new demographic. This narrowcasting, demographic shift also aligns with greater youth- and teen-focused programming. Narrowcasting toward teens and edutainment further heightened during the rise of cable in the 1990s. However, nationally sponsored public broadcasting programming remained the exception rather than the rule in the US.[7] Certain episodic series in teen TV have historically included topical public service announcement-oriented narrative arcs with issues such as teen pregnancy, drug and alcohol abuse, and suicide.

Yet, entertainment and selling to advertisers remain industry priorities. ABC's *Afterschool Specials* aired from 1972 to 1997, and during this time, family-friendly situational comedies also incorporated moralistic messages in "very special episodes." This stands in contrast to many public service-oriented global TV programs that attempt to instill education and cultural weight with entertainment to teach moral lessons and promote nationalistic values. In many ways, with the first season funded by a nonprofit organization, Hulu's *East Los High* shifted the norm for American teen TV by straying from a primary commercial motivation.

As Ouelette asserts, the US public sector is minimally involved in commercial programming. Nonprofits in America have taken up the goals and missions of public sector work in other countries in relation to social issues. Nonprofits previously partnered with studios, networks, or individual series to convey messages. *ABC Afterschool Specials,* which were produced and aired by ABC, is a slight parallel. Amanda Keeler discusses the similar case of the *Gilmore Girls* as the "first advertiser advocated show" funded by the Family Friendly Programming Forum (FFPF), a group consisting of major US corporations who offered up a million dollars to "fund 'family friendly' programming." She states that this funding was solely based on the idea that lead protagonist Lorelai Gilmore is a single mother, and decided to keep her child when she was pregnant as a teen.[8] Unlike *East Los High*, the funding and creative side did not collaborate on program content.

On the surface, the first English-language series with an entirely Latino cast is a teen version of popular telenovelas mixed with narrative milestones of popular high school dramas. Before Bedoya came on board, the series was created by the PMC, a nonprofit organization that funds and produces "entertainment-education soap operas" that focus explicitly on population stabilization through family planning and women's rights. The PMC is a US-based, yet global-reaching, nonprofit company dedicated to sustainability and conquering overpopulation by promoting safe sex and family planning. The PMC previously produced series dedicated to reducing unwanted pregnancies in 53 other countries, using the so-called "Sabido Method," a technique for soap operas to deliver topical messages in Mexico in the 1970s and 1980s. The creator of the Sabido Method, Miguel Sabido, is also attributed as having developed entertainment education.[9]

McMurria argues that grassroots communities and fan activism can work to democratize a highly conglomerated, monolithic television landscape in which "fans can challenge conglomerates to be more accountable to consumer interests."[10] He connects this to Henry Jenkins's argument that grassroots fan communities actively challenge commercial programming by building their own meanings, referencing Pierre Levy's notions of "collective intelligence" and "knowledge communities."[11] As social justice issues in the US primarily deal with marginalized groups, the lack of minorities who own and produce media in the US could be a direct cause for less representation of these issues. Civil rights organizations call for the media to portray minorities responsibly, but this only serves as a proverbial watchdog.

The PMC functions as a parallel to the grassroots fan communities, but one that has managed to crossover into commercial television. In a phone interview, PMC president Bill Ryerson asserted that the organization stalled investing in a US series due to the sheer competition.[12] The small nonprofit produced a first season of the series, received several offers, and ultimately picked Hulu, knowing that teens are more likely to stream. The research for *East Los High* development was extensive. Ryerson explained that they found one of the highest teen pregnancy demographics in the US is Hispanic Americans, and they wanted to focus in on that. Future shows similar to *East Los High* will air in other high teen pregnancy areas, Harlem New York and the rural south. PMC taught the writing team the foundations of the

Sabido methodology, US government policies, positive and negative values, transitional characters, and role models. They also incorporated social learning theory, works from Albert Brandera, Solomon Asch's conformism and people driven to the norm, and the idea that charismatic characters change perceptions. Ryerson stated that teen television programming in the US tended to unintentionally romanticize teen moms, as American television historically took few risks to depict abortions in prime time.

Once the series was passed on to Bedoya and Portugal, the two showrunners expanded beyond the Sabido Method to include more issues and other storytelling modes. This was partly because *East Los High* would not be a telenovela, which airs daily on weekdays, but instead would be released weekly on Hulu. However, viewers could still binge-watch on the platform. Bedoya stated:

> We created our own formula. We chose to keep all the dramatic elements of the telenovelas that we love and include the social issues in a more nuanced manner. We kept what worked well and reinvented the rest. And every season, we adjusted the issues as needed. If we were going to accurately depict Latino youth growing up in East LA, we had to discuss other social issues impacting them such as the criminalization of people of color and immigration.

Further, the research to incorporate socially conscious issues mirrors that of *Degrassi*. Bedoya recognizes the effort behind preliminary research, and that a creative team must agree with the decisions and efforts to establish the mandate. The series also cumulated feedback from viewers to expand upon the characters and topics that mattered to the young demographic. On making the impact feasible, Bedoya believes:

> Teen pregnancy, domestic violence, substance abuse, incarceration and many other challenges faced by youth of color in this country are complicated issues impacted by other social

and political factors that need time and space to be portrayed in a thoughtful, open manner. It's about taking that extra step—connecting viewers to resources—which makes all the difference. Presenting issues that are complicated in a way that is not black or white but with many other shades of color can be an important vehicle to open awareness, change perspective and even impact behavior.

## Past Treatment of Teen TV Abortions

Television plots around abortion and teen mothers are historically ambivalent to political and social stances, with a few exceptions. The first TV narrative incorporating an abortion occurred with Norman Lear's *Maude*, in a two-part arc entitled "Maude's Dilemma." The middle-aged protagonist decided to have an abortion due to her age and desire not to have any more children, as she was already a grandmother. The titular protagonist is known for being straightforward and unapologetically progressive. Ahead of its time, this episode aired in 1972, a year before the Roe v. Wade Supreme Court case. However, abortion was legal in New York state at the time, Maude's location. Franchise showrunner Shonda Rhimes, a publicly fierce supporter of Planned Parenthood, has included abortions in her widely popular series *Grey's Anatomy* and its spinoff *Private Practice*. To date, one of the only prime-time television abortion narratives for a teen is Jason Katims' *Friday Night Lights*. In *The O.C.*, Ryan may have impregnated his hometown sweetheart. She and Ryan both hail from a neighborhood not unlike East Los Angeles, and the difficulties of teenage parenthood is shown for both mother and father. While she lies to Ryan about her abortion, she ultimately keeps the baby.

Teen TV teenage moms, even those who do proceed with an abortion, historically have a safety net to fall back on. Jason Katims' *Friday Night Lights* and *Parenthood* most recently show the potential repercussions and the choice of young female teens to terminate their pregnancy. In *Lights*, lower-class Becky decides not to follow in the path of her mother, who was a teen mom herself. The repercussions of the abortion are shown in the small-town conservative Christian community's backlash toward Tami Taylor (Connie Britton), who ethically points out all of Becky's options. However, the town, and Becky's boyfriend's Christian mother, use Taylor as a scapegoat and the reason behind the abortion. In *Parenthood*, a Katims series that faced fewer ratings troubles than *Lights* and centers on an upper-middle-class family from Berkeley, California, the abortion is for a tertiary character who is ready to embark on college at an elite university. The financial strain in *Parenthood* is less prevalent, although the issue of choice is stressed, and the visibility of Planned Parenthood emphasized in the episode.

The central conflict in the first season of *East Los High* is a geek-ish teenage girl Jessie's unplanned pregnancy after losing her virginity. Her life unravels as her mother dies of cancer in debt, and her boyfriend falls in love with her cousin. Her ambitious best friend, successful aunt, and mother's doctor serve as educational supplements to encourage the protagonist to question her choices and careers. *East Los High* became the first all Latino cast, English-speaking series. The cast and crew were 100% Hispanic, and its "creators" after PMC were Carlos Portugal and Kathleen Bedoya. Portugal stated that he had three rules for the writers of *East Los High*—no gardeners, no gang members, and no maids—"My hope is that people from East LA get to see themselves in the show portrayed as diverse human beings and not the typical Latino stereotypes we see in TV and films."[13]

The intersection of race, class, and location is crucial in *East Los High*. Recent series *Fresh Off the Boat* and *Black-ish*, both on ABC, provide a more auteurist perspective of Asian immigrants, and identity struggles of the black experience once upwardly mobile, respectively. Even with *Fresh off the Boat*, in which the Asian-American family is in the early stages of upward mobility, viewers see it from the perspective of the fictionalized narrator, a young Eddie Huang, a real-life immigrant success story. *East Los High* focuses on a lower-class neighborhood filled with predominantly Mexican-American residents who constantly battle socioeconomic struggles. This is why the consequences of teen pregnancy are more vivid than most other televisual representations. As of 2010, more than 90% of Boyle Heights are Latinos and close to

73% live in a rental property. These residents are also more likely to rely on government resources than the rest of the country, thus less likely to use private coverage.[14] The neighborhood has also historically held higher teen pregnancy statistics than the rest of Los Angeles county. While this is not the first "anthropology shot," as Roz Kavney would call it, it is one of the most nuanced looks at teens who are not middle-class or upper-middle-class, considering some of the most popular teen TV shows of the past 20 years are *Beverly Hills 90210*, *The O.C.*, *Gossip Girl*, and *Pretty Little Liars*.[15] The non-commercial incentive of focusing a teen series on a Latino, lower-class neighborhood is thus crucial when contrasting *East Los High* to its teen TV peers.

Katie Elmore Mota was the first main producer of *East Los High* when she worked for PMC. After the successful first season, she realized she needed a full team to support her, and founded production company Wise Entertainment, geared at socially conscious programming for women. In terms of writing, the series has expanded beyond just reproductive responsibility and the principles of the Sabido Method. Mota stated that the characters and their situations are more complex and nuanced, in a gray area rather than a black and white, good versus bad binary.[16] After the first season, Mota's Wise Entertainment took over production for *East Los High* under the funding and further supervision of Hulu. The series also began to show a heightened production value and incorporated product placement.

After the initial success of *East Los High*'s first season, several trade press publications noted that Hulu had won over the Latino demographic. During this same time, Hulu shifted from an ad-supported model for $7.99 a month, to a new $11.99 premium plan with no commercials. This began to mirror HBO, Netflix and Amazon more than the basic cable model Hulu initially imitated. Further, in the years leading up to the series premiere of *East Los High*, media marketers began to realize the potential for an untapped audience. In the 1990s and early 2000s, content creators and distributors focused on Spanish-language content and niche targeting through Hulu Latino, FX Latino, and HBO Latino. While the 2000s began to acknowledge the growing potential of Latino audiences, bilingual Millennials were overlooked until much later. Latinos accounted for 54% of US population growth between 2000 and 2014, with the highest concentration of Latinos in the US in California, followed by Texas.[17]

Latino voters were also considered paramount to Barack Obama's second presidential domination in 2012. Statistics on US Latinos' buying power and viewing habits soon followed. According to the 2016 *Ad Age* Hispanic Fact Pack, 56.6 million Hispanics live in the US, comprising 17.6% of the population, with a buying power of 11.3%. Hispanics are more than 20% of the 10–39 years population. Major media spending across traditional and digital platforms added up to $7.83 billion. While Univision remains the key player, new content creators and distributors are tapping into the demographic.

This new research on Latinos in the US homed in on the bilingual Millennial consumer who also sought out English-language media. A 2012 study from Nielsen Media stated that Hispanic Americans were the largest growing minority segment in the country and their spending power was not a passing niche, but a newfound mainstay. The study reported that "Hispanics spend 68 percent more time watching video on the Internet and 20 percent more time watching video on their mobile phones compared to non-Hispanic Whites."[18] Nielsen further stated that successful marketers would need to provide transmedia platforms for the new targeted Hispanic consumer. Toyota proved to be one of the most invested companies in the demographic, as research showed it was among the most persistent brands Hispanics purchased, favoring American imports over foreign cars.[19] Hulu Latino first launched in 2011, premiering original Spanish-language series and acquired content from Univision. Announced at the launch were the five companies invested in the streaming platform: Corona, Modelo, Toyota, Pantene, and Volkswagen of America.[20] A majority of the programming was in Spanish, not catered toward bilingual Millennials who grew up speaking English.

In addition to Hulu subscriptions, profit from *East Los High* is achieved through one of the most traditional television mechanisms: integrated product placement. By the second season, the Toyota RAV4, which male protagonist Jacob drives, sponsored the series. Portugal made sure this transition was believable and convincing within the world of the show. Mota agreed, citing in an interview with *Stream Daily*: "He's now graduated from East Los and gone back to being the assistant football coach and is running his father's taqueria, so he's got a professional career going on that would allow him to have that car."[21] The use of Toyota for the series is also strategic for the demographic. As of 2015, Toyota, the world's largest car manufacturer, has been the top automobile brand for Hispanic consumers for the past ten years. The brand used Spanish-language and culturally specific campaigns to target consumers, even creating the tag line "Mas Que Un Auto," or "More Than A Car," catering to the family and community-driven nature of US Latinos.[22] This strategy reflects that of PMC, Wise Entertainment, and Hulu. Like Toyota, Hulu began early marketing toward the demographic upon realizing its buying potential.

Indeed, this model is a much more subtle form of integrated product placement than most TV series. While the camera does emphasize Jacob's car often, an elevated form would revolve around each cast member driving the same car and perhaps discussing it in depth. This often occurs with cell phone products, whereby every character on a show such as *The O.C.* will use the same mobile. Therefore, Jacob's use of the RAV4 creates more verisimilitude than most product placements. Even after splitting with PMC for production and funding, the series continues to work with local and national nonprofits, such as Vota Latino in a Season 4 story arc about Latino rights during the 2018 presidential election.

The next prominent Latino-centered US series came in 2014 with *Jane the Virgin* on the youth-centered CW network. The integrated Target product placement serves as part of the titular character Jane's personal brand. By the fifth episode, her mother states, "Jane's not impressed with money or power. She likes going to the movies or shopping at Target. That kind of thing. Low-key stuff." Unsurprisingly, the company's collaboration with the series revolved around a greater push to appeal to Latino Millennials. The initial product placement coincided with a new campaign aimed at Spanish-speaking customers, #SinTraduccion, meaning "without translation." The *Ad Age* Data Center reported that Target spent $51 million on Hispanic-based media in the US in 2013 alone.[23] Like *Ugly Betty* before it, *Jane the Virgin* was adapted from a Spanish-language soap opera and achieved crossover critical and commercial success. It adheres to tongue-in-cheek telenovela style drama, but with a focus on family and social consciousness.

In "Episode Forty-Six" from 2016, Jane's mother Xiomara gets an abortion after a one-night stand, and openly tells her religious mother and ex-boyfriend. She is straightforward yet thoughtful about the decision, which is rarely shown on US television, whether network, premium, or streaming. The series also openly supported Planned Parenthood by inserting a #StandWithPlannedParenthood onscreen in a 2017 Valentine's Day episode, "Chapter Fifty-Five."

The series also tackled immigration reform with an ongoing storyline around Jane's beloved grandmother, Alba, and her status as an undocumented immigrant from Venezuela. When Alba must go to the hospital, she is terrified she will be deported if she cannot provide sufficient properties. Through the use of its frequent onscreen narrative and appeal to youth, viewers see "Yes, this really happens. Look it up. #ImmigrationReform" ("Chapter 10"). Humanizing an undocumented immigrant proved to be an exercise in empathy and tolerance for the series. *Jane the Virgin's* ratings average at 1.06 million viewers with an 0.4/1 share.[24] However, the series has won Peabody, Paleyfest, Imagen, American Film Institute, and Golden Globe awards. It may not be a high-rating success for the CW, but this is made up by the show's critical acclaim and awards accolades.

In 2017, Netflix debuted the reboot of Norman Lear's *One Day at a Time*, which Lear also spearheaded. The latest version revolves around a Cuban-American family in the rapidly gentrifying Echo Park neighborhood of Los Angeles. This was Lear's first "new" TV series in 20 years, and it received generally positive reviews from critics, averaging 8.1/10 on IMDB.com, 4/6 with Common Sense Media, 96% on reviews aggregator *Rotten Tomatoes*, and 79% on another aggregator, *Metacritic*. The show has already won a National Hispanic Media Coalition Award for Outstanding Series and was renewed by Netflix for Season 2. Because the streaming platform does not release any form of ratings, no viewership statistics are available.

As well as these successes, several Latino-focused series have failed over the past five years, including FX's *The Bridge* (2013–2014), ABC's *Cristela* (2014–2015), and the Eva Longoria-fueled *Telenovela* on NBC (2015–2016). *Cristela*'s first season averaged 5.23 million viewers with a 1.0 rating for adults aged 18–49 years. Latina women were behind both sitcoms, but the rigidity of broadcast TV's ratings system led to both demises.

While Latino-centered shows are not always successful, their stars often thrive. In 2016, *Modern Family*'s Sofia Vergara was TV's highest-paid actress, gaining an annual $43 million and holding the title for five years. For her role in the highly successful ABC drama *Desperate Housewives*, Eva Longoria received $375,000 per episode.[25] By 2016, approximately 11 television series predominantly featured Latino characters, from Netflix's *Orange is the New Black*, *Narcos*, and *The Get Down* to Starz's *Power* and ABC Family's *The Fosters*. Still, despite the success of *Fresh Off the Boat* and *Black-ish*, no broadcast network succeeded with a Latino-based prime-time series. This could mean that Latino viewers are still too "niche" for the most mainstream TV outlets, or that the broadcast representations fall flat for audiences seeking authenticity and heterogeneity.

Measuring the success of *East Los High* is difficult and elusive for several reasons. While the show is not necessarily only concerned with ratings, the impact and influence are important. First, Ryerson noted in an interview that 27,000 people linked from the show to share Planned Parenthood via social media or email. A study in the *American Journal of Public Health* also revealed that young teens are impacted by the content in the series, and most of all, learn about reproductive health and social issues.[26] While Hulu does not release viewership statistics, Hulu acting CEO Andy Forssell stated that it became a top 15 show on the platform in its premiere month, stayed in the top 10 after reruns, and established itself as the most-watched show for Latino viewers. Forssell asserted that the series was just as popular as staples such as *Grey's Anatomy* and the *Daily Show*.[27]

The TV democratization in *East Los High* is also akin to a generation of digital disruptors—mostly from marginalized groups—who produce and create their own web series that get picked up by mainstream outlets. This includes Abbi Jacoson and Illana Glazer's *Broad City* (Comedy Central), Issa Rae's *Insecure* (HBO), and Katja Blichfeld Ben Sinclair's *High Maintenance* (HBO). While these web series are focused around diverse representation rather than social justice, I associate them as overall disruptors of traditional US programming, because diverse representations is a political pillar of discussions about television programming. Many of these series feature storylines around social and political issues woven into professional and personal narratives, similar to *East Los High*. Jacobson and Glazer featured then-presidential nominee Hilary Clinton in an episode of *Broad City*, remained fierce supporters throughout her election, and subsequent public dissenters of Donald Trump's presidency. And while the economic model for distributing, marketing, and sustaining the series is a digital transmedia update of a traditional product placement standard, the content and cultural impact of the series is still new territory for social issues in the mainstream US television landscape. *East Los High* is undeniably part of a movement toward democratizing television and inciting social change.

## Asian and Asian-American Protagonists in Teen TV: A Brief Overview

Asian and Asian-American representations in US media scarcely place them as leading protagonists, but 2014 marked increased visibility. The box office success of *Crazy Rich Asians* (2018), based on the eponymous 2013 novel written by Kevin Kwan, also helped push for more representation. Previously, *The Mystery Files of Shelby Woo* (1996–1998) was one of the only children/tween/teen series with an Asian protagonist. Asians and Asian-Americans were more likely to play secondary characters, such as Lane Kim in *Gilmore Girls*. She is the best friend of co-lead Rory, and is an indie and alternative rock aficionado. She hides her collection from her strict Christian Korean mother under her floorboards. Soon, Lane learns the drums in secret, joins a band, and falls for bandmate Dave (Adam Brody). Brody would leave the secondary role to co-star in *The O.C.*, and Lane's character would form an unlikely relationship with another bandmate.

While several elements of John Hughes's teen films are much beloved and emulated, the racist depiction of foreign exchange student Long Duk Dong (Gedde Watanabe) in *Sixteen Candles* (1984) is stark. On the role's place in the John Hughes filmography, Susannah Gora writes:

> The only significant non-white character in any of these films is also the basest caricature of all: Long Duk Dong… A heightened national sense of cultural sensitivity (or political correctness, depending on how you look at it) swept America and the movie studios in the early nineties, and so the 1980s were, in many ways, the last moment when racially questionable jokes regularly found their place in mainstream comedies.[28]

*Glee* (2009–2015, Fox) featured two Asian teens in its ensemble cast. Tina Cohen-Chang (Jenna Ushkowitz) is initially a shy outcast who comes into her own after finding a sense of belonging in Glee Club. Tina and Mike Chang begin a romance when they are both counselors at "Asian camp." They have one of the longest relationships in the series. Mike Chang (Harry Shum Jr.) is one of the many popular football players who join Glee Club despite the inevitable "social suicide." The jocks and cheerleaders who join the club find the same sense of belonging that the outsiders do, and they eventually form a utopian social group no longer dominated by the hierarchies of popularity. As his character developed, Mike became a "main cast" member of the club, which concurrently gave Shum Jr more screen time. As a cute football player, talented dancer, and good boyfriend, Mike represents an Asian boy as a teen dream. Before *Fresh Off the Boat* (2015–2020, ABC), the only previous Asian-centered network series was comedian Margaret Cho's short-lived *All American Girl* (1994–1995, ABC).

Gen Z Asians in the US account for 6% of the total population, marking a 2% increase from their Millennial predecessors.[29] *Never*

*Have I Ever* (2020–, Netflix) became a milestone series because of its focus on an American teenager with immigrant parents from India. Based on creator Mindy Kaling's own experiences, the series was praised for defying South Asian stereotypes while still acknowledging cultural heritage, and balancing two national identities with varying cultural norms and expectations. The success of the young adult trilogy written by Jenny Han turned Netflix film adaptation with a teen Asian protagonist, *To All The Boys I've Loved Before* (2018), was both critically acclaimed and one of the platform's most-watched original movies. The first film shows an introverted and precocious Korean-American high school student, Laura Jean (Lana Condor), and her unlikely romance with the most popular boy at her school, Peter Kavinsky (Noah Centineo). While her Korean heritage is discussed further in the book, given the space provided, it is a small subplot in the films.

Netflix's 2020 reboot of *The Baby-Sitters Club* also adopted a more inclusive cast, and both carried over original characters storylines and dealt with issues for Gen Z girls. In the original books and adaptations, the only non-white characters were Japanese-American Claudia and secondary character, African-American Jessi. In Netflix's adaptation, original central character Mary Anne is bi-racial, and Dawn, who moves from California, is Latinx. Claudia's Japanese-American identity is emphasized in the first season reboot. As with past versions, Claudia is a talented artist who struggles in math and science, much to her parents' dismay, while her older sister Janine appears to excel in all subjects and has a photographic memory. In Season 1, Episode 6, directed by Linda Mendoza and written by Jade Chang, Claudia's grandmother has a stroke, and upon waking, she recounts disparate memories from her time at a Japanese Internment Camp during World War II. The episode unites Claudia and her sister, as they parse their memories together to understand her recollection. Claudia states she could not believe the American government imprisoned people in the camps. Janine makes a topical comment by responding she cannot believe it is still happening, a reference to undocumented immigrants' inhumane conditions in detention facilities.

## Genre Hybridity: Teen Crime Drama

The transformation of the B-movie teen horror flick of the 1950s to the "quality" teen series of the post-network era is important to note. The critical reception for teen series, whether they are earnest and realistic, or dark and crime-fueled, remains mixed throughout the 2000s. Genre hybridity, such as teen crime drama, became the norm for American television in the late 20th century. Michael Newman refers to the hybridity of episodic and serial formats, among other things, as prime time serials (PTS); a genre style since the 1980s MTM productions such as *Hill Street Blues*. He writes that the most distinguishing factor of the PTS is investment in character, through the character arc device.[30]

*Pretty Little Liars*, *Riverdale*, and *13 Reasons Why* are the most recent teen crime dramas to incorporate a "whodunit?" plot as the main focal point, and serialized component, of the series. Smaller serializations, from love triangles to family drama, contribute to making these series relevant to topical teen issues.

In *Pretty Little Liars*, a missing best friend, Alison DiLaurentis, turns into an unsolved homicide case the Liars embark upon outside of the unreliable police authorities. They investigate their own friends and family members for the murder. Meanwhile, the four Liars are brought back together when an anonymous bully, who goes by "A," taunts, threatens, and perpetrates acts of revenge. The Liars find that Alison blackmailed, threatened, or taunted several residents of Rosewood, who could all be potential murderers or possibly A. Even when Alison resurfaces as alive midway through the series, A's identity is constantly questioned and shifted. Each season follows a main suspect, which mostly remain false. Newman addresses the centrality of season acts in the PTS, with *Pretty Little Liars* as a clear example. By the Season 2 finale, "Unmasked," viewers see that former geek turned popular girl who was once ridiculed by Alison, Mona Vanderwaal is A. She reveals her plan to Spencer Hastings while driving, asking if she will join the "A-Team" or she will drive them off a cliff. When Spencer asks how Mona was able to be "everywhere" and "always one step ahead" of them, she replies, "You're not the only genius in the car. You bitches underestimated me." Mona played the shopaholic bimbo disguised as an evil genius, all while remaining best friends with Liar Hanna. Throughout the series, each Liar is confronted with deceit surrounding Alison's disappearance, attempted murder, and A's identity.

When Mona is committed to Radley Sanitarium, the psychiatrist states:

> She was living in a perpetual state of hyper-reality. The adrenaline rush that accompanied her feelings of empowerment and her high level of intelligence fueled Mona's ability to be seemingly all-knowing and omnipresent.

When Hanna asks if she will always be in this state, the doctor responds that those with her type of personality disorder can improve with treatment and the right medications. While Mona smirks in a confined room in the sanitarium, her voiceover indicates her institutionalization is hardly the end of A. Although one mystery is temporarily unsolved, the finale ends with two new cliffhangers. First, Liar Emily's girlfriend Maya's body is found buried. Second, Mona receives a visit from an unidentified guest wearing a red cape. The subservient teenager looks up and states, "I did everything you asked me to" in the final seconds of the Season 2 finale, indicating that Mona did not act alone as A, nor is she the mastermind behind the aforementioned "A-Team." By the Season 3 finale, Spencer joins her boyfriend, who was undercover for the A-Team to protect her, so they can finally find the anonymous nightmare that has caused death and destruction in their lives. Mona promises to present the four Liars to the mysterious A mastermind, now known as Red Coat. When the Liars are one step ahead of her for the first time, another vengeful player attempts to kill them by setting their building on fire. Mona divulges that not even she knows who the elusive Red Coat is. It is in the Season 3 finale that the girls start to believe Alison is alive, because she saved them from the fire and ran off.

The Season 4 opener, narrated by Mona, serves as a refresher for fans on the first three instalments. Throughout this season, the Liars suspect fellow Liar Aria's boyfriend Ezra Fitz could be A. However, he was simply using the girls to write a book on Alison, her disappearance, and the subsequent crimes that surrounded Rosewood. He then helps the Liars with clues and evidence on A's identity and Alison's potential whereabouts. The girls find their lost friend, who reveals someone threw a rock at her head in her front yard, and that her mother buried her shortly after to keep the murder a secret. She does not know who hit her, and cannot trust her mother, who buried her alive when she was left for dead.

The Liars and Alison find a mutual meeting ground, but a new A attempts to kill them. Ezra, who followed the girls, takes the bullet for them, reinforcing his love and loyalty for Aria. Meanwhile, a mysterious killer buries Alison's mother alive. The girls try to catch A one last time, with no success. While Aria waits for Ezra at the hospital after his gunshot wound, Shana, a friend of Alison's comes to comfort her. Aria then later joins the rest of the Liars in a secret hiding spot. After tampering with Ezra's stabilizer at the hospital, she follows Aria to the rest of the girls to kill them all. Although she was initially Alison's friend, she fell in love with one of the many people the mean girl hurt. Jenna Marshall, a new girl in town, became blind when Alison threw a "stink bomb" into her garage. The rest of the Liars became accessories to the unintentional crime, which was one of the principal reasons they were too frightened to confront the police when A first approached them. A seemed to know all of their secrets. Shana explains she took on the role of A to enact revenge for her lover, but Aria is able to kill her. Just as Hanna, Spencer, and Emily faced grief and violence in past seasons, Aria must now confront taking someone's life and keeping the secret.

At the onset of Season 5, Alison returns to Rosewood with a false claim of kidnapping to keep her escape and suspicion a secret. Mona then enacts an A army, full of Alison's former victims, to protect themselves from the mean girl. Mona then later fakes her death and frames Alison to prove her loyalty to the A mastermind. The Liars are charged as accomplices and accessories to the murder. A then kidnaps them, keeping the girls in an underground dollhouse. Throughout the series, we see A "playing" with dolls that are identical to the girls. Mona is also trapped, as is a mysterious new player, Sara Harvey, who is eventually revealed to be A's partner in revenge. While trapped, the girls find a secret room of A's childhood memories. They learn that A is somehow related to Alison, going by the name Charles DiLaurentis.

In the Season 5 mid-season finale, the girls find out who A/Charles is. They return to A's lair to find Alison, her father, and brother, trapped. Charles is the transgender CeCe Drake, who the Liars met when she introduced herself as Alison's friend from a summer in Cape May. Drake was a patient at the sanitarium who escaped to be with her relatives, the DiLaurentis Family. Charles was Alison's cousin, birthed by Alison's mother's twin while she was at Radley Sanitarium.

The family took Charles in as an adopted son, until he tried to give baby Alison a bath, almost drowning her. Frightened he may have the same mental instability as his mother, they placed Charles at Radley for the foreseeable future. Alison's mother continued to visit him regularly, buying him the same dresses as her own daughter. Charles's only friend at Radley, Bethany, framed him for murder when he was still a young boy. Bethany pushed a woman inmate off the roof, blaming it on Charles, "the boy wearing a dress." His subsequent years were spent on heavy tranquilizers.

Alison's mother eventually let "Charles" die and "Charlotte" live, suggesting a sex change process that is not discussed in any great depth or detail. Charlotte was also forced back to Radley, however. She spent her time focused on math, became a genius, and was allowed to take classes at the local college. This is when she fled and took on the CeCe Drake identity to befriend her family. Charlotte/CeCe soon found out that Bethany, her patient friend who framed her, snuck out of the institution to hurt Alison's mother upon hearing she had an affair with her own father. Charlotte followed Bethany and hit her with a rock, only to find out it was actually Alison she attempted to murder. Alison then realizes her own mother buried her to save her mentally disturbed adopted daughter/niece. In the past, the Liars and Alison suspected Alison's brother Jason committed the act, knowing a mother would only cover her own child's murder to protect her other child.

When Charlotte returned to Radley, she met a heavily drugged Mona, and planned the "A" scheme to enact revenge on the Liars who seemed content Alison was missing/gone. For Charlotte, being A was a game, and the Liars were her dolls she would "never hurt." And Mona became her outside contact and liaison for the A army/team. The series previously placed progressive examples of LGBTG teen issues, with principal Liar Emily's coming out, dealing with her family's view on her sexuality, acceptance from her friends, reliability in her relationships. However, the case of Charles/Charlotte DiLaurentis as a transgender child, then teen, then twenty-something is glossed over in Season 6, Episode 10, "Game Over, Charles." Further, the main purpose of this reveal is to expose Charlotte as A, although the Liars and Alison empathize with her struggles. It seemed that the bathtub issue that first put Charles away was an innocent child's mistake, but placing him at Radley is what caused his real mental health problems. Charlotte hints that Alison's father used the bathtub incident as an excuse to get rid of him, as he was always disturbed by the young boy's proclivity toward girls' clothing. This does show the harsh realities and prejudice transgender citizens face, and how society chooses to hide or ostracize them instead of accepting them. However, again, this is mostly glossed over.

So the question remains: why choose to make the principal antagonist/villain of *Pretty Little Liars* a transgender woman? Charlotte had no friends, was isolated, repressed, and wanted to have her "dolls" to play with in lieu of social interaction. Ultimately, the series does place Charlotte as more of a product of her situation. This is how Alison feels for her cousin, who she takes care of after the Season 6 reveal.

Instead of a potentially awkward college years transition after the big A reveal, Season 6, Episode 11, "Of Late I Think of Rosewood," flashes forward five years. Alison asks the Liars to return home to speak on behalf of Charlotte, allowing her to leave Radley. All the now 20-something Liars, besides Aria, state they are no longer afraid of her in front of a judge. Mona also tells Spencer she still has nightmares, despites therapy and medication. Later, Hannah calls Aria "the only honest woman in town" for speaking out about her trauma. In Seasons 6 and 7, an "Uber A," is revealed when the girls return to Rosewood, ready to enact revenge again. Alison learns that Charlotte's doctor was also her boyfriend, and tricked Alison into marrying her so he could take the family's fortunes. Charlotte's mother then mysteriously returns to town, having worked with the doctor to get part of her family inheritance that her sister supposedly stole.

With the Liars now at legal drinking age and Radley Sanitarium closed for its poor practices, Hanna's mom turned the site into a boutique hotel and bar. This is now the main site of the series, where the girls try to uncover past secrets from the mental institution still lurking.

Instead of mean girls fighting against each other, *Pretty Little Liars* focused on close friends who battled bullying and practiced good citizenship. It also set the stage for future teen crime dramas. Several writers noted the series' references to *Twin Peaks*, which is often described as a "quality" series due to David Lynch's participation. However, the teen characters are less discussed, even if the series revolves around the death of a pretty, popular teen girl in a small town. Her death marks the death of innocence for the town, and uncovers the dark underbelly of its residents. Similarly, *Pretty Little Liars* reveals a small, affluent suburb of Philadelphia's true darkness and loss of innocence.

Louisa Stein considers how *Pretty Little Liars* fuses elements of both *Veronica Mars* and *Gossip Girl*, stating:

> Channeling *Veronica Mars* we have the themes of male power and female vulnerability; female strength and male disconnectedness; the strength of millennial networks (in this case—and in contrast to *Veronica Mars*—mostly female networks); and the fascinatingly repeated trope of the dead, sexually-promiscuous girl at the center of the mystery, who haunts the narrative in potent flashback.[31]

In the same year of Pretty *Little Liars*' finale, two new crime teen dramas with similar intentions debuted: *Riverdale*, which premiered in January 2017, and *13 ReasonsWhy*, which followed in March 2017. Both enjoyed instant critical and commercial success.

*Riverdale* is loosely based on the characters from the Archie comic series, although the plot is distinct. The headline for an article in *Slate* reads, "Archie Meets *Twin Peaks* Meets Live Action Meets *Gossip Girl*," showing further genre hybridity and intertextuality.[32] The author Willa Paskin goes on to state that it falls into the category of "an enjoyable and moody teen series for adults who love teen series."[33] For Paskin, part of the appeal is the subversive, self-reflexive nature of the principal characters, which reinforces Newman's argument on character arcs and the PTS.

*Riverdale's* appeal to adults can account for the mass critical acclaim from TV critics. However, unlike the focus on Lynch in *Twin Peaks* or Schwartz in *The O.C.*, focus on the auteur-showrunner figure is dismissed in favor of new interests. In a *New York Times* roundup of critics' responses, Judy Berman uses sections based on "It has a retro, Lynchian aesthetic," "It updates 'Archie Comics' archetypes for the 21st century," "Archie is hot (and sidelined)," and "It's incredibly self aware."[34] Genre hybridity, production values, and self-reflexivity—all markers of "quality TV"—are at the forefront of praise for *Riverdale*.

Its retro reliance also harks back to *Clueless*, a film still praised for its use of fashion and teen-speak. One way to measure interest in a series in the digital post-network era, especially for the Millennial consumer, is the social media response. With teen- or youth-centered series, Tumblr is the ideal platform for grassroots fan responses.

The backdrop of *Riverdale* is the decline of small town America, along with its traditional adolescence and patriarchal structures. Like Twin Peaks, we see a tiny hamlet exposed. In this post-recession climate, literal and figurative Middle America is forgotten. The quintessential welcome town sign of both series lingers in the introduction, with a flurry of tall, ominous forests. As Veronica Lodge arrives in town from Manhattan, she meets Betty and Archie at local diner hangout Pop's Choc'Lit Shop. Always full of literary references, she states, "Are you familiar with the works of Truman Capote? I'm *Breakfast at Tiffany's* and this town is *In Cold Blood*." She is reluctant to be in her mother's hometown but also decides to forego her previous mean girls way after the Bernie Madoff-like scandal her imprisoned father caused. When her new friends Kevin, Archie, and Betty tell her everyone knows about the scandal, she calls herself the *Blue Jasmine* of Riverdale.

The 2013 Woody Allen film (which won Cate Blanchett a best actress Academy Award) is inspired by the story of Bernie Madoff's wife, who lost her fortune and settled for a downgraded lifestyle with her working-class sister. After sticking up for Veronica in front of the series' troubled mean girl Cheryl Blossom during cheerleader tryouts, she tells the team captain she is living proof everyone will receive their reckoning based on their behavior toward others. Veronica's mother later tells Archie's mother (played by 1980s teen star Molly Ringwald of *Sixteen Candles*, *The Breakfast Club* and *Pretty in Pink*) that her misfortunes are due to the cosmic karma of being a mean girl in high school.

Former teen stars playing current parents are prevalent in the series. *90210*'s Luke Perry (Dylan McKay) plays Archie's dad, Fred Andrews; Mädchen E. Amick of both the original and revival *Twin Peaks* (NBC, Showtime, 2017) is Betty's mother Alice Cooper; and Skeet Ulrich of 1990s teen horror films *Scream* and *The Craft* reprises his bad-boy roles as a gang member and father to Jughead. Veronica's mother is played by Marisol Nichols, who held minor parts in *Beverly Hills 90210*, *Scream 2*, and *Can't Hardly Wait*. The intertextual trend even includes minor characters, with recurring actors such as Shannon Purser (who portrays the beloved teen girl nerd Barb on *Stranger Things*), Robin Givens (of ABC's *Head of the Class*, 1986–1991), Tiera Skovbye (who portrayed Elizabeth Berkeley in the 2014 Lifetime film *The Unauthorized Saved By The Bell Story*), and Sarah Habel (who portrayed a young roller derby player in the 2009 film *Whip It*). Similarly, *13 Reason Why* also featured former teen TV stars—from Lane Kim of *Gilmore Girls* to Ricky of *My-So-Called Life*. Although they are two minor characters, their casting is purposeful. Both actors played beloved minor roles and are also minorities: an Asian-American, music lover and drummer with an overly protective Christian mother and secret CD collection; and a once homeless Latino gay teen.

Several actors who portray teens on *Riverdale* also hold child star pedigrees. Jughead is portrayed by Dylan Thomas Sprouse, who is half of the twin acting duo with this brother Cole Mitchell Sprouse. The two co-starred with *Adam Sandler* in Big Daddy in 1999, and later reached Disney Channel fame for *The Suite Life of Zac & Cody* (2005–2008) franchise.

In 2011, MSN Money projected the Sprouses to be among the richest teenagers in the US, and the most famous acting twins since the Olsen sisters of *Full House* and fashion empire fame.[35] Mirroring Ashley and Mary-Kate Olsen, they attended New York University and subsequently pursued acting. Ross Butler, who plays Archie's football rival, starred in films like The Disney Channel's *Teen Beach 2* and *Perfect High* on Lifetime, and will not renew his role in Season 2 because of commitments to *13 Reasons Why*. Ashley Murray, who plays Josie, will be co-starring in the musical adaptation of the 1980s teen cult classic *Valley Girl*.

Part of the intertextuality (and appeal to older audiences) of *Riverdale* is the use of nods to other teen series and revered film, TV, and literature. David Silver of *90210* served as the hip-hop expert; Lane Kim of *Gilmore Girls* as the rock maven; Seth Cohen in *The O.C.* was the indie rock/pop culture/comic book oracle; Veronica Mars functioned as not only a genius detective but fan of cult classics like *The Big Lebowski*; and Dan Humphrey of *Gossip Girl* was the literary ingénue. Similarly, each main character in *Riverdale* holds a talent and/or encyclopedic knowledge of their given passion. As with many other cosmopolitan-minded female protagonists, from *Gossip Girl*'s Blair Waldorf to *Pretty Little Liar*'s Hanna, Veronica is also a fashionista with a lust for designer bags and subscription to *Vogue*. Yet, this does not play down her intelligence. While Archie is a star football player and talented fledgling musician, his elders mock him for not being familiar with legends like Bob Dylan. The eponymous Josie and the Pussycats frontwoman is named after Josephine Baker, by her jazz musician father. Although the band is award-winning and popular, he chastises his daughter for her commercial pop proclivities and focus on branding.

The entire series is founded on Jughead Jones's voiceover narration, based on a book he is writing about Riverdale's decline since the death of Jason Bloom. Each episode is named after a chapter in his non-fiction tome. While Jughead writes for the school paper with Betty, she is the talented "Lois Lane" journalist, and her parents run the local newspaper. Although Jughead is writing a book, his true passion is film: he references Quentin Tarantino as the king of indie film, and protests the closure of his beloved drive-in theater. As he comes from a troubled family in the gang-led south side of Riverdale, the movies served as an escape. Most of all, we find out that Jughead fears the end of the theater because it served as his temporary home.

### *Twin Peaks* and its Teen Crime Drama Successors

David Lynch's *Twin Peaks* is praised for making several shifts in the TV landscape, and is an early example of the auteur-showrunner figure. Of course, other non-teen related crime series, from *Desperate Housewives* to *The Killing* to *Fargo*, have also been considered as clear successors to *Twin Peaks*. However, the high school setting, loss of the innocence of youth, and small-town America locale of *Twin Peaks* makes it a natural predecessor to the teen crime dramas it would later influence.

Matthew Gilbert of *The Boston Globe* writes that *Twin Peaks* "ushered TV drama—then symbolized by the highly predictable 'Murder, She Wrote' and 'Matlock', both Top 20 shows in 1989–1990—onto another level of sophistication" and "purposefully undid every dull convention of TV storytelling at the time—linear plotting, neat conclusions, flat atmospherics."[36] In regards to the crime genre component, he states it aimed to "redefine TV's whodunit game, [and] Lynch and Frost kept the tone inconsistent and defiant, veering from murder mystery to soap spoof to supernatural drama and back around again." Gilbert also points out that it began a new surge of auteur-driven TV, due to Lynch's reputation as a highbrow art cinema director. Even if *Twin Peaks* is not often considered a teen series on its own, its influence on the genre, as well as crime drama, cannot be overlooked. Lynch's take on small-town America is also highlighted by subverting many of its teen protagonists over a retro, warped *Happy Days* aesthetic.

Therefore, any teen series with a darker view on high school, especially coupled with a murder, is inherently likened to the retro Lynchian auteurism. This likening to *Twin Peaks* nearly always serves as a tribute to the teen crime genre, from *Veronica Mars* and *Pretty Little Liars* to *Riverdale* and *13 Reasons Why*.

*Veronica Mars* also involves noir nods, solving the murder of dead teen girl and surrealist dream sequences from the murder victim to series protagonist Veronica. Both idyllic settings, coupled with a gruesome high school experience, punctate the connections between the two. Many critics view the first season of *Veronica Mars* as a homage to Lynch's series. As Daniel Kurland of *Den of Geek* states:

> *Mars'* Lilly Kane, the victim whose murder must be solved, is a Laura Palmer amalgam to the point where some of her behavior seems to be intentionally aping the character ("I loved Lilly, and Lilly loved boys"). *Veronica Mars* even used "Who killed Lilly Kane?" as an advertising slogan, much like *Peaks'* "Who killed Laura Palmer?" mantra.[37]

*Pretty Little Liars* also draws on a formerly safe suburb where the death of a pretty, blonde teenage girl exposes the underbelly of its residents, including its teenagers. The ABC turned Freeform series was a huge commercial success, and a substantial draw for women audiences based on its female-centered protagonists. Feminist media scholar Alyx Vesey states that both the murder cases of Laura Palmer in *Twin Peaks* and Alison DiLaurentis of *Pretty Little Liars* "reveal the contradictions that popular young white girls often embody to achieve some modicum of social power," while "their absences also reveal the horrors under the gleaming surfaces of high school suburbia."[38] However, female friendship, rather than mean girls, is at the core of the latter. Vesey goes on to state:

> Girl friendship is a much stronger force for good in *PLL* than in *Twin Peaks*. Both shows are interested in affairs and love triangles, but *Twin Peaks* never explored female bonding and thus had no insight into how girlfriends can be sources of support. Conversely, *Twin Peaks* is far more unsettling in how it aestheticizes kitsch than *PLL*.[39]

## It's Not (Teen) TV: It's HBO

### Key Series: *Euphoria*

The range of issues *Euphoria* deals with, such as addiction, mental health, body image, toxic masculinity, sexuality as a spectrum, gender identity, and domestic violence, are not new, nor solely impact Gen Z teens. Yet, they are told through very specific characters with fleshed out and nuanced narrative arcs and elaborate backstories to properly depict their psyche and evolving troubles and traits. The series also hired an intimacy coordinator and transgender consultant.

In summer 2019, HBO premiered *Euphoria*, its first original series about teens. Although set in a vaguely middle-class Southern California suburb of East Highland, its premium cable pre-production development and high budget, along with its close consideration of Gen Z specificity, marked a shift in the future of the genre. While UK and European programs such as *Skins* and *Skam* previously allowed creative liberties, streaming platforms Netflix and Hulu took the lead on original teen TV programming. HBO previously commissioned late-20 to early-30-something Millennial-specific coming-of-age programming such as *Girls, High Maintenance, Insecure*, and in the summer of 2020, a co-production with BBC, Michaela Cole's (formerly of Channel 4 series *Chewing Gum*) *I May Destroy You*.

Therefore, HBO's first teen TV series would have to set itself apart. *Euphoria's* development was announced in 2017, with Sam Levinson attached as the showrunner. As a loose adaptation of Israel's eponymous 2012 series, its original creators Ron Leshem, Daphna Levin, and Tmira Yardeni also were included as producers. By 2018, former child star of *Degrassi* turned rapper Drake, along with his collaborator rapper Future the Prince, were included as co-executive producers. A24, an independent production company (known for critically acclaimed films such as *Get Out, Moonlight, Ladybird, The Farwell, Midsommar*, and *Uncut Gems*) also became involved with the production in 2018.

Whereas HBO's adaptation is contemporary, the original Israeli *Euphoria* was set in the 1990s and includes a murder subplot. While some characters in the HBO version are inspired by the original, the greatest influence is the treatment of mature teenagers and subsequent subject matter. Levinson, a Millennial born in 1985, used his own teenage battles with addiction to fuel the central character's development. Played by former child star Zendaya, born in 1996 on the cusp of Gen Z, Rue provides the omniscient narration of the series. Each episode begins with a different character's back story with Rue's voiceover before the title credits, and shift to the present. The pilot episode focuses on Rue's return home from rehab at the end of summer, where she was sent after her younger sister, Gia (Storm Reid), found her unconscious from an overdose.

In a voiceover monologue, Rue embarks on a tirade against slut-shaming and the nature of sexuality online and her generation:

> Here's the fucking thing that pisses me off about the world. Like, every time someone shit gets leaked, whether it's [celebrities] J Law [Jennifer Lawrence] or Leslie Jones, the whole world's like, "well if you don't want it out there, don't take the nudes in the first place." I'm sorry, I know your generation relied on flowers and fathers' permission, but it's 2019. And unless you're Amish, [sharing digital] nudes are the currency of love, so stop shaming us. Shame the assholes who create password-protected online directories of underage girls.

When Rue returns to her hometown, she finds ways to cheat the drug tests her mother administers and easily states she is sleeping over at a friend's while she attends a party. At first, Rue is a loner who walks the suburban streets alone, although her friends welcome her return, even if they privately admit they assumed she might have died from the overdose. One of her first stops back home is to her friend and drug dealer, Fez. Instead of a one-dimensional teen dropout, even his character is developed to show how his socioeconomic circumstances led him to his current illegal job. He also balances his role as a dealer and friend to Rue, as he tries to protect her from his dangerous boss and will not sell to her. It is also Fez who first tells Rue about the requisite new girl Jules, as he has a feeling they could be friends. For a teen drug dealer, Fez sacrifices his future to support his sick grandmother, does not seek profit from one of his most in-demand clients, and is shown to protect those to whom he is loyal.

The first five minutes of the *Euphoria* pilot features Rue narrating her early life in a dry, unaffected, tone. A life that began with fear and pending violence, followed by anxiety and mental health, years of numbness, and panic attacks. Generational specificity is shown, such as early diagnosis of a variety mental health conditions and an abundance of prescriptions, exposure to sex through pornography, random threats of violence through text messaging, body image issues, school shooting drills, the US healthcare system, and blatant sexual abuse from a classmate. The next two minutes show Rue's way of dealing with both her internal and external conflict, after providing an existential teen narrative of her life to date. The two-minute montage reveals the formal aesthetics of *Euphoria*: its eclectic party mixtape-like soundtrack with electronic, hip-hop, and R&B; the flashing neon lights reminiscent of both *Spring Breakers* and *Moonlight*; and the glittery eyeshadow and matching bright fluorescent makeup. This introduction presents the viewer with *Euphoria*: part stark reality of adolescence and the 21st century, part drug-fueled fantasy and hyper-realism rooted in intertextuality and teenage visions of bliss, in a nondescript, far suburb of Los Angeles. Like many teen shows before it, the classmates appear a bit older, are dressed better, and have perfect hair and makeup. But unlike these earlier series, beneath the surface-level neon shine and aspirational Instagram-worthy color palettes and effortless coolness, are the perpetual, serialized, turmoil of teenage life in America.

Rue's backstories deal with her mental health and addiction, which are established in the series pilot, and the first introductory backstory. Seventeen-year-old Rue narrates the world of anxiety, fear, and easy access to pharmaceutical drugs, she was born into. She begins by stating, "I was born three days after 9/11," as a baby emerges out of her mother's womb in a hospital room, while President George W. Bush rallies over a megaphone, preparing to declare war. She states, "I can hear you, I can hear you, I can hear you, the rest of the world hears you, and the people who knocked these buildings down will hear all of us soon." The newborn appears to be intently watching the boxy TV set attached to the hospital wall, and begins crying after Bush's crowd cheers and chants "USA! USA! USA." As the wars Bush initiated in the Middle East continued in 2019, Gen Z never knew a time their nation was not involved in war. Rue then states her mother and father stayed in the hospital for two days after her birth, keeping her "under the soft glow of the television, watching those towers fall over, and over, and over, again, until the feelings of grief gave way into numbness." This repetition later mirrors many of the characters' relationship with various addictions and Rue's mental health. While Gen Z is often associated with mobile phones and personal laptops, the *Euphoria* flashbacks reveal childhoods dominated by 24-hour-television.

The narration then cuts to images of suburban homes and Rue's voiceover: "and then, without warning, a middle-class childhood in America begins." Next, Rue's mental health is chronicled from an early age. A young Rue is shown seated at the kitchen table during dinner, counting boxed fluorescent lights on the ceiling. When her mother interrupts her to ask what she is doing, she begins to cry, to the confusion of both her parents. The next scene cuts to the family seated in a doctor's office as Rue is diagnosed with "Obsessive Compulsive Disorder, Attention Deficit Disorder, and General Anxiety Disorder, and possibly Bipolar Disorder, but she's a little too young to tell." Rue's teenage voiceover concurrently acknowledges her privilege, imagining "worse" childhood troubles: "It's not like I was physically abused, or had a shortage of clean water, or was molested by a family member." The next scene cuts to Rue dryly remarking, "So, explain this shit to me," as her mother attempts to assuage her: "Honey, it's just how your brain is hardwired," over the image of multiple pills divided in a plastic container. Her mother continues, positively, "Plenty of great, intelligent, funny, interesting and creative people have struggled with the same things you're struggling with." A preteen Rue sits in front of her chocolate-covered puff cereal watching her mom pile up the pills and asks, dubiously, for examples. After some stalling, an "Uh.." and hand twitching, her mother calls names with a montage of their demise: "Vincent Van Gogh" (shooting his ear off), "Sylvia Plath" (placing her head in an oven), "and your favorite, Britney Spears" (accompanied by a bystander video of the living pop star during her 2008 mental breakdown, bald, while getting a tattoo). Young Rue sighs, stating she does not "remember much between the ages of eight and 12," in a more subdued, numbed manner, likely due to the overmedication, as she passes the school highways. She continues, "just that the world moved fast, and my brain moved slow." The camera pans to Rue panting at her desk, experiencing a panic attack while a teacher recites a lesson, because "every once in a while, if I focused too clearly on the way I breathed, I'd die." The classroom fades to black as she faints on the floor and her peers turn around in unison. A match cut follows with Rue on the floor, breathing through a brown paper bag while her teacher instructs her, and her classmates look down on her and take photos with their mobile phone. Rue finishes the sentence with, "until every second of every day, you find yourself trying to outrun your anxiety." Preteen Rue is then shown looking at herself in the mirror, tucking her belly in. She receives an anonymous text message on an early model iPhone that reads "Imma gonna rape you cunt", and responds to her mother's, "What's wrong?" by synching the past mouthing with her present voiceover, "I'm fucking exhausted."

The next sequence follows a now teenage Rue as her mother is on the phone with their health insurance company, asking for logistics about in-network providers. She joins her younger sister at the table who asks if she saw the viral video of a "beauty queen that had acid thrown on her face," and that it was "pretty fucked up." Then, as she embarks on her ritual of flushing her prescribed anti-anxiety Xanax down the toilet, she states, "And at some point you make a choice, about who you are, and what you want", as she grabs her parents' wedding photo. Her mother, still on the phone, proclaims she cannot pay the $300 co-payment, and asks Rue, who is now rail thin, wearing a crop top, if she ate breakfast, as the sisters leave their home. They take a selfie at the back of the school bus, seemingly happy, as an overhead shot of a palm tree-lined neighborhood appears with the Los Angeles skyline in the far distant background. Rue continues with, "I just showed up one day without a map or a compass," as she participates in a school shooting drill, "or to be honest, anyone capable of giving one iota of good fucking advice." As Rue shifts her head, a classmate looks at her, mimicking fellatio as he watches the act on his cell phone. She concludes, "And I know it all may seem sad, but guess what? I didn't build this system. Nor did I fuck it up."

Shortly after five minutes, another montage follows, of surreal, neon lights as Rue partakes in her ritual that renders her numb. Rue snorts a white powdery substance in her bedroom, then swigs a bottle of vodka at a house party filled with flashing lights. She describes the feeling of getting high, the respite from real life, accompanied by a close-up of Rue's made-up face and loose curls as she experiences it: "And then it happens. That moment when your breath starts to slow. And every time you breathe, everything stops: your heart, your lung, and finally, your brain. And everything you feel, and wish, and want to forget, it all just sinks." She recounts the first time she experienced the high. She feared she would die and wanted to be taken to the hospital, but did not want to "ruin everyone's night." After her first high, the addiction began, and "over time, it's all I wanted. Those two seconds of nothingness." Briefly, a home video shot of a childhood Rue in pure joy, hula hooping is shown before the title credits appear accompanied by Beyoncé's "Lemonade."

Sexuality is not told through a "coming out" lens if the teen protagonists are not strictly straight; indeed, no character's sexuality appears stagnant. While Rue is clearly taken by Jules, she recounts her past sexual experiences were with teen boys. Jules seeks out cis-gender older men on Tinder, but is also infatuated by their younger counterparts. Her friendship with Rue is pure, but her sexual and romantic feelings toward her new best friend are unsure.

In *Euphoria*, traditional high school popularity and attractiveness reveal a seedy underbelly. The jock character is not only hiding his gay identity, he also sneaks into his father's secret sex tapes that also reveal his hidden sexuality. And perceived outsiders and outcasts hold a place in the Gen Z high school. Nate is initially depicted as a stereotypical obnoxious, overconfident high school football player who drives around in an oversized truck and catcalls Rue upon her return to East Highland. By Season 1, Episode 2, "Stuntin' Like My Daddy," his repressed gay sexuality turns him into a hyper-masculine jock. As the series progresses, his behavior turns violent and vengeful. He beats a college student half to death, abuses his girlfriend Maddy, and frames Jules for sharing her own naked pictures, which is considered child pornography by California law, to cover up his own crimes. Like Nate, Maddy is obsessed with her image. Her flashbacks, in Season 1, Episode 5, "03 Bonnie and Clyde," reveal that she competed in beauty pageants at a young age and saw her immigrant Latinx mother work tirelessly as a nail salon artist in the service of white upper-middle-class women. In becoming a popular cheerleader in high school and dating Nate, Maddy possesses social mobility and a desire to separate from her parents' lower-class identity. She is frustrated by her socioeconomic standing, is hardly at her parents' apartment (rather than larger houses that her friends have), and appears disgusted by spending their free time in front of a television. In the previous episode, Season 1, Episode 4, "Shook Ones Pt. II," Nate asks her to change into a more covered up outfit at the town carnival because his family will be in attendance. He admits that his parents already dislike her, which leaves her infuriated, and she is determined to humiliate him in front of their chilli stand. By the end of the carnival, Maddy confronts her boyfriend about the photos of male genitalia on his phone, which leads him to strangle and threaten her. By Episode 5 it is clear Nate abuses Maddy, and that she is in a codependent relationship with him. Although the police question her about the marks he left around her neck, she refuses to tell them the truth. They meet in the same motel that Jules encountered Nate's dad in the season pilot, and appear together at a Halloween party as an act of couple solidarity after Nate and his family are denied service at a local restaurant due to his pending charges. The abusive relationship between Nate and Maddy show the complex nature of violence, repressed sexuality, codependent relationships, and how domestic violence can begin during the teenage years.

In stark contrast to Nate, the other athlete in *Euphoria* (Christopher), McKay, is sensitive and intelligent. He is struggling during his first year of college, which is within driving distance of his hometown where all of his friends and girlfriend Cassie still live and attend high school. McKay's backstory, shown in Season 1, Episode 6, "The Next Episode," reveals the pressures he faced as his father pushed him to be a star athlete in high school to gain a college football scholarship. A bright math student, McKay calculates his unlikely odds of actually playing in college and going on to the NFL. Yet, his father is determined to see his son thrive, and simply tells him he must move on and persevere, even if he is not playing during his freshman year. With his glory days behind him, McKay has trouble adjusting to feeling below average. His fraternity initiation process proves particularly strange and cruel. Unlike Maddy and Nate's relationship, McKay and his high school girlfriend Cassie genuinely like, even love, each other. Yet, McKay's friends share Cassie's naked photos and videos she previously shared with past relationships aggravated on a website, and they call her a vapid slut. In *Euphoria*, the teen boys, rather than the girls, slut-shame. McKay is then embarrassed by Cassie when she shows her skin in her Halloween costume while visiting him at college. He urges her to cover up, like Nate does with Maddy, and provides his football jersey as an alternate costume. In his first initiation process, McKay is challenged to eat a live goldfish, which Cassie does before him for encouragement. However, the process exacerbates as a group of fraternity brothers open his dorm room when he and Cassie begin having sex, and brutally anally rape him while calling him "McGay." Like many other characters, he is unwilling to show any sign of vulnerability and retreats to his bathroom to cry. Upon his return, he proceeds to turn Cassie around to have anal sex with her. Cassie does not verbally express her consent or urge him to stop, as in a previous instance, but this scene contrasts with past sexual experiences where the two communicated and enjoyed sex together. With McKay growing distant toward Cassie, she embarks on a flirtation with another boy at school. When she does not have sex with him, he belittles her, stating men will only want her for sex. In Season 1, Episode 7, "The Trials and Tribulations of Trying to Pee While Depressed," Cassie's flashback deals with the complexity of her parents' divorce, and father's eventual absence. It also highlights how men perceive her following puberty, noticing their wandering eyes and inappropriate touching and side comments. Both Cassie and McKay struggle with adults' expectations of them: McKay as a good looking and talented football star in high school who cannot continue his social or athletic achievements to his first year of college; and Cassie, who grows into a traditionally beautiful blonde white teenager is not valued beyond her looks by the opposite sex. McKay is the only exception, but with their relationship unclear, she is left spiraling. In contrast to McKay's over-involved father, Cassie's mother is rarely shown outside her home and is depicted as an alcoholic. While McKay is black and Cassie is white, their interracial relationship is never commented on. This is also the case for Rue's parents, and Rue's relationship with Jules. This is not to say that the series suggests a post-racial America; rather, that racialized prejudices are dominated by micro-aggressions rather than large-scale admonishment. However, McKay does not introduce his parents to Cassie, but Cassie's mom remarks on her boyfriend's attractiveness and encourages the relationship. In fact, Cassie's mother even asks Rue if she "met any cute boys" while in rehab.

The perceived "fat" outsider turned body-confident heroine, Kat, is taunted at a house party in the pilot, which leads her to lose her virginity. The initial conversation asks Kat if her friend, then if she, is a "prude or a slut," perpetuating the virgin/whore dichotomy. Soon after, she learns that the event was recorded and distributed to her entire high school, although she denies it. In her dedicated flashback, in Season 1, Episode 3, "Made You Look," her weight gain is chronicled from a middle school trip to the Caribbean that led her to drink bottomless virgin tropical drinks. Upon her return to school, her first boyfriend breaks up with her. She deals with the heartache by binge-watching TV series with various soul mate plot lines, from *True Blood* to *Gilmore Girls*. She soon becomes active online. Her timidity from tweendom to the beginning of the episode is contrasted with her fierce following on Tumblr, for her fanfiction focused on a backstage romance between members of the boy band group One Direction. Yet, Kat dreads that her online fans will be disappointed when they see she is overweight. However, after she notices her unsolicited pornographic video yields to laudatory sexual comments, she decides to embrace her body. After giving herself a teen dominatrix makeover at the local mall, she gains confidence, and money from online "sugar daddies" who want to be insulted and dominated by her pseudonym, "Kitty Kat." She sees adult men who fetishize her body, and the illegal self-exposure to child pornography and subsequent financial gains gives her confidence to be sexually explorative in high school and social gatherings. Yet, her first heartbreak, other forms of judgment that led her to feel unworthy of love and affection, and online dominatrix behavior also lead her to doubt any boy who genuinely likes her. When she allows Ethan, a new student, into her life, she quickly dismisses him when her insecurities rise, as Kat sees him speaking to a skinny blonde woman. Critics praised the role of Kat for defying the "fat best friend" stereotype and fatphobic tropes common on television. In her journey of self-exploration and validation, Kat experiences a multitude of emotions and turmoil that do not always yield to simple, clean-cut solutions and closure of network teen TV: "*Euphoria*, after all, is a teen drama about fucking up, the systemic traumas that often drive those fuck-ups, and what comes after—not always redemption, but exploration and personal development."[40,41]

Season 1, Episode 3, "Shook Ones, Part I," begins with Jules' backstory: at the age of 11, her mother admits her into a children's psychiatric unit. During her time there, she self-harms and is given medication that numbs her. Eventually, however, her father is supportive of her trans identity and desire to physically transform. This explains why Jules lives only with her father and is estranged from her mother. Alongside her peers, she does not experience transphobia. Hunter Schaefer, who plays Jules, explains her proclivity toward sleeping with men who claim they are not gay or queer, as well as older men.

## *Gen Z Stardom and* Euphoria

The *Euphoria* cast includes a variety of established, up and coming, and new actors. Zendaya's career consists of modeling, dancing, singing, acting, and writing. As the star and face of the series in its promotional material, she first became known for her role on the Disney Channel original *Shake it Up* (2010–2013). She later appeared on *Dancing with the Stars* and released a pop album.

Following her Oscar appearance in 2015, the next presenter inserted a racialized joke that her hair smelled of "patchouli oil" and "weed." Zendaya took to Instagram to say that several successful people have the loc hairstyle, and it does not equate to drug use. She became celebrated as an outspoken, socially conscious young celebrity. That same year, Mattel subsequently released a Barbie of her in her Oscar ensemble, in honor of her "standing up for her culture." She was 19 at the time.

By 2016, at the beginning of her 20s, Zendaya's feature film career began. She was lauded as a scene-stealer and MVP, despite her brief debut in the box office success *Spider-Man: Homecoming* (2017). Later that year, she co-starred in the musical *The Greatest Showman* alongside Hugh Jackman, Zac Efron, Michelle Williams, and Rebecca Ferguson. Throughout her career, she has been praised for her fashion choices. Net-a-Porter ranked her as one of the best-dressed women in 2018, and she was a frequent guest host for various iterations of *Project Runway*. *Vogue* magazine dubbed her the new "Gen Z poster girl" for the coveted Tommy Hilfiger global ambassador role. In addition to appearing in their campaigns, she collaborated on a line with Hilfiger.[42] Despite her previous roles and recognition, at the age of 22, *Euphoria* was Zendaya's first star project.

Aside from Zendaya, several of the other actors first debuted on television in *Euphoria*, although many had online personas and original content, and strong fan followings. In addition to Zendaya's established and expanding fandom and social awareness, Hutcher Schaefer and Barbie Ferriera are also stars with model backgrounds, strong social media followings, and champion socially conscious issues in their public life that reflect their characters.

Hunter Schaefer made her TV debut on *Euphoria* as Jules. As a trans actress, she spoke of the importance of a trans consultant on the series as an ally and resource:

> That was really nice to know that I had another trans person around to be able to support me through moments where

there might be a lot of other cisgender people around who might not be able to completely understand where I'm coming from. I think having some sense of community, even on a super-safe space like our set, it's really important and that should be involved on any set.[43]

The 22-year-old Brazilian-American model turned actor who plays Kat, Barbie Ferriera, has been vocal about body positivity both before and after her television debut in *Euphoria*. On her unprecedented role, Ferriera states, "you don't get fat girl roles where you're allowed to explore sexuality, where you're not just the tragic, dowdy, chubby girl."[44] She first gained recognition at the age of 18 for her non-photoshopped images for an Aeirie lingerie campaign and went on to model for brands such as American Apparel. She then became a body-positive advocate and created her own Vice video series, *How to Breathe*, about self-care. By 2016, with millions of Instagram followers, she was named one of *Time* magazine's Most Influential Teens.[45]

Ferriera began working toward an acting career when she was 13, which coincides with her burgeoning social media presence. In interviews, Ferriera praises the positive benefits of working hard to achieve her goals, which took her nearly a decade, through community platforms like Instagram:

> I hope they see that if you really work hard, treat people well, [and] take risks things can happen, and it's not like only a select few people who already have a one-up that can get where they want to be … I've been talking about wanting to be an actor since I was literally 13 on the Internet. Now I get messages from friends saying, "Oh my god, I can't believe you did that because you've been talking about it for almost 10 years," and I'm like, yeah, and I worked my butt off to get here! I think it's not as unheard of as people make it seem.

Reid, who plays as a tertiary character who is still in middle school, was born in 2003 and is one of the youngest actors involved in the series.

However, the 17-year-old's resume includes roles in Oscar-winning *12 Years A Slave*, Ava Duvernay's *Wrinkle in Time* and Netflix original series *When They See Us*, as well as a cameo in Jay-Z and Beyoncé's 2017 video for "Family Feud."

Nearly a year after *Euphoria* first premiered, it received six 2020 Emmy nominations for Zendaya's performance as Leading Actress in a Drama Series; Contemporary Costume; Contemporary Makeup; Original Lyrics and Music; Music Composition and Scoring and Music Supervision.[46]

## Kathleen Bedoya Interview

### East Los High *Co-Creator & Executive Producer*

*Stefania Marghitu:* One of the first series you worked on is *Los Beltran*, and it really establishes your initial interest in showing progressive content in Latino-American TV programming. Can you talk about the development of the series and your early interest in this?

*Kathleen Bedoya:* I was working at Telemundo in programming development when the project of *Los Beltrán* was presented to the network. When the series went into production, I joined the creative team as Co-Executive Producer and got a taste of what it takes to create a sitcom from the other side of the process. It was a ground-breaking series in many ways—it was a sitcom on a Spanish-language network during primetime, with original scripts, and we tackled themes about the immigrant experience, what it's like to be caught between two worlds, the conflicting perspective of the children of immigrants in the U.S. and the humor behind it. The series spoke to me on many levels because I was raised in a working-class Latino community, which was predominantly Cuban. And after living so many years in Los Angeles, I developed a real affinity and respect for

| | |
|---|---|
| | the Mexican-American and Central American communities. The show was a unique and hilarious combination of the two. It filled a gap, a sitcom written specifically for the U.S. Latino market, in Spanish, and people loved it. That's why it's so great to see *Los Beltran* airing on Hulu now and being exposed to a new audience. |
| SM: | What was the transition to Fox and LA like? |
| KB: | The transition to living in Los Angeles was a very intense time for me. I missed New York and my family a great deal and had to get used to driving on huge freeways instead of using public transportation. When I first started working in television, I realized how much we [the Latino American Community] were not in the picture. At the time, there were few, if any, Latino executives making big programming decisions. |
| SM: | Were there other interests in the Latino market during this time? |
| | There was definitely an interest in Hollywood for the Latino market but not necessarily a true financial and creative commitment on behalf of the top networks to reach the audience in an innovative, authentic, and resonating manner. |
| SM: | Did *Betty La Fea* (Colombia, 1999–2001)/*Ugly Betty* (ABC, 2006–2010) have any influence on this? |
| KB: | The telenovela, *Betty La Fea* broke the mold of traditional telenovelas by presenting a love story with humor featuring an atypical protagonist. In a similar manner, *Ugly Betty* succeeded in adapting a Latin American telenovela into a popular US network series with a Mexican American actress as the protagonist and a Latina executive producer behind the scenes. It was exciting to see the growth and novelty of both programs. I think when programming that thinks out of the box succeeds, it opens the door a bit wider for more originality to follow. |

SM: You later worked on an MTV Latin America telenovela, *Ultimo Año* (2012). Was this your first foray in teen TV?

KB: No, I had worked years before at MTV Tr3s so I was already familiar with programming for the young Latino demographic. My role on the telenovela was to work with the writers on incorporating social issues related to teens' sexual health and well-being. I traveled to Mexico, did a lot of research, met with youth groups and organizations. We reviewed the existing storylines and found ways to seamlessly integrate messaging regarding sexual consent, STDs, HIV, domestic violence, and contraception among other topics. The writers did an amazing job and we managed to address many social issues impacting Mexican and other Latin American youth.

SM: With *East Los High*, you came on fairly early, in contrast. It was about sexual health awareness from beginning.

KB: Yes, on East Los High, I was there from its inception. It was myself, Carlos Portugal ([my]co-creator) and Katie Elmore Mota (Executive Producer). Carlos and I were hired to create a show that addressed the high rate of teen pregnancy among Latinas in the U.S. We based it in Los Angeles and created characters whose stories were close to our hearts and personal experiences as Latinos growing up in the U.S. We began by addressing sexual health issues and eventually opened up storylines over 4 seasons (60 episodes + the final movie) to discuss many other issues impacting Latino youth such as immigration, domestic violence, gentrification, access to health care, and criminalization.

SM: I understand that you also recruited the entire cast and crew, and that they were mostly Latino as well.

KB: Yes, we made it a point to create a diverse team and particularly wanted our cast to reflect an authentic picture of the world we had created. Mota's production company, Wise Entertainment, made it a priority every season to create a top-notch cast, crew and writer's room, inclusive of women, Latinas/os and other people of color. I think that's part of what makes the show feel authentic and real—from casting to locations to music—it was just second nature to us.

SM: How do you feel about the genre or title of edu-tainment? Do you think about it instinctually, in writing or developing?

KB: I honestly didn't know about the field of edu-tainment until I started working on *East Los High* and we didn't really refer to the show as such. Our main objective was to create, first and foremost, an entertaining dramatic series that integrated positive messaging in a new way. We developed the series with the social messaging in mind but also allowed space for the storylines to develop with their own dramatic weight so that they could deliver that messaging in a way that was instinctual and natural. It was hard work and required a good deal of research and negotiation with the writing team on the development and resolution of important character storylines but it was all worthwhile.

SM: Do you think there are other series doing this?

KB: There are definitely other great series that have taken on serious issues impacting youth in the US—*The Secret Life of the American Teenager*, *Glee*, *The Fosters*, and *13 Reasons Why* to name a few off the top of my head. What set *East Los High* apart was that we began as an original streaming show at a time when *House of Cards* had just premiered. We were an unconventional package with an all Latino cast, an advisory committee and a transmedia world that offered extensive resources to our viewers. I think just like there is a place for drama, suspense and comedy in a show, there's a place for social responsibility. Media is so unbelievably powerful. Especially when dealing with youth and knowing how much television impacts their awareness, perception and behavior—as a writer and producer, it's my personal desire to have a place for social responsibility and I bring it to everything I do in one way or another. It's not easy—it can be difficult to know when to pull it back. As a team, on *East Los*, it was something we often discussed, the push and pull, what was too much or too little. That's when you need a good writing team to work through those moments.

SM: I showed the pilot to a group of very savvy college seniors at USC who did not feel it was too much. I asked them if they would be bothered if a show tried to have some underlining message, and some of them said yeah, and some of them said it's not that different from advertising or a writer/creator's point of view. But they ultimately didn't think *East Los* was heavy handed about its sexual health issues. Not like the kind of videos or movies we would watch in health class that were moralistic, and conservative, or talking down to kids. So I think the balance in *East Los* is really incredible.

KB: That's great to hear! We were actually surprised after receiving audience feedback on Season 1 that viewers were asking for more information, not less. We had a scene where the doctor talks to Jessie about the different options to consider when she finds out she has an unplanned pregnancy. Many viewers appreciated the honesty of that scene and the information provided in it. Others wrote about Plan B, putting on a condom properly and Vanessa's HIV status. Viewers

SM:     didn't know about the many great websites available for information about all of these issues.

SM:     It's amazing to see just how many organizations you work with in the show.

KB:     One of the most gratifying aspects of working on this show has been meeting the partners we worked with in sexual health, social justice, domestic violence, and immigration. To me, that's where the real stars are— people working passionately on these causes day in and out. And the young people who volunteer to do it on their own. We learned so much as writers. There were times we were perpetuating stigmas and stereotypes without being aware of it so we learned ways to avoid that while still telling the story we wanted to tell. We had both non-profit and academic partners working with us, schooling us, supporting us and we supporting them in social media campaigns and events. It was a unique and ground breaking collaboration.

SM:     I spoke with Katie Elmore Mota about expanding beyond the Sabido Methodology practiced by PMC, to include other issues you mentioned such as domestic violence and immigration. Could you talk about developing that after Season One?

KB:     The Sabido Methodology was a starting point that launched us in the right direction. However, since we were not following the standard telenovela format (120 episodes which air daily on weekdays) and we knew we were creating a show in a media world on the precipice of a major transition (as it was in 2010 when we were developing the show), we created our own formula. We chose to keep all the dramatic elements of the telenovelas that we love and include the social issues in a more nuanced manner. We kept what worked well and reinvented the rest. And every season, we adjusted the issues as needed. If we were going to accurately depict Latino youth growing up in East LA, we had to discuss other social issues impacting them such as the criminalization of people of color and immigration.

*SM:* Did the timeliness of it impact you all? I remember in Season 4, some characters were watching TV and discussing a Trump-like candidate.

*KB:* It was unbelievably timely. Some of the issues we were including in Season 4 started coming up in the news during the presidential primaries. It wasn't even planned that way. We just wanted to raise awareness and conversation about the hate crimes going on, especially in Latino neighborhoods in East LA.

*SM:* And I think some of the most powerful episodes revolve around one of the main characters in the immigration detention center. The Voto Latino element felt very real too, living in LA and seeing the signs and grassroots communication and organizations.

*KB:* We met many Latino youth who were passionate, brave and hard-working advocates for their communities. That's why we created the Sofia character, to see a politically active, smart, motivated teenager speaking out for what she believes in and helping others around her. Having her volunteer for Voto Latino was a natural and realistic connection since the organization does great work on immigration issues and Sofia's parents were deported when she was younger. It was important for us to have that character as well as Eddie's character, who presents the storyline of an undocumented youth and all the challenges he encounters on a daily basis with his mother's lack of access to health care, deportation, applying for DACA, etc. We consulted with several other key organizations for his storyline such as United We Dream.

*SM:* Could you talk about the transmedia elements of the show?

*KB:* The initial transmedia strategy of East Los High was created by our creative team at Wise Entertainment and The Alchemist. We developed the transmedia experience from the very beginning as the show was written and produced so it informed the series in a very powerful manner. We built an entire site dedicated to providing viewers with an expanded universe of the show by having a fictional East Los High newspaper called, The Siren, many bonus videos per season and resources on every issue raised within the episodes (www.eastloshigh.com).

*SM:* And did the transmedia component change after Season One?

*KB:* After Season One, we increased our presence in social media while maintaining the site and continuing to produce more bonus content where we could dig deeper into the social issues of the show. We reached more viewers this way and increased awareness working with our partners and their social media campaigns. It was all about learning the best way to get the message out there and collaborating with our partners.

*SM:* It makes me wonder why social consciousness is not a mandate for every show. I can see a producer thinking, "that's a lot of work." But it seems so important and worthwhile.

*KB:* It does take a good deal of work to do the research and requires consensus on behalf of the creative team and decision-makers to see it through to the page and the screen. For example, in the first season of *East Los High*, Ceci gets pregnant while in high school, has the baby and becomes a single, working mom. Four seasons later, we are still seeing the impact and consequences of her decisions, looking at her issues around dating, work, dreams, parenting issues and watching her growth throughout. Ceci's character grew as the series grew and evolved. So based on the feedback we have received from viewers in research studies and on social media about characters like Ceci's and how the show has impacted their lives in a positive manner, it is definitely worth it!

SM: And Ceci wasn't really a likeable character in the first season, she was a mean girl. But it wasn't framed as Ceci is the "bad pregnant teen" and Jessie is the "good pregnant teen," it wasn't black and white like you mentioned.

KB: No, we don't present issues in a simplistic way because they are all very complex. Teen pregnancy, domestic violence, substance abuse, incarceration and many other challenges faced by youth of color in this country are complicated issues impacted by other social and political factors that need time and space to be portrayed in a thoughtful, open manner. It's about taking that extra step—connecting viewers to resources—which makes all the difference. Presenting issues that are complicated in a way that is not black or white but with many other shades of color can be an important vehicle to open awareness, change perspective and even impact behavior.

SM: I know you all picked Hulu as your distributor for several reasons, one of which was knowing your audience was more likely to watch streaming content. Do you think working for Hulu rather than the traditional networks, or even the CW, would be different?

KB: Hulu was an ideal home for *East Los High* and we were very fortunate to have been their longest running original show as of this year (2017). We had a great deal of creative freedom, which I think would have been different at the big networks. And when we premiered Season One in June 2013, we were at the forefront of the changing television landscape, when streaming networks began to be taken seriously. It was a very exciting time for television and it was particularly exciting to have our show, which is about Latinos, created and produced by Latinos and featuring a cast of unknown Latino talent to be one of Hulu's first original shows. It was just the right place at the right time—an innovative show at an innovative network.

## Notes

1. Michael Dimock, "Defining generations: Where Millennials end and Generation Z Begins," Pew Research Center, January 17, 2019, accessed February 3, 2019, https://www.pewresearch.org/fact-tank/2019/01/17/where-millennials-end-and-generation-z-begins/
2. Richard Fry and Kim Parker, "Early Benchmarks Show 'Post-Millennials' on Track to Be Most Diverse, Best-Educated Generation Yet," Pew Research Center, November 15, 2018, accessed March 3, 2019, https://www.pewsocialtrends.org/2018/11/15/early-benchmarks-show-post-millennials-on-track-to-be-most-diverse-best-educated-generation-yet/
3. Ibid.
4. Laurie Ouelette, "Citizen Brand: ABC and the Do Good Turn in US Television," in *Commodity Activism: Cultural Resistance in Neoliberal Times*, eds. Sarah Banet-Weiser and Roopalo Mukherjee (New York: New York University Press, 2012), 57.
5. Ouelette, "Citizen Brand," 58.
6. Stefania Marghitu, Interview with Jessica Kumai Scott, Los Angeles, CA, April 7, 2017.
7. Michela Addis, "New Technologies and Cultural Consumption—Edutainment Born!" *European Journal of Marketing* 39, no. 7/8 (2005): 732.
8. Amanda Keeler, "Branding the Family Drama: Genre Formations and Critical Perspectives on *Gilmore Girls*," in *Screwball Television: Critical Perspectives on Gilmore Girls*, eds. David Scott Diffrient and David Lavery (Syracuse, NY: Syracuse University Press), 19–35.
9. Arvind Singhal, Michael J. Cody, Everett M. Rogers, and Miguel Sabido, *Entertainment Education and Social Change* (Mahwah, NJ: Lawrence Erlbaum, 2004), 61.
10. John McMurria. "Pay-for Culture: Television Activism in a Neoliberal Digital Age," in *Commodity Activism: Cultural Resistance in Neoliberal Times*, eds. Sarah Banet-Weiser and Roopalo Mukherjee (New York: New York University Press), 254.

11 McMurria "Television Activism," 267.
12 Stefania Marghitu, Interview with Bill Ryerson, Los Angeles, CA, February 9, 2017.
13 Tony Castro "*East Los High* on Hulu is First English Language Show with All Latino Cast," *The Huffington Post*, June 6, 2013, http://www.huffingtonpost.com/2013/06/06/east-los-high-hulu_n_3395762.html
14 Ali Modarres, "Boyle Heights: A Brief Demographic and Health Profile," Pat Brown Institute of Public Affairs at California State University, Los Angeles, 2013, https://www.patbrowninstitute.org/up/documents/publications/BoyleHeightsReport2013ModarresFINAL.pdf
15 Roz Kaveney, *Teen Dreams: Reading Teen Film and Television from 'Heather' to 'Veronica Mars'* (London and New York: I.B. Taurus, 2006).
16 Stefania Marghitu, Interview with Katie Elmore Mota, Los Angeles, CA, March 1, 2017.
17 Jens Manuel Krogstad. "Key Facts About How the U.S. Hispanic Population is Changing," Pew Research Center, 2016, http://www.pewresearch.org/facttank/2016/09/08/key-facts-about-how-the-u-s-hispanic-population-is-changing/
18 Nielsen Media. "State of the Hispanic Consumer: The Hispanic Market Imperative," *Nielsen*, Quarter 2, 2012, http://www.nielsen.com/content/dam/corporate/us/en/reports-downloads/2012-Reports/State-of-the-Hispanic-Consumer.pdf
19 Nielsen, "Hispanic Market," 2012.
20 Meg James, "Hulu Launches Latino Service with Spanish-language Programming," *Los Angeles Times*, December 13, 2011.
21 Todd Longwell, "With Bigger Budget, *East Los High* is Splashy Yet Sincere," *Stream Daily*, July 14, 2014, http://streamdaily.tv/2014/07/14/with-bigger-budget-east-lost-high-is-splashy-yet-sincere/
22 Toyota Press Room, "Toyota Celebrates Milestone as No. 1 Automotive Brand in Hispanic Market for 10 Years," March 18, 2015, http://corporatenews.pressroom.toyota.com/releases/toyota+celebrates+10+year+milestone+hispanic+market.htm
23 Claire Carussillo, "*Jane the Virgin* and Target's Televised Push for Millennial Latinas," *Racked*, October 12, 2015, accessed February 13, 2017, http://www.racked.com/2015/10/12/9497359/jane-the-virgin-target-product-placement
24 *TV By the Numbers*, "Monday Final Ratings: *The Voice* and *Big Bang Theory* adjusted up, *Castle*, *Life in Pieces* and *Scorpion* Adjusted Down," *TV By the Numbers*, October 13, 2015, accessed February 3, 2017, http://tvbythenumbers.zap2it.com/featured/monday-final-ratings-oct-12-15/478481/.
25 Madeliene Berg. "The World's Highest-Paid TV Actresses 2016: Sofia Vergara Stays the Queen of the Small Screen with $43 Million," *Forbes*, September 14, 2016, accessed February 3, 2017, https://www.forbes.com/sites/maddieberg/2016/09/14/the-worlds-highest-paid-tv-actresses-2016-sofia-vergara-stays-the-queen-of-the-small-screen-with-43-million/#23140a5965a4
26 Hua Wang and Arvand Singhal, "East Los High: Transmedia Edutainment to Promote the Sexual and Reproductive Health of Young Latina/o

Americans," *American Journal of Public Health* 106, no. 6 (April 14, 2016): 1002–1010, accessed February 3, 2017, https://www.ncbi.nlm.nih.gov/pubmed/27077336

27 Alex Ben Block, "How Hulu Lured Latinos to *East Los High*," *The Hollywood Reporter*, July 26, 2013, accessed February 3, 2017, http://www.hollywoodreporter.com/news/east-los-high-how-hulu-590957#sthash.eV9xvzXR.dpuf

28 Susannah Gora, *You Couldn't Ignore Me If You Tried: The Brat Pack, John Hughes, and Their Impact on a Generation* (New York: Three Rivers Press, 2011), 320–322.

29 Fry and Parker, "Post-Millennials," 2019.

30 Michael Newman, "From Beats to Arcs: Towards a Poetic of Television Narrative," *The Velvet Light Trap*, no. 58 (Fall 2006): 16–28.

31 Louisa Stein, "From Veronica Mars to Pretty Little Liars," *Antenna*, January 29, 2011, accessed June 7, 2016, http://blog.commarts.wisc.edu/2011/01/29/from-veronica-mars-to-pretty-little-liars/

32 Willa Paskin, "Archie Meets *Twin Peaks* Meets Live Action Meets *Gossip Girl*," *Slate*, January 26, 2017, January 26, 2017, http://www.slate.com/articles/arts/television/2017/01/the_cw_s_riverdale_based_on_the_archie_comics_reviewed.html

33 Ibid.

34 Judy Berman, "What Are Critics Saying About 'Riverdale,' CW's Dark Archie Comics Drama?" *The New York Times*, January 26, 2017, accessed January 26, 2017, https://www.nytimes.com/2017/01/26/watching/riverdale-what-are-critics-saying.html

35 https://web.archive.org/web/20110720143427/http://money.uk.msn.com/your-cash/salary-centre/photos.aspx?cp-documentid=153707371&page=9

36 Matthew Gilbert, "Yes, 'Twin Peaks' Changed TV, and Yet . . .," *The Boston Globe*, May 19, 2017, accessed May 19, 2017, https://www.bostonglobe.com/arts/television/2017/05/18/yes-twin-peaks-changed-and-yet/fijeOlAkquUaE4qJZtXQGL/story.html

37 Daniel Kurland, "Twin Peaks: The 25 Year Influence of the David Lynch TV Series," *Den of Geek*, April 8, 2015, accessed June 1, 2016, http://www.denofgeek.com/us/tv/twin-peaks/239941/twin-peaks-the-25-year-influence-of-the-david-lynch-tv-series

38 Stefania Marghitu, Interview with Alyx Vesey, Los Angeles, May 17, 2017.

39 Ibid.

40 Clarkisha Kent, "Euphoria's Kat is Not Your Stereotypical 'Fat Best Friend'," *Entertainment Weekly*, July 16, 2019, accessed July 17, 2019, https://ew.com/tv/2019/07/16/euphorias-kat-not-your-fat-best-friend/

41 P. Claire Dodson, "Barbie Ferreira: Inside Her Euphoric Rise," *Them*, September 10, 2019, accessed September 12, 2019, https://www.them.us/story/barbie-ferreira-euphoria-cover-story

42 Alice Newbold, "Tommy Hilfiger Taps Zendaya For Next Collaboration Vogue," October 16, 2018, accessed September 3, 2019, https://www.vogue.co.uk/article/zendaya-tommy-hilfiger-collaboration

43 Kirsten Chuba, "'Euphoria's' Hunter Schafer on Exploring Trans Identity Onscreen," *Hollywood Reporter*, July 7, 2019, accessed September 3, 2019, https://www.hollywoodreporter.com/live-feed/hunter-schafer-trans-portrayal-euphoria-1222500
44 Claire P. Dodson, "Barbie Ferriera: Inside Her Euphoric Rise," *Them*, September 10, 2019, accessed September 12, 2018, https://www.them.us/story/barbie-ferreira-euphoria-cover-story
45 Ibid
46 Television Academy, "72nd Emmy Awards Nominations and Winners," September 20, 2020, accessed September 20, 2020, https://www.emmys.com/awards/nominees-winners/2020?page=1

# DISCUSSION QUESTIONS

## Chapter 1

1. Describe how teens were an early target for mass media advertising for specific demographics.
2. What are the four core archetypes found in Teen TV? Discuss how they have shifted and.
3. How did the coming-of-age narrative in Teen TV align with network TV's serialized soaps and episodic situational comedies?
4. How were ideas from the Civil Rights Movement of the 1960s both included and pushed back in Teen TV catered toward Baby Boomers?
5. What are the racial dynamics of musical programming such as *American Bandstand* and *Soul Train*? How much of the concept of Least Objectionable Programming (LOP) was determined by race and class?

## Chapter 2

1. How does the construct of the Gen Xer fit alongside their identity toward media consumption, both in terms of what they consume and how they do so?
2. Discuss how topics of sex and sexuality, and drugs and alcohol, shifted in Teen TV for Gen X?

3. What were the key factors that made the nighttime teen soap accessible, and subsequently successful, both to teen audiences and a larger audience?
4. How do series like *My So-Called Life* and *Freaks and Geeks* align more closely with the idea of nichecasting over broadcasting and Least Objectionable Programming (LOP)?
5. How did Teen TV catered toward Gen X set the foundation for themes of moral ambiguity in post-network TV?

## Chapter 3

1. What is the relationship between Millennials, participatory culture, and politics?
2. Can you discern the authorship of Josh Schwartz across *The O.C.* and *Gossip Girl*?
3. How does Teen TV catered toward Millennials both conform to and subvert traditional heteronormative notions of sex and sexuality?
4. Describe the transnational relationship and exchange of influences between UK and US teen series catered toward Millennials in the post-network era?

## Chapter 4

1. How does *East Los High* differ from traditional modes of production in US television?
2. Where do you imagine the "Do Good Turn" progressing to in future representations on teen television?
3. In what ways is the representation of Gen Z a continuation of that of Millennials, and how have they also forged new ideas about identity?
4. Analyze how the stardom of a Gen Z star such as Zendaya moves across several media forms.

# TEEN TV FILMOGRAPHY

**Organized by Decade and Network/Platform**

*Longest Running Teen Drama:*

*Grange Hill* (1978–2008, BBC)

### 1950s

*Meet Corliss Archer* (1951, CBS)
*The Many Loves of Dobbie Gillis* (1959–1963, CBS)
*The Ozzie and Harriet* Show (1952–1966, ABC)

### 1960s

*Never Too Young* (1965–1966, ABC)
*Gidget* (1965–1966, ABC)
*Bachelor Father* (1957–1962, ABC, CBS, NBC)
*Soul Train* (1971–2016, WCIU-TV/WGN)
*American Bandstand* (1962–1989, ABC, USA)

### 1970s

*Room 222* (1969–1974, ABC)
*What's Happening!!!* (1976–1979, ABC)
    Based on *Cooley High* (1975 film)

*Happy Days* (1974–1984, ABC)
*James at 15* (1977–1978, NBC)
*The Facts of Life* (1979–1988, ABC)
*Welcome Back, Kotter* (1975–1979, ABC)

## 1980s

### *MTV Premiered 1981*

*Network TV (ABC, CBS, NBC)*

*The Wonder Years* (1988–2993, ABC)
*Saved by the Bell* (1989–1993, NBC)
*A Different World* (1987–1993, NBC)

*Family Network TV with Teen Characters*

*Growing Pains* (1985–1992, ABC)
*Full House* (1987–1995, ABC)
*Family Matters* (1989–1997, ABC, 1997–1998, CBS)

*The Disney Channel*

*The All New Mickey Mouse Club* (1989–1995)
*Good Morning Miss Bliss* (1988–1989) *Saved by the Bell* is a spinoff
*Teen Angel* (1989)
*Teen Angel Returns* (1989)

### *International*

*Canada*

DEGRASSI

*Degrassi Junior High* (1987–1989, CBC)
*Degrassi High* (1989–1991, CBC)
*Degrassi: The Next Generation*

Original network
CTV (2001–2009)
MuchMusic (2010–2013)
MTV Canada (2013–2015)

*UK*

*Press Gang* (1989–1993, Children's ITV)

### 1990s

### *Network TV (ABC, CBS, NBC, Fox)*

*Fresh Prince of Bel-Air* (1990–1996, ABC)
*Boy Meets World* (1993–2000, ABC)
High School Season 2–5, 1994–1998
*Beverly Hills 90210* (1990–2000, Fox)
    Reboots: *90210* (2008–2013, Fox)
          *BH90210* (2019, Fox)
*Blossom* (1990–1995, NBC)
*Sabrina The Teenage Witch* (ABC, 1996–2000, The WB, 2000–2003)
*Clueless* (1996–1997, ABC, UPN, 1997–1999)
*My So-Called Life* (1994–1995, ABC, syndicated later on MTV)
    Adaptation:
    *Mein Leben & Ich* (RTL, 2001–2009)
*Freaks and Geeks,* (1999–2000, NBC)
*That 70's Show* (1998–2006, Fox)
*Malcom in the Middle* (2000–2006, Fox)

### *The WB / UPN*

*Sister, Sister* (1994–1995, ABC; 1995–1999, WB)
*Moesha* (1996–2001, UPN)
*Buffy, the Vampire Slayer* (1997–2001, WB; 2001–2003, UPN)
*Charmed* (1998–2006, The WB)
*Dawson's Creek* (1998–2003, The WB)

*Popular* (1999–2001, The WB)
*Roswell* (1999–2002)
    Revival: *Roswell, New Mexico*, 2019–, CW)

## *MTV*

*Daria* (1997–2002)
Spinoff of *Beavis and Butthead* (1993–1997)

### Nickelodeon

*Are You Afraid of the Dark?* (1990–1996; revived 1999–2000)
*Doug* (1991–1994, MTV; 1996–1999, ABC)
*The Adventures of Pete and Pete* (1991–1996)
*Hey Dude* (1989–1991)
*Welcome Freshmen* (1991–1993)
*Salute Your Shorts* (1991–1992)
*Clarissa Explains it All* (1991–1994)
*The Secret World of Alex Mack* (1994–1998)
*All That* (variety) (1994–2005)
    *Keenan and Kel* (1996–2000)
    *The Amanda Show* (1999–2002)
*The Mystery Files of Shelby Woo* (1996–1998)

### Disney

*The Famous Jett Jackson* (1998–2001)
*Flash Forward* (1995–1997)

## 2000s

### Network Television

*American Dreams* (ABC, 2002–2005)
*The O.C.* (2003–2007, Fox)

*Friday Night Lights* (2006–2011, NBC, The 101 Network)
*Glee* (Fox, 2009–2015)
*Joan of Arcadia* (CBS/CTV, 2003–2005)
*Scream Queens* (Fox, 2015)

### *Tween / Family Series: ABC Family, Disney Channel, Nickelodeon, The CW/WB*

*ABC Family*

*Greek* (2007–2011)
*The Secret Life of the American Teenager* (2008–2013)
*Make It or Break It* (2009–2012)
*10 Things I Hate About You* (2009–2010)
*Pretty Little Liars* (2010–2015) Freeform (2016–2017)
*The Fosters* (2013–2018)
**Freeform** relaunch (2016)
*Grown-ish* (2018–)

*The CW/WB*

*Gilmore Girls* (2000–2007)
*Smallville* (2001–2011)
*Veronica Mars* (2004–2007)
*Gossip Girl* (2007–2012) (Reboot: HBO Max)
*One Tree Hill* (2003–2012)
*The Vampire Diaries* (2009–2017)
*The Flash* (2014–)
*Riverdale* (2017–)
*The 100* (2019–2020)

*Disney Channel*

*Even Stevens* (2000–2003)
*Lizzie McGuire* (2001–2004)

*That's So Raven* (2003–2007)
*Hannah Montana* (2006–2011)

### Nickelodeon

*Drake and Josh* (2004–2007)
*iCarly* (2007–2012)

### Hulu

*East Los High*
*Looking for Alaska* (2019)

### HBO

*Euphoria* (2019–)
    Adapted from Israeli series *Euphoria* (2012–2013)

### MTV

*Laguna Beach: The Real Orange County* (2004–2006)

SCRIPTED:

*The Hard Times of RJ Berger* (2010–2011)
*Skins* (2011)
*Awkward* (2011–2016)
*Teen Wolf* (2011–2017)
*Faking It* (2014–2016)

MTV REALITY TV:

*Teen Cribs* (2009, Snapchat, CMT)
*My Super Sweet 16* (2005–2008)

*16 and Pregnant* (2009–)
*Teen Mom* (2009–)

*Netflix US*

*The Get Down* (2016–2017)
*Stranger Things* (2016–)
*Haters Back Off* (2016)
*American Vandal* (2017–2018)
*13 Reasons Why* (2017–2020)
*The Chilling Adventures of Sabrina* (2017–)
*Atypical* (2017–2021)
*On My Block* (2018–)
*Insatiable* (2018)
*Sex Education* (UK Co-production) (2019–)
*Anne with an "E"* (2017–2019)
*Big Mouth* (2017–)
*The End of the F***king World* (2018–)
*Everything Sucks!* (2018)
*Alexa and Katie* (2018–2020)
*Daybreak* (2019)
*The Order* (2019)
*The Society* (2019–)
*The Umbrella Academy* (2019)
*The Politician* (2019–)
*Trinkets* (2019–)
*I Am Not Okay with This* (2020–)
*Never Have I Ever* (2020–)
*Outer Banks* (2020–)
*The Expanding World of Alex Garcia* (2020–)

*Netflix International*

*Elite* (2018–, Spain)
*Baby* (2020, Italy)

## Apple TV

*Dickinson* (2019)

## *International*

### United Kingdom

#### CHANNEL 4 UK

*Bromwell High* (2005)
*Sugar Rush* (2005–2006)
*Skins* (2007–2013)
*Misfits* (2009–2013)
*My Mad Fat Diary* (2013–2015)
*The End of The Fucking World* (2018–)
*Derry Girls* (2018–)

#### BBC

*Normal People* (2020)

### Korea

*All of Us Are Dead* (Netflix, 2021–)
*Andante* (KBS1, 2017–)
*At Eighteen* (JTBC, 2019)
*Boys Over Flowers* (2007)
        Based on original Japanese *Boys Over Flowers* (1992–2008)
*Dream High* (KBS2, 2011)
*Dream High 2* (KBS, 2012)
*Flower Band* (KST, 2012)
*Girls' Generation 1979* (KBST, 2017)
*The Heirs* (SBS, 2013)
*Monstar* (Mnet, 2013)
*Orange Marmalade* (KBS, 2015)

*Puberty Medley* (KBS2, 2013)
*Reply 1997* (tvN, 2012)
*School 2013* (KBS, 2013)
*School 2017* (KBS, 2017)
*Schoolgirl Detectives* (jTBC, 2014–2015)
*Sweet Revenge* (Oksusu/BTV, 2017–2018)
*Sweet Revenge 2* (XtvN/Oksusu, 2018)

METEOR GARDEN/BOYS OVER FLOWERS INTERNATIONAL ADAPTATIONS

*Meteor Garden* (CTS, Taiwan, 2001)
*Meteor Garden II* (CTS, Taiwan, 2002)
*Hana Yori Dango* (TBS, Japan, 2005)
*Hana Yori Dango Returns* (TBS, Japan 2007)
*Hana Yori Dango Final* (film, Japan, 2008)
*Boys Over Flowers* (KBS2, South Korea, 2009)
*Meteor Shower* (Hunan TV, China, 2009)
*Kaisi Yeh Yaariaan* (MTV India, India, 2014)
*Siapa Takut Jatuh Cinta* (SCTV, Indonesia, 2017)
*Meteor Garden* (Hunan TV/ Netflix Original, China, 2018)

*Skam International Adaptations:*

*Skam* (Norway, NRK, 2015–2017)
*Skam Austin* (Facebook Watch, US, 2018–)
*Skam España* (Movistar, Spain, 2018–)
*Skam France/ Skam Belgique* (France.tv, Slash/France 4; RTBF Auvio/La Trois, France/Belgium (Wallonia, co-production, 2018–)
*Druck* (funk, ZDFneo, Germany, 2018–)
*Skam Italia* (TIMvision/Netflix, Italy, 2018–)
*Skam NL* (The Netherlands, NTR, 2018–)
*wtFock* (VIER/VIJF/wtfock.be, Belgium (Flanders) 2018–)

# INDEX

Abdul, Paula 70
*Ad Age* 170–171
*The Adventures of Ozzie and Harriet* 32
*Advertising and Marketing to Young People* (Gilbert) 44
*Afterschool Specials* 160, 164
Aguilera, Christina 13, 71
AIDS epidemic 66–67
Akil, Mara Brok 88–89, 96
Akil, Salam 89, 96
Albee, Edward 38
Alcoholics Anonymous (AA) 74
Alcott, Louisa May 5
*All American Girl* 175
*All in The Family* 42, 68
*All My Children* 32
*The All-New Mickey Mouse Club* 13
*The Amazing Spider-Man* 38
*The Amazing Spider-Man 2: Rise of Electro* 38
Amazon 19, 161, 169
American Association of School Administrators 92
*American Bandstand* 16, 23, 44, 47–51, 69
American Broadcasting Company (ABC) 25–26, 37, 50, 67, 70, 73, 89, 91, 110–112, 162, 164, 168, 187
*American Crime Story* 108
*American Graffiti* 43
*American Horror Story* 108

American International Pictures 37
antiwar movement 27
AOL Instant Messenger 105
Apatow, Judd 17, 75, 84
Archer, Corliss 25
*Archie Comics* 25–26
*Archie Comics, Riverdale* 1
Arnold, Beatrice 112
Asch, Solomon 166
Asian-American protagonists in teen TV 174–176
Asian protagonists in teen TV 174–176
Austen, Jane: *Emma* 5; *Pride and Prejudice* 5
auteurism 9, 186

Baby Boomers 4, 17, 23, 25
Baby Boomer teen TV 23–60; *American Bandstand* 47–51; Dobie Gillis' lasting influence on teen TV 36–37; early Music TV for teen Baby Boomers 43–47; early teen soaps 32–33; early teen TV sitcoms 33–36; *Gidget* 33–36; *Gidget* and Baby Boomer stardom 37–41; *The Hardy Boys* and *Nancy Drew* 25–28; Linda Schuyler 51–60; literary precedents from 1940s to 1960s 25–28; *The Many Loves of Dobbie Gillis* 33–36; overview 23–25; Sally Field 37–41; *Soul Train* 47–51; targeting teen consumer and

## INDEX

early broadcast TV 28–32; *Welcome Back Kotter* (1975–1979, ABC) 41–43
*The Baby-Sitters Club* 176
Badgley, Penn 124
Barton, Mischa 89
BBC 134, 136, 188
The Beatles 23–24, 27, 44, 46–47
*Beavis and Butthead* 69
Bedoya, Kathleen 1, 160, 161, 166, 168, 200–209
*Being Mary Jane* 96
Bell, Kristen 123
Berridge, Susan 136–139
*Beverly Hills 90210* 5, 17, 37, 40, 67, 73–74, 76–78, 80, 86, 114, 169, 184
Beyoncé 70, 193, 200
*The Big Lebowski* 185
Bilson, Rachel 77
Black Entertainment Television (BET) 67, 93, 96
*Black-ish* 93, 168, 173
*Black Lightning* 89, 96
#BlackLivesMatter 159
Black R&B 47
Blanchett, Cate 184
*Bloodline* 85
Bloom, Jason 185
*Blue Jasmine* 183
Bodroghkozy, Aniko 26
*The Bodyguard* 43
*Bonnie and Clyde* 30
*Booksmart* 120
Braff, Zach 121
Brandera, Albert 166
*Breaker High* 18
*Breakfast at Tiffany* 183
*The Breakfast Club* 16, 110, 184
*Bridesmaids* 84
*The Bridge* 173
Bright Eyes 121
Britton, Connie 113, 167
broadcast 2; live 48; programming 24; rules of LOP and 32; teen consumer and early broadcast TV 28–32
*Broad City* 174

Brody, Adam 77, 89, 114, 174
Bronte, Emily: *Wuthering Heights* 5
*Brothers and Sisters* 38
Brown, Helen Gurley 30
Brown, Millie Bobby 111, 142
*Brown v. Board of Education* 50
*Buffy the Vampire Slayer* 18, 74, 75, 77, 131
The Buggles 68
Bush, George W. 106, 191
*Busy Tonight* 85
Butler, Ross 185
Buttigieg, Pete 106

*Cabaret* 34
Cable News Network (CNN) 68
Caldwell, John T. 12
campus protests 27
Canadian Broadcasting Channel (CBC) 91
*Can't Hardly Wait* 184
Cardellini, Linda 75, 84–85
Cardi B 70
Carey, Mariah 70
Caro, Cindy 37
*The Carrie Diaries* 4
Carter, Jimmy 71
The Castaways 32
*Casual* 163
"Catalano Generation" 106
*Catcher in the Rye* (Sallinger) 3
CBS 18, 36, 44, 50, 68, 94
Centineo, Noah 176
Chapman University 2
*Charlie's Angels* 73
*Charmed* 18
Chasez, J. C. 71
*Cheers* 89
Cher Papa 37
*Chicago* 34
*Chico and the Man* 42
The Chiffons 47
*The Chilling Adventures of Sabrina* 26
Cho, Margaret 175
*Cinderella* 94

# INDEX

civil rights movements 16, 26
civil rights organizations 165
Clark, Dick 47, 50
Clinton, Bill 71, 106
Clinton, Hilary 174
*Clueless* 79, 83, 128, 183
Cobain, Kurt 70
Coco Chanel 125
Colantoni, Enrico 129
Cold War 67
Cole, Michaela 188
"collective intelligence" 165
Collins, Phil 69
Columbia Broadcasting Company (CBS) 67
Columbia Pictures 37
Comack, James 42
coming of age: genre 3–5; narratives 21; programming 188; series 77; story 2–5, 43
*Commodity Activism: Cultural Resistance in Neoliberal Times* 162
Condor, Lana 176
*Cookie Goes to the Hospital* 91
The Cookies 47
Cornelius, Don 27, 51
Corona 170
Cosby, Bill 67
*The Cosby Show* 89
*Cosmopolitan* 30
*Cougar Town* 85
COVID-19 pandemic 2, 159
*The Craft* 184
Crawford, Chace 126
*Crazy Rich Asians* 174
*Cristela* 173
Cruz, Wilson 79
"cultural specificity" 21
CW Network 1, 18, 26, 88–89, 94, 96, 110, 122–123, 136–137, 171–172
*Cycle of Outrage* (Gilbert) 3
Cyrus, Miley 13

*Daily Show* 173
*Dallas* 67

*Dallas Buyers Club* 83
Daman, Eric 12, 18, 128, 143–155
*Dancing with the Stars* 198
Danes, Claire 17, 71, 79
*Daria* 69, 120
*Dawson's Creek* 4, 18, 74, 75, 85–89, 107, 129, 137
*Dead to Me* 85
Dean, James 23, 46, 74, 89, 114
"decoding" 6
Dee, Sandra 37
*Degrassi Junior High* 92
*Degrassi: The Next Class* 91, 93
*Degrassi: The Next Generation* 5, 13, 18, 51–60, 89, 90–93, 105, 134–135, 139, 140, 166
Delmont, Matthew F. 47, 48–50
*Den of Geek* 187
Denver, Bob 35
*Desperate Housewives* 115, 173, 186
DiCaprio, Leonardo 13, 76, 82
*A Different World* 75, 89, 93
*Dirty Dancing* 43
Disney Channel 13, 18, 50, 185, 197
The Dixie Cups 47
*Dobie Gillis* 24; lasting influence on teen TV 36–37
Dohring, Jason 129
Dunn, Teddy 129
Dunst, Kristen 82
Duvernay, Ava 200
Dyer, Richard 14–15, 49
Dylan, Bob 185
*Dynasty* 67, 73

early Music TV for teen Baby Boomers 43–47
early teen soaps 32–33
early teen TV sitcoms 33–36
*East Los High* 1, 19, 160–167
*Easy Rider* 30, 47
*The Ed Sullivan Show* 16, 23, 27, 44, 45
Efron, Zac 198
Eichner, Billy 163
Eilish, Billie 142

Elan, Priya 109
*Elite* 137
Elliot, Mia 33
Elliot, Missy 70
Elsley, Bryan 134
Elvis 23, 27, 44–45
*Emma* (Austen) 5
Entertainment and Sports Programming Network (ESPN) 68
*Entertainment Tonight* 69
*Entertainment Weekly* 112
*ER* 38, 85
*Esquire* 44
*Euphoria* 1–2, 5, 19, 80, 83, 160, 188–197
Ewing, J. R. 109

Facebook 105, 151
Family Friendly Programming Forum (FFPF) 164
*The Famous Jett Jackson* 75
fans/fandom 1, 7, 11, 12, 15, 17, 23, 46, 48, 50, 59–60, 70, 83, 85, 118, 120, 142, 165, 178, 196
*Fargo* 186
Farquhar, Ralph 94, 95
*The Farwell* 188
*Father Knows Best* 31
Feig, Paul 17
*The Feminine Mystique* (Friedan) 31
Ferguson, Rebecca 198
Ferriera, Barbie 198, 199
*Ferris Bueller's Day Off* 110
*Feud* 108
Fieg, Paul 75
Field, Sally 5, 16
Fiske, John 7
Flippen, Ruth Brooks 37
*The Flying Nun* 38
*Forbes* magazine 141
*Forgetting Sarah Marshall* 84
*For Keeps* 110
Forssell, Andy 173
Fosse, Bob 34
*The Fosters* 173

Foucault, Michel 10
Fox 17, 46, 88, 96, 110, 136, 163
Fox Corporation 73–74
Franco, James 13, 17, 84
Frankfurt School 6, 8
*Frank's Place* 75
*Freaks and Geeks* 5, 13, 17, 68, 70, 72, 75, 88, 120
*Fresh Off the Boat* 89, 168, 173, 175
*The Fresh Prince of Bel-Air* 75
*Friday Night Lights* 89, 112–113, 167
Friedan, Betty: *The Feminine Mystique* 31
*Fringe* 88
Frost, Mark 75
*Full House* 185

*The Game* 96, 97
*Game of Throne* 3
*Garden State* 121
Gaye, Marvin 32
Generation Xers 65–67
*Generation X: Tales for an Accelerated Culture* (Coupland) 66
Generation X teen TV 65–101; *Beverly Hills 90210* 76–78; Brandy Norwood 93–97; Claire Danes and Jared Leto 82–83; *Dawson's Creek* 86–89; *Degrassi* 90–93; Gen Z stardom 82–83; Gen Z stardom and *Freaks and Geeks* 84–85; *My So-Called Life* 78–81; and narrowcasting in post-network Era 86–89; nostalgia and Gen X in Middle Age 86; overview 65–76; rise and fall of WB 86–89; stardom and *Moesha* 93–97; Winnie Holzman 97–101
genre hybridity 68, 177–186; teen crime drama 177–186
genres: case of teen TV 6–7; as cultural categories 6–7
Gen Z 4; Claire Danes and Jared Leto 82–83; stardom 82–83; stardom and *Euphoria* 197–200; stardom and *Freaks and Geeks* 84–85
Gen Z teen TV 159–209; Asian and Asian-American protagonists in teen

TV 174–176; *East Los High* 160–167; *Euphoria* 188–197; genre hybridity 177–186; Gen Z stardom and *Euphoria* 197–200; HBO 188–197; Kathleen Bedoya 200–209; overview 159–160; past treatment of teen TV abortions 167–174; teen crime drama 177–186; *Twin Peaks* and its teen crime drama successors 186–187
*The Get Down* 173
*Get Out* 188
*Gidget* 4–5, 16, 24, 31, 33–36; and Baby Boomer stardom 37–41; and Sally Field 37–41
*Gidget, the Little Girl with Big Ideas* (Kohner) 37
*Gidget Gets Married* 40
*Gidget Goes Hawaiian* 37
*Gidget Goes New York* 37
*Gidget Goes Parisienne* 37
*Gidget Goes to Rome* 37
*Gidget in Love* 37
*Gidget: Origins of a Teen Girl Transmedia Franchise* (Wojcik) 24
Gilbert, Eugene 29; *Advertising and Marketing to Young People* 44
Gilbert, James: *Cycle of Outrage* 3
Gilbert, Matthew 186
*Gillis* 44
*Gilmore Girls* 18, 77, 129, 164, 174, 185, 196
*Girlfriends* 76, 88, 96
*Girls* 84, 188
The Girls 32
*The Girl with Something Extra* 38
Gitlin, Todd 4, 9, 74
Givens, Robin 184
*The Glass Menagerie* 38
Glazer, Illana 174
*Glee* 79, 106–108, 136, 137, 175
Glee Club 175
*The Goat, or Who Is Sylvia?* 38
*The Goldbergs* 31–32, 42
Gomez, Selena 13
Gora, Susannah 175

Gosling, Ryan 13, 18
*Gossip Girl* 4, 5, 12, 13, 18, 40, 77, 80, 89, 105, 109, 113–115, 122–129, 143–155, 169, 182–183
Graham, Aubrey Drake 5, 13, 18, 140–142
Grande, Ariana 70
Gray, Jonathan 12
*Grease* 43
*The Greatest Showman* 198
*Great Gatsby* 124
*Grey's Anatomy* 112, 122, 167, 173
*Growing Pains* 13, 76, 82
*Grown-ish* 89, 93
guerilla civil rights 27
Guttenberg, Steve 132

Habel, Sarah 184
Hall, Stuart 6, 10
Hamlin, Harry 130
Hampton, Brenda 112
Han, Jenny 176
*The Handmaid's Tale* 163
*Hannah Montana* 13
Hannigan, Alyson 131
*Happy Days* 43, 186
*The Hardy Boys* book series 25–28
*Harry Potter* 3
*Hart to Hart* 73
HBO 1, 169, 188–197
Hepburn, Audrey 125
Herbert, F. Hugh 25
Herskovitz, Marshall 78
Hickman, Dwayne 34
*High Maintenance* 174, 188
high school 3, 5–6, 17, 35, 39, 41–42, 69, 72, 75, 78, 81, 84, 89–91, 107–111, 114, 123, 125, 129–136, 164, 176, 184, 186–187, 193–197
*The Hills* 110
*Hill Street Blues* 68, 177
hippie counterculture 27
Holmes, Katie 86, 87
Holzman, Winnie 17, 75, 78–79, 81–82, 97–101

## INDEX

*Homeland* 82–83
*Hormones* 136
Hoult, Nicholas 13, 135
Houston, Whitney 43, 70, 94
*How to Breathe* 199
Hughes, John 110, 175
Hulu 19, 105, 160–163, 165–166, 169–173, 188

*Ida Makes a Movie* 91
ideology, defined 14
indie rock 120–122
*Insecure* 96, 174, 188
Instagram 199
interviews and production studies 7–13
*Irene Moves In* 91
*It's Always Sunny in Philadelphia* 89

Jackman, Hugh 198
Jackson, Janet 70
Jackson, Joshua 86, 87, 88
Jackson, Michael 69–70
Jacoson, Abbi 174
*The Jamie Foxx Show* 88
*Jane the Virgin* 171–172
Jay-Z 200
*The Jeffersons* 43
Jenkins, Henry 7, 71, 165
*Jezebel* 110
Jones, Caroline 77
*Journal of Consumer Marketing* 66
*Jughead Jones* 26
*Juno* 111
"Juno Effect" 111–112

Kaling, Mindy 176
Kaplan, Gabe 42
Katims, Jason 112–113, 167
Kavney, Roz 169
Keeler, Amanda 164
Kelley, Andrea 47
Kennedy, John F. 71
*The Kids of Degrassi Street* 91
*The Killing* 186
*Kiss and Tell* 25

*A Kiss for Corliss* 25
Klausner, Julie 163
*Knocked Up* 84
"knowledge communities" 165
Kohner, Frederick: *Gidget, the Little Girl with Big Ideas* 37
Kun, Josh 49
Kurland, Daniel 187
Kwan, Kevin 174

*La Dolce Vita* 24
*Ladybird* 188
Lady Gaga 70
Lagerfield, Karl 128
*Laguna Beach* 110
Langer, A. J. 79
Latino Millennials 171
Lear, Norman 42, 112, 167, 172
Least Objectionable Programming (LOP) 30
*Leave it to Beaver* 32
Leshem, Ron 188
Leto, Danes 71
Leto, Jared 71
Levin, Daphna 188
Levinson, Sam 188–189
Levy, Pierre 165
Lewis, Jenny 121
LGBTQIA+ 107, 108
*Life* 17, 44
*Lifestyles of the Rich and Famous* 69
*Lifestyle Television* (Ouellette) 15
Lil' Kim 70
*Lincoln* 38
*Lion* 135
literary precedents: from the 1940s 25–28; from the 1960s 25–28
*Little Women* (Alcott) 5, 82
Lively, Blake 13, 125, 128
*Living Single* 76
Long, Shelley 121
Longoria, Eva 173
*Look* 44
*Los Angeles Times* 91
*The Love Boat* 73

# INDEX

*Love Is a Many Splendored Thing* 32–33
Lowell, Chris 133
Luhrman, Baz 82
Lukeba, Merveille 136
Lynch, David 71, 75, 186

*Mademoiselle* 28
*Mad Men* 85, 128
Madonna 7, 69
"Mainstream Tech" 106
*The Many Loves of Dobie Gillis* 4, 16, 33–36
*Many-Splendoured Thing* (Suyin) 33
Martha and the Vandellas 47
Martin, Alfred L., Jr. 93–94
*Mary Tyler Moore Show* 31, 68, 79
*Maude* 112, 167
"Maude's Dilemma" 112, 167
*The Max* 72
Mayer, Vicki 12
McConaughey, Matthew 83
McKay, Dylan 184
McMurria, John 162, 163, 165
*Mean Girls* 105, 109–110, 109–113
Meester, Leighton 77, 125
*Meet Corliss Archer* 25
*Metacritic* 172
#MeToo movement 85, 142, 159
*Miami Vice* 68
*Mickey Mouse Club* 71
*Midsommar* 188
*Mighty Ducks* 88
*Millennial Fandom* 105
Millennials 65, 159; stardom and *Degrassi* 140–142
Millennial teen TV 105–155; Aubrey Drake Graham 140–142; Eric Daman 143–155; *Gossip Girl* 122–129; indie rock and *The O.C.* 120–122; *Mean Girls* and reality teen moms 109–113; Millennial stardom and *Degrassi* 140–142; *The O.C.* 113–120; overview 105–109; *Skins* 134–139; *Veronica Mars* and suicide 129–134
Miller, Mark Crispin 8

*The Milton Berle Show* 45
*The Mindy Project* 163
*The Mitch Thomas Show* 49, 50
Mittell, Jason 7, 21
Modelo 170
*Modern Family* 173
*Moesha* 5, 75, 107
Mo-G 142
Momsen, Taylor 127
Monroe, Marilyn 69
Monroe, Meredith 87
*Moonlight* 188, 190
*Moon Pilot* 37
Mota, Katie Elmore 161, 169, 171
Motion Picture Production Code 30
Motown's The Marvelettes 47
MSN Money 185
MTM Productions 68
*Much Music* 92
Mukherjee, Roopalo 162
Murdoch, Rupert 73
Murphy, Ryan 108
Murray, Ashley 185
Murray, Hannah 135
Murray, Susan 13
Music Television (MTV) 17, 67, 69, 105, 112
*My So-Called Life* 17, 67–68, 70, 72, 75, 78–81, 82, 83, 97–101, 106, 107, 120, 137
*The Mystery Files of Shelby Woo* 174

Nancy Drew 25–28
*The Nancy Drew Mystery Stories* 26
*Narcos* 173
narrowcasting in post-network era 86–89
Nash, Ilana 47
National Association of Broadcasters 30
National Broadcasting Company (NBC) 71
National Campaign to Prevent Teen & Unplanned Pregnancy 112
National Education Association 92
*The Nat King Cole Show* 50

# INDEX

Nelson, Rickie 32
Netflix 1, 19–20, 26, 85, 93, 108, 137, 142, 161, 169, 172, 173, 176, 188, 200
Network TV 67
*Never Have I Ever* 175–176
*Never Too Young* 32, 120
New American Cinema 30
Newcomb, Horace 9
Newman, Michael 68, 177, 183
*Newsweek* 44
*New York* magazine 124, 127
*New York Times* 83, 86, 183
*Next Generation* 90
niche-casting 68
Nichols, Marisol 184
Nickelodeon 18, 68
Nicki Minaj 70
Nielsen Media 170
*Nip Tuck* 108
*Nirvana* 80
Nixon, Agnes 32
*Noel Buys a Suit* 91
*Norma Rae* 38
Norris, Patrick 81
Norwood, Brandy 5, 71, 94, 96–97
nostalgia and Gen X in Middle Age 86
Noway 137
NWA 70

Oakes, Jonathon I. 66
Obama, Barack 79, 106, 159, 170
*The O.C.* 4, 18, 37, 72, 77, 88, 89, 105, 107, 109–110, 112, 113–120, 125, 127–130, 167, 169, 171, 175, 183, 185; indie rock and 120–122
Ocasio-Cortez, Alexandria 106
O'Connell, Jack 13
O'Connor, Carroll 42
*O.C. Weekly Review* 121
Odessa, Devon 80
"OK Boomer" 2
"OMFG" campaign 123
*One Day at a Time* 172
*One Life to Live* 32

*Orange is the New Black* 173
"The Oregon Trail Generation" 106
Ortner, Sherry B. 65–66
Ouelette, Laurie 15, 160, 162, 164
*Ozzie and Harriet* 89

Palin, Bristol 111
Palin, Sarah 111
Palladino, Grace 28, 30, 44, 47
Pantene 170
"paratexts" 12
*Parenthood* 113
Parents Television Council (PTC) 123
*Paris is Burning* 108
Parker, Tom 46
Paskin, Willa 183
past treatment of teen TV abortions 167–174
Patel, Dev 13, 135
Paterson, Mark 27–28
*The Path* 163
Patsavas, Alexandra 122
Pattinson, Robert 122
*The Patty Duke Show* 24
Payton, Philana 95
*Pearl Jam* 80
*Pen 15* 105
Pepsi 44
*Perfect High* 185
Pew Research Center 159
Phillips, Busy 84–85, 88
Phillips, Irma 32
*Pineapple Express* 84
Pitzer College 2
*Places in the Heart* 38
Planned Parenthood 112–113, 167–168, 172, 173
*The Politician* 108
*Popular* 18, 108
Population Media Center (PMC) 161, 165, 169, 171
Portman, Natalie 121
Portugal, Carlos 161, 166, 168
The Postal Service 121
post-network cable 16, 78

INDEX

*Power* 173
*Pretty in Pink* 184
*Pretty Little Liars* 5, 109, 122, 169, 177, 181–182, 185, 187
*Pride and Prejudice* (Austen) 5
print journalism 122
*Private Practice* 112, 167
*Project Runway* 128
Public Enemy 70
*Purple Rain* 43
Purser, Shannon 184

*Queen Bees and Wannabes: Helping Your Daughter Survive Cliques, Gossip, Boyfriends, and the New Realities of Girl World* (Wiseman) 109
Queen Latifah 94, 96
Questlove 51
Quintanilla, Selena 70

race 7, 21, 33, 48, 69, 95, 106–107, 130, 136, 168
Rae, Issa 96, 174
The Raiders 32
Reagan, Ronald 17
Reaganism 67
*The Real Housewives* 115
*Reality Bites* 67
reality teen moms 109–113
*The Real OC: Laguna Beach* 115
*Real World* 105
*Rebel Without A Cause* 76, 117
"recombinant culture" 4
Reid, Tim 75
Reiner, Rob 42
Renner, Lisa 130
*Requiem for a Dream* 83
Revere, Paul 32
Reynolds, Debbie 34
Rhimes, Shonda 112, 122, 167
Ringwald, Molly 110–111, 184
*Riverdale* 26, 87, 88, 89, 177, 182–183, 185, 187
*Roadies* 81
rock 'n' roll music 17, 26, 28, 43–50

*Roe v. Wade* 112, 167
Rogen, Seth 17, 84
*Rolling Stone* magazine 70
*Romeo and Juliet* (Shakespeare) 3
*Romeo + Juliet* 82
The Ronettes (The Spectrum Sound) 47
Roosevelt, Franklin D. 71
*Rotten Tomatoes* 172
Russell, Keri 13
Ryder, Winona 67, 82
Ryerson, Bill 165–166, 173

Sabido, Miguel 165
Sabido Method 165–166, 169
*Sabrina, The Animated Series* 26
*Sabrina: The Secrets of a Teenage Witch* 26
*Sabrina the Teenage Witch* 26
Saddle Creek Records 121
Sallinger, J. D. 3
same-sex marriage 79
Sarandon, Susan 82
Sarkissian, Raffi 107–108
Sarris, Andrew 9
*Saturday Night Fever* 43
*Saturday Night Live* 51, 141
*Saved by the Bell* 17, 37, 67, 71, 72, 73, 78, 80, 117, 133
Schaefer, Hutcher 198
Schuyler, Linda 18, 51–60, 90–92
Schwartz, Jason 17
Schwartz, Josh 105, 108, 113–114, 122–123
Schwartz, Joshua 88
Scodelario, Kaya 135
*Scooby-Doo, Where Are You!* 25–26, 36
Scott, A. O. 86
Scott, Jessica Kumai 162
*Scream* 4, 184
*Scream 2* 184
*Scream Queens* 108
*The Secret Life of the American Teenager* 111–112
Segel, Jason 17, 84
September 11 terrorist attacks 159
*Sesame Street* 51

*Seventeen* magazine 28–29, 39, 94
sex 18–19, 36, 46, 70, 74, 76–79, 88, 110–112, 123, 126–128, 131, 134
*Sex and the City* 128
sexuality 3, 7, 19, 21, 31, 45, 76, 79, 90, 93, 106–109, 121, 133, 136–139, 142, 160, 181, 188–189, 193
*Shake it Up* 198
Shakespeare, William: *Romeo and Juliet* 3
The Shangri-Las 47
The Shins 121
The Shirelles 47
Shulman, Max 33–35
Shum, Harry, Jr. 175
Shumway, David R. 45–46
Silverstone, Alicia 79, 128
Sinatra, Frank 44
Sinclair, Katja Blichfeld Ben 174
*Singin' in the Rain* 34
*Sister, Sister* 75, 97
"situated authorship" 10
*16 and Pregnant* 112
*Sixteen Candles* 110, 175, 184
*Skam* 1, 137, 188
*Skins* 4, 5, 13, 19, 89, 134–139, 188
Skovbye, Tiera 184
*Slate* 182
*Slumdog Millionaire* 135
*Smallville* 18
Smith, Kerr 87
Smith, Will 71
social media 12, 20, 109, 123–124, 173, 183, 198–199
*Soul Train* 16, 23, 27, 44, 47–51
Spears, Britney 13, 70, 71
Spelling, Aaron 73–74
*The Spice Girls* 71
*Spider-Man: Homecoming* 198
Spielberg, Steven 38, 86
*Splendored Thing* 41
*Splendor in the Grass* 76
Spotify 122
*Spring Breakers* 190
Stallion, Meg Thee 70
#StandWithPlannedParenthood 172

*Stars* (Dyer) 14
stars/stardom: and Brandy Norwood 93–97; and celebrity 13–16; and *Euphoria* 197–200; and *Freaks and Geeks* 84–85; Gen Z 82–83; and *Moesha* 93–97
Stein, Louisa E. 105, 106, 123–124, 136
*The Steve Allen Show* 45
Stewart, Kristen 122
*Stranger Things* 1, 142, 184
*Stream Daily* 171
streaming 2, 4, 13, 19–20, 48, 75, 85, 91, 93, 106, 124, 142, 160–163, 170, 172, 188
Struthers, Sally 42
*The Suite Life of Zac & Cody* 184
The Sunrays 32
*Superbad* 84
*Supernatural* 18
The Supremes 47
Suyin, Han: *Many-Splendoured Thing* 33
*Sweet Valley High* 18
*Sybil* 38
Sykes, Wanda 96

Tarantino, Quentin 185
teenagers 3, 17, 25, 29–31, 34–35, 44, 46–49, 74, 76, 81, 124, 134–135
*Teen Beach 2* 185
*Teen Canteen* 47
teen consumer and early broadcast TV 28–32
*Teen Mom* 112
*Teen Mom 2* 112
*Teen Mom 3* 112
*Telenovela* 173
Temple, Shirley 25
*Temple Grandin* 82
*Thank Me Later* 141
*That Girl* 31, 37
*They Shall Be Heard* 48, 50
*13 Reasons Why* 1, 89, 177, 182, 184–185, 187
*Thirtysomething* 78

## INDEX

*This Will Only Hurt a Little* 85
Thomas, Marlo 37, 50
Thomas, Rob 133
Timberlake, Justin 13, 71
*Time* magazine 44, 199
#TimesUp movement 85, 142
*Titanic* 43, 82
*To All The Boys I've Loved Before* 176
Toyota 170–171
Travolta, John 43
*Troop Beverly Hills* 121
*True Blood* 196
Trump, Donald 106, 174
Tucker, Ken 112
Tumblr 1, 109
Turnbull, Sue 130
Turner, Ted 68
TV sitcoms 33–36
*12 Years A Slave* 200
*Twilight* trilogy 122
*Twin Peaks* 7, 70, 71, 75, 182, 183, 184; and its teen crime drama successors 186–187
Twitter 109, 163
*Two and a Half Men* 89

*Ugly Betty* 172
*The Unauthorized Saved By The Bell Story* 184
*Uncut Gems* 188
*Undeclared* 84
Union, Gabrielle 96
United Paramount Network (UPN) 18, 72, 74, 75, 88, 95
University of Southern California 2
Univision 170
Ushkowitz, Jenna 175

Valentine, Helen 28–30
*Valley Girl* 185
*The Vampire Diaries* 122
Van, Bobby 34
Van Der Beek, James 87
*Variety* magazine 12, 112
Vergara, Sofia 173

*Veronica Mars* 26, 77, 89, 107, 109, 119, 182, 187; and suicide 129–134
Vesey, Alyx 187
Viacom 18
Vietnam War 42
*Views* 141
*Vogue* 185
Volkswagen of America 170
Voorhies, Lark 73
*Vulture* 92

"Walk This Way" 70
Walley, Deborah 37
*Wanda at Large* 96
Warner, Kristen 21
Warner Brothers (WB) 18, 72, 74, 86; and narrowcasting in post-network era 86–89; rise and fall of 86–89
War on Drugs 67
Watanabe, Gedde 175
*Welcome Back Kotter* 24, 41–43
Westwick, Ed 77, 126, 128
*Whatever Happened to Dobie Gillis?* 35
*When They See Us* 200
*Whip It* 184
White Anglo-Saxon Protestant (WASP) 31–32
*Wicked* 81
Wiig, Kristen 84
Wilde, Olivia 120
*Will & Grace* 79
Williams, Michelle 87, 198
Williams, Tennessee 38
Williamson, Kevin 88
Willis, Ellen 28
*Will Smith* 94
Wilson, Carl 86
Wilson, Hugh 75
Wilson, Larissa 135
Wise Entertainment 169, 171
Wiseman, Rosalind: *Queen Bees and Wannabes: Helping Your Daughter Survive Cliques, Gossip, Boyfriends, and the New Realities of GirlWorld* 109
*Wizards of Waverly Place* 13

Wojcik, Pamela Robertson: *Gidget: Origins of a Teen Girl Transmedia Franchise* 24
*The Wonder Years* 43
Woodley, Shailene 111
Woods, Faye 136–138
Woods, Georgie 49–50
World Trade Center 105
World War II 24–25, 176
*Wrinkle in Time* 200

Writers Guild of America 11
*Wuthering Heights* (Bronte) 5

Y2K 105
Yardeni, Tmira 188
YouTube 13

Zendaya 5, 189, 197–198, 200
Ziegesar, Cecily von 122
Zwick, Ed 78